Real Gangstas

CRITICAL ISSUES IN CRIME AND SOCIETY
Raymond J. Michalowski, Series Editor

Critical Issues in Crime and Society is oriented toward critical analysis of contemporary problems in crime and justice. The series is open to a broad range of topics including specific types of crime, wrongful behavior by economically or politically powerful actors, controversies over justice system practices, and issues related to the intersection of identity, crime, and justice. It is committed to offering thoughtful works that will be accessible to scholars and professional criminologists, general readers, and students.

For a list of titles in the series, see the last page of the book.

Real Gangstas

LEGITIMACY, REPUTATION, AND VIOLENCE IN THE INTERGANG ENVIRONMENT

TIMOTHY R. LAUGER

RUTGERS UNIVERSITY PRESS

New Brunswick, New Jersey, and London

LIBRARY OF CONGRESS CATALOGING-IN-PUBLICATION DATA

Lauger, Timothy R.
   Real gangstas : legitimacy, reputation, and violence in the intergang
environment / Timothy R. Lauger.
      p. cm. — (Critical issues in crime and society)
   Includes bibliographical references and index.
   ISBN 978–0–8135–5373–3 (hbk. : alk. paper) — ISBN 978–0–8135–5374–0
(pbk. : alk. paper) — ISBN 978–0–8135–5375–7 (e-book)
   1. Gangs—United States.   2. Gang members—United States.   3. Youth
and violence—United States.   I. Title.
   HV6439.U5L39   2011
   364.106′60973—dc23

                                                            2011048989

   A British Cataloging-in-Publication record for this book is available
                        from the British Library.

Copyright © 2012 by Timothy R. Lauger

Visit our website: http://rutgerspress.rutgers.edu

Manufactured in the United States of America

Contents

ACKNOWLEDGMENTS

THIS BOOK IS THE END RESULT of a lifetime of learning and countless interactions with people who shaped my personal and intellectual growth. I must first thank my parents, Richard and Marjorie Lauger, who provided a home environment that encouraged me to pursue my own interests and helped develop the intrinsic motivation to take on this project. They also made great financial sacrifices to help send their four children to college. This sacrifice led to me Calvin College, where I first became genuinely interested in academic endeavors. Although many faculty members contributed to my intellectual growth in college, Scott Richeson and Robert Butler fostered my interest in criminology and, more importantly, first identified my potential for academic success. Without their encouragement, I would never have thought about going to graduate school. My years pursuing a doctorate in criminal justice at Indiana University were also filled with individuals who contributed to this book in some manner. Greg Lindsteadt served as an invaluable peer mentor during my first years of graduate school. Without his moral support, I might not have finished my studies. For providing me ample freedom and encouragement to pursue the research for this book, I want to thank Steve Chermak, Kip Schlegel, Bill Pridemore, Richard Spano, and Veronica Herrera. Over the years, Kip, especially, fostered my intellectual development, as his door was always open to provide intellectual discussion and emotional support.

I am especially thankful to Steve Chermak for being the kind of mentor who steered me through uncertainties, insecurities, overconfidence, and those inevitable bad first drafts of papers. Steve's encouragement, guidance, and patience over the years have been immeasurably vital to the development of this book. He identified and understood my strengths before I did, and he guided my growth as a scholar. For this I am grateful.

A number of other people read and commented on earlier versions of this book. I specifically want to thank Stephen Tillotson, Frank Hagan, Peter Benekos, and Sue Godboldt for their editorial contributions. The latter three also provided a work environment at Mercyhurst College that was conducive to writing this book. In this manner, Tina Fryling was also especially considerate, as she constructed my teaching schedule so that I could find time to write. I also want to thank Peter Mickulas, my editor at Rutgers University Press. His support of this project has been vital to the publication of the book. His advice about preparing the final manuscript has been extremely helpful, and his efforts have led to a better book. In addition, I am grateful for careful attention that Willa Speiser gave to editing the final version of this book. My anonymous peer reviewers also gave me numerous ideas for how to improve the book. Thank you.

Of course this book could not have been written without the help of the individuals in Indianapolis who allowed me to observe their daily routines. I wish I could publicly thank them, but they shall remain anonymous, and I will always be thankful for their efforts.

My wife, Heidi, also deserves a lot of credit for this book. Without her constant support and unrelenting patience during the last nine years, this book could not have been written. Moreover, her editorial contributions over the years have been immeasurably helpful, as she has willingly been involved in editing and commenting on multiple drafts of this book.

Real Gangstas

Introduction

ON THE NORTHEAST SIDE of Indianapolis, along a busy highway, large spray-painted letters mar an unremarkable brick building. Plainly written in black paint, without much creativity or attention to style, the letters spell out the name of a local street gang—DFW Boyz. Lacking traditional gang signifiers like bright colors, numbers, pitchforks, a crown, the Star of David, or other discernable gang jargon, the writing does not resemble stereotypical gang graffiti. If one is bound by preconceptions of gang signifiers, the writing can be easily mistaken for the work of a preadolescent child or a wannabe playing the part of a gang member. Drivers passing through the area may not notice the writing; it probably blends into the tapestry of the surrounding urban environment. Perhaps it is just another symbol reminding them of what goes on in the poorer neighborhoods that are adjacent to the highway. Yet to the tagger and his peers, the name is meaningful. The moniker "DFW Boyz" represents a defining element of the gang's collective identity; they are down for whatever.[1] Being down for whatever means taking advantage of opportunities for such activities as robbery, burglary, or overt manipulations of weaker peers to obtain money. It also implies a willingness and ability to fight whenever necessary. The letters on the building are an outward manifestation of an identity that many of the gang's members embrace and enact on a day-to-day basis.

By publicly displaying "DFW Boyz" on the side of the building, the tagger, an active gang member named Layboy, was not simply expressing a salient part of his identity; he intended for peers to see his work. Only a few days after tagging the building, Layboy proudly showed me the graffiti. He boasted about how nearby surveillance cameras recorded the act, but the black hood on his sweatshirt provided enough of a disguise to foil authorities. His motivation for the act, although simple, was illustrative of the day-to-day concerns of many gang members. The graffiti was not intended to mark gang territory. Although a few members of the DFW Boyz lived nearby, this location only served as a temporary hangout for gang members, and it was also home to a few other gangs that invariably encountered the DFW Boyz. The graffiti was also not intended to send a secret message to other gang members, as its content was clear to anyone in the area. Instead, it merely announced the presence of the DFW Boyz. It was a crude and largely unplanned effort to maintain or increase the gang's visibility in this northeast side neighborhood. Being known in the streets of Indianapolis is vitally important to the gang member's daily negotiation of his or her social environment, and so the name was displayed on the brick building for all to see.

Understanding the everyday concerns of gang members is essential for gaining insight into some of their more troubling activities. Spray painting "DFW Boyz" on a building was not the most serious crime that I had been exposed to while hanging out with members of the street gang. For months, members of the gang had regaled me with tales of robbery, fighting, and intimidation. On a few occasions, I was more involved in those activities than I would have liked. Yet the motivation and rationale for such behavior was often revealed through the banality and tedium of their daily lives. My exposure to serious criminal behavior was accompanied by seemingly endless hours of boredom and inactivity, as I observed gang members go about their daily routines. Yet such observations increased my familiarity with both members of the DFW Boyz and the Indianapolis streets. Conversations between gang members that had previously seemed trite became consequential, and I became more attuned to whom they were interacting with and talking about. Their conversations and interactions, which initially seemed mundane, revealed numerous insights that helped explain why gang members were so willing to rob, fight, and intimidate.

My exposure to active gang members occurred during an eighteen-month ethnographic study in the streets of Indianapolis. My research began February 2007 and ended in early August 2008. I spent much, but not all, of that time with Layboy, his brother Shawn, and some of their closest associates within the DFW Boyz. These active gang members play a central role in this book, and, as will be evident in the ensuing chapters, they gave me unlimited access to their lives. This exposure revealed that gang members were immersed in a complex social environment that heavily influenced their behavior. More specifically, they routinely engaged in meaningful social interactions with members of other gangs, and these intergang interactions often produced the motivation for an array of problematic behaviors. Indeed, Layboy's graffiti, his need to be known in the streets of Indianapolis, and his gang's violent behavior were largely produced by awareness of and interactions with other gangs. Yet a more nuanced examination of these intergang interactions also demonstrated that gang members were not passive figures in the face of overpowering peer pressure or cultural values. They actively interpreted the nature of each encounter with other gangs. They constructed the meaning of each intergang interaction and created characterizations of their counterparts. This book examines how complex intergang interactions influenced gang members' behavior.

THE INTERGANG ENVIRONMENT

In Indianapolis, and in many other cities, select neighborhoods provide ideal settings for the formation and proliferation of street gangs. Yet street gangs rarely evolve into large-scale organizations that dominate extensive geographical areas within a city. They are, more commonly, smaller collections of loosely organized youths that may or may not control a small amount of turf (Decker and Van Winkle 1996; Klein and Maxson 2006), and poorer sections of the city tend to be home to numerous intersecting street gangs. Multiple gangs share space within the urban landscape, and interactions between these groups are common, yet varied. The resulting network of interactions between these street gangs produces the intergang environment, which is vital to understanding the daily concerns of gang members. Quite simply, gangs are not islands in the street.[2] They engage in meaningful interactions with other gangs in their respective communities. Through this book I hope to develop a more thorough understanding of the intergang environment and demonstrate that intergang interactions significantly influence the perceptions and behaviors of gang members. In short, I argue that intergang interactions involve a process whereby gang members observe, interpret, and assess the behaviors of their peers. Understanding this process provides insight into some of the motivating factors that can produce violence, and to further this understanding the material that follows closely examines the nature and consequences of intergang interactions.[3]

The notion of an intergang environment accounts for the collection of gangs within a given area. With the exception of research on conflict or threat between gangs (see Decker 1996; Decker and Van Winkle 1996), scholars have largely ignored the influence that intergang interactions have on gang members. In fact, as I entered the research field, my interest in such interactions was nonexistent, and I realized their significance only after months of research. As gang members consistently talked about peers and provided frequent commentary about other local gangs, I unexpectedly began to appreciate the creative potential of their routine social interactions. They were actively involved in constructing social boundaries, interpreting and creating meaning during social interactions, and labeling peers. This book relies on my personal observations of active gang members, interview data, and recorded conversations between gang members to capture this creativity, and it substantially enhances an otherwise barren conception of intergang interactions.

Gang members spend much of their time observing and assessing the behavior of their peers. This attentiveness to peer behavior commonly extends beyond the internal social dynamics of a single gang and becomes an enduring characteristic of intergang interactions. In fact, the gang members in this study did not spend much time or energy evaluating the behaviors of their close associates. They looked outward to assess the actions of peers who were claiming membership to an array of gangs, cliques, or hoods. Although at times the dynamic of threat or conflict characterized intergang interactions, a subtler, but equally important, dynamic between gangs often influenced gang member behavior. Gang members observed their peers with a degree of skepticism, as they believed that too many supposed gang members were not real gang members. They were known as wannabes who were perpetrating a fraud. This belief dramatically affected intergang interactions.

The notion of "being real" was a central concern of the gang members in this study, and it is, therefore, a central theme in this book. In Indianapolis, a gang member's definition of "real" was socially constructed through his or her experiences and interactions with close associates. Each gang formed a collective identity that was embraced and enacted by members and then publicly displayed to peers. Self-defined gang members were fully confident in their status as real gang members. Yet considerations of "real" became problematic when a gang or gang member's internal certainty was not consistent with the evaluations of others. What happened when self-defined gang members were confident in their status as real gang members but some peers disagreed? What happened when pervasive skepticism in the intergang environment created widespread disagreement about who was and who was not real? These questions were particularly important in Indianapolis, where intergang interactions were often permeated by doubt and derision.

Confronted with skepticism that was often publicly expressed by peers, gang members in Indianapolis struggled to gain and maintain legitimacy in the intergang environment. To gain legitimacy and minimize dismissive appraisals, gang members had to develop well-known reputations for violence. Other forms of verifying legitimacy were ineffective. For example, superficial signifiers of gang membership such as signs, colors, and codes could not be used for validation. They were too easily mimicked and were often viewed with skepticism. Consequently, gang members used routine conversations and street gossip to disseminate their violent exploits throughout the intergang environment. They developed violent self-characterizations and openly disparaged peers during public and private conversations. As gossip circulated and peers heard about these disparaging comments, intergang hostilities were either born or intensified. Intergang conflict, therefore, began as a slowly evolving process between two gangs that were attentive to street gossip and motivated by the struggle for legitimacy in the intergang environment.

Researching Gangs by Becoming Marginal: The Emergence of Tim Tim

"Tim Tim," said TJ, as he emerged from an apartment complex. The greeting had been a ritualized element of our interactions for a few months.

"What what," I responded accordingly, much to TJ's delight. This had become my routine retort.

"Hey, you want to be down with us?" asked Layboy as we stood outside. "We can jump you in. You can bang."

The question reflected a desire to observe my response more than an actual invitation to join the gang. I turned toward Layboy and simply looked at him with a raised brow in an attempt to communicate, "You have got to be joking."

Laughter erupted from a couple of gang members behind us and Shawn said, "He could be an assassin."

This was not the first time Shawn had characterized me this way. My role as a researcher often caused me to quietly watch and listen to the boys as they went about their daily activities. Although most of these activities were mundane, my unwavering behavior in the occasional tense situation was apparently consistent with individuals in the street who listened first and acted with little warning. I never corrected Shawn's mischaracterization, but I was pleased that my role with the gang had transitioned from outsider to marginal insider. After months of frustration, mistakes, awkward situations, and failed attempts to access gang members, this newfound comfort coincided with a sense of familiarity for Shawn, Layboy, TJ, and the DFW Boyz.

The success of a qualitative study is largely contingent on the researcher's ability to establish relationships with selected research participants. Most researchers begin at a point of complete detachment and must work their way into being a recognized and trusted community participant. At some point, individuals allow the researcher to peer into their lives, record conversations, and participate in their activities. Still, the degree of involvement needed for a successful study is debatable (Adler, Adler, and Rochford 1986). Too much inclusion places the researcher at risk for "going native," or uncritically embracing and accepting the views of others as his or her own (ibid.; Gold 1958; Hammersley and Atkinson 1995; Monti 1992). This can reduce the researcher's ability to analytically engage his or her research environment, and it can lead to description without analysis. But with too little inclusion the researcher cannot become sufficiently familiar with research participants or the subject matter. Qualitative researchers must struggle to find an imperfect balance between the conflicting needs of intimacy and objectivity.

Achieving intimacy is the researcher's first concern, and perhaps my biggest challenge was getting access to a substantial number of gang members who were willing to participate in the study. A major flaw in my research design hindered this process: I originally relied too heavily on one community leader who promised, and repeatedly failed, to put me in contact with active gang members. For too long I patiently trusted his assurances that gang members were going to come by and talk to me. He did occasionally have people stop by his community center for interviews, but a few months into the research I had not established consistent relationships with gang members. Although I spent much of this time passively sitting around the center, naively waiting for the research to come to me, I was unknowingly establishing connections that would later lead to successful research. Despite his deficiencies, the aforementioned community leader did have diverse contacts. I became familiar with the local community by working at nonprofit organizations, talking with residents, and canvassing northeast Indianapolis neighborhoods by car and foot.

Within the confines of one community organization, I had a serendipitous encounter with someone who greatly influenced my understanding of the Indianapolis streets. One evening, while I waited for an interview, an unfamiliar man named Sidney came by to talk to the organization's executive director. Given that Sidney was unemployed and looking for a job, he proudly showed me some job application materials that drastically underrepresented his work capabilities. After some discussion, I offered to help him create a more professional résumé that would greatly aid his job search. This simple gesture, which initially served to alleviate my boredom, provided the foundation for a long and productive relationship. Although only in his mid-forties, Sidney had been arrested twenty-seven times as an adult, and he had spent much of his adult life in state and federal prison. He had never been a gang member, but he had been heavily involved with various criminal activities that ranged from selling pharmaceuticals to routinely robbing drug dealers. For the duration of my research, Sidney, who was an uneducated, intelligent, and skilled laborer, struggled to find and maintain gainful employment. When I met Sidney, he was still dealing with some minor court cases, owed several thousand dollars in child support payments, and was living in a broken-down RV. He was also struggling with his desire to desist from the criminal lifestyle, and he often lamented the temptation to get fast money illegally.

In the following months, Sidney became my first reliable contact. My relationship with Sidney not only led to a number of additional research participants and new theoretical insights, but it also established a basic model for relating to the individuals in this study. My role in the research field was not necessarily guided by a job description or a specific activity but by an ascribed identity that arose when I interacted with research participants (see Venkatesh 2002). To Sidney I was a symbol of an external and unreachable world that was taking a rare glimpse into the conditions of inner-city life. Although I never expressed any political views, I was a sign of hope and a possible political ally. In fact, Sidney often tried to motivate me to run for political office. Although he was excited about the project, Sidney was also keenly aware of being manipulated, and he resented anyone who leveraged his disadvantageous life circumstances for selfish gain. Some community leaders promised Sidney jobs and politically orchestrated court leniency in return for unconditional obedience to their work demands. Given that he was typically unpaid and often unrewarded, Sidney dramatically compared himself to a slave and told me that he was treated better in prison. Accordingly, I had to demonstrate a genuine concern for his life and for the community, or he could have quickly labeled me as a slave master.

I could only demonstrate such concern with short-term contributions to the lives of Sidney and other individuals participating in this study. At times these contributions can violate the idealistic ethic that researchers should not disturb the natural processes they study, but they can also mute the self-serving nature of qualitative research. When pursuing the goals of research, the researcher continually tries to get generally unmotivated individuals to talk about the intimate and often illegal aspects of their lives without promising much in return. After a given period of time, the researcher leaves the research site to further his or her academic career and advance the scientific understanding of an issue only to leave participants in the study with very little for their efforts. In the case of adolescent gang members, this dynamic of the research process may cause them to be abandoned by another adult, this time in the person of the researcher.

The participants in this study seemed to understand that I would be the one to benefit most from this study, and they often talked about helping me with my research. Yet such altruism would not have sustained productive field research. For example, Sidney's lack of income severely hindered some basic requirements for the research. He did not have the ability to buy, maintain, and operate his own vehicle. Although I usually provided transportation for Sidney, when he did have to find transportation it usually cost him money. Given that he used a pay-by-the-minute phone, each phone conversation cost money that Sidney did not have. For such things I provided him with meager and informal monetary reimbursements. I also periodically took him out to eat and paid for his meal. Sidney perceived these small gestures as adequate reimbursements for his efforts rather than charity, and he did not try to exploit our growing relationship by asking for more.

Over the course of the project, my role in Sidney's life transitioned from outsider, to marginal insider, to friend and confidant. By the end of the research, I had driven him to court numerous times, been a character witness for him during a sentencing hearing, visited with his mother multiple times, and kept him company while he was on house arrest. Sidney provided me with moral support when I dealt with frustrating community members. He changed his life dramatically during my time in the research field and, during one conversation, he noted my role in his transformation by saying that I had been a pallbearer for his former self. My departure from field research was not easy for Sidney, as I moved eight hours away to begin my career, and in our last phone conversation he spoke of visiting me the following summer. He died in a freak accident only a few weeks later.

My relationships with other research participants did not equal my friendship with Sidney, as I more effectively balanced the need to remain somewhat detached and objective while gathering data about the more intimate aspects of gang members' lives. Numerous scholars advocate that researchers achieve a marginal role with the individuals they study (Gold 1958; Hammersley and Atkinson 1995; Horowitz 1986; Junker 1960). If the researcher is successful in achieving a marginal role, he or she becomes a known and accepted part of a new social world but is not bound by relational obligations. He or she is free to enter and exit the research participant's life as needed. As such, there is an established unidirectional intimacy so that studied individuals are willing to discuss sensitive aspects of their lives without expecting the researcher to reciprocate. In effect, individuals experience no social consequences for talking openly with the researcher, as the information is not going to be used in a socially manipulative way or be spread through a social grapevine. This marginal role ensures the researcher access to research participants and reduces the emotional involvement that might hinder analysis and theory construction.

Marginality in this study, however, was contingent on routine contact with established gang members, and for months I relied on a chain referral system that produced in-depth interviews but did not provide opportunities for extensive observation of active gang members. During this time, I volunteered at a small nonprofit youth organization and interacted with a group of gang members. I oversaw their activities at the community center, but I did not inquire about their gang activities. Selecting key informants was vital to this study, and failing to pick the best informants would have led to a problematic study (Fleisher 1998). Given that I needed to find a few key informants who were knowledgeable, connected, and willing to participate in the study for an extended period of time, this decision signified a key juncture in the research. After I observed and interacted with Shawn and Layboy for a few months, they seemed to be the best candidates to serve as key informants. They were both intelligent and articulate teenagers, natural leaders who garnered respect from younger and older peers. Furthermore, most of their extended family members were heavily invested in gang life.

I eventually discussed the study with Shawn and Layboy, who were willing to provide access to their daily routines and social connections. Although my preexisting relationship with Shawn and Layboy increased their willingness to participate in this study, they also perceived the study to be beneficial. Given that Layboy, Shawn, and many other gang members in this study were accustomed to constant lectures from adults, their relationship with me transcended their usual interactions with adults. They appreciated the opportunity to be heard. As in other studies, some of the gang members in this study suggested that their participation was cathartic (see Decker and Van Winkle 1996). More importantly, gang members were enamored with the idea of being the focus of a possible book. As I will discuss in later chapters, they were fixated on becoming known entities in the streets of Indianapolis, and being the subject matter of a book reinforced their significance.

Similar to Sidney, Shawn and Layboy's initial interest in the study would have been short-lived if I had not been sensitive to their life conditions. They desired summer jobs, and, after their mentor had repeatedly ignored their pleas for assistance, I volunteered to help them. My offer to help led to a lengthy process of driving to prospective employers, filling out applications, and hoping for interviews. They were granted a few interviews and some places seemed interested in hiring the boys, but they never found jobs. Such failure was personally disappointing, but the effort substantially increased their comfort with me and proved vital to the research process. These outings often led to lengthy and informal discussions about life, the streets, and gangs. Their efforts in this study also warranted nominal monetary reimbursement. Although no one was paid for participating in the study, I gave Layboy and Shawn varying small amounts of money for tracking down prospective research participants. Often this compensation occurred when one of their pay-by-the-minute cell phones was out of minutes and they needed to contact people. Shawn and Layboy understood this informal arrangement to be equitable compensation for both their sacrificed time and the expenses that accompanied their efforts.

My time with the DFW Boyz and other research participants was generally spent observing mundane activities. I often drove the boys around the city in search of job opportunities or other gang members to interview. We frequently hung out in various apartment complexes, houses, or street corners and talked about an array of topics. During these times I was usually content to simply listen to the natural flow of teenage conversation, but, at times, I asked pointed questions about the topic of their discussions. Sometimes I conducted in-depth, though unstructured, one-on-one interviews with select individuals. I use both forms of data in this book, as they both provided unique insights into members' lives. In total, I interviewed and/or observed fifty-five street offenders, most of whom were active gang members. Some of these individuals were not affiliated with the DFW Boyz, but I spent most of my time with members of that particular street gang.

As I gradually became closer to Layboy, Shawn, and a core group of the DFW Boyz, I became familiar with an expanding network of gang members and was able to access some of the more privileged details about their activities. Members of the DFW Boyz initially seemed to withhold information from me, but by the end of my research they openly discussed specific instances of gunplay by gang members. They allowed me to examine the more intimate areas of their life through lengthy conversations about childhood anger, sex, and violence. By that point in the research, I had established a pattern of routinely interacting with a core group of gang members. Even members who were not close to me accepted my role among their peers, and they did not seem bothered by my presence. Only a few members viewed me as a potential snitch and were guarded in my presence. Still, the group did not grant me full insider status. There were times when they held conversations behind closed doors, and in some instances they asked me to stay behind while they confronted members of other gangs (see chapter 7). As I exited the research field, I realized with regret that another year of field research might have enhanced the research experience, but after eighteen months of data collection, conversations had become redundant, and time had run out.

THE ORGANIZATION OF THE BOOK

The theoretical argument that unfolds over the course of this study is grounded in observation and interview data. True to the ideals of grounded theory and theoretical emergence (Glaser and Strauss 2006), these data largely guided the development of the argument in this book. Few, if any, of the ideas in this study existed before research began. They were slowly constructed, as I became more familiar with the salient concerns of the individuals in this study. The components of the argument were not subtle aspects of members' lives that I selected to fit a previously constructed argument. Instead, they represented consistent themes that reemerged throughout the research process.

Chapter 1 introduces the reader to the research site, Indianapolis gangs, and the DFW Boyz. Largely inspired by Elijah Anderson's (1999) trip down Philadelphia's Germantown Avenue, it discusses the ecological or socioeconomic conditions within the research area that provide an ideal environment for developing and maintaining street gangs. Not surprisingly, the area is poor. This chapter also reintroduces the reader to the notion of the intergang environment and discusses the concepts of an intergang field (which is produced when individuals attempt to establish boundaries for the intergang environment), intergang interactions, and legitimacy.

Chapters 2, 3, and 4 demonstrate how gang members become immersed in a paradox of legitimacy. Chapter 2 combines observational and interview data from this study with the findings of the broader gang literature to explain why individuals join gangs. The rationale for joining a gang further illuminates the false promises of gang membership, and it helps explain why gang members remain invested in gang life. Youths often join gangs because they falsely believe that gangs will help them resolve a set of problems related to street activity. The prospective gang member views the gang as a source of protection, respect, and friendship, or as a collectivity that will increase one's ability to make fast money through illicit activities.

Chapter 3 looks more closely at gang members' confidence in their position within the boundaries of the intergang field and the contrasting general skepticism of the intergang environment. The individual labels himself or herself as being a real gang member, but peers often disagree and subsequently belittle his or her claims to gang membership. This disagreement typically does not occur between members of the same gang, but between members of different gangs, and it reflects a basic contradiction in the intergang environment. Individuals join gangs that exhibit high levels of certainty about their gang status, but the broader intergang environment is dubious about those claims. In effect, all self-defined gang members believe that they are real gang members, but they also believe that many other self-defined gang members falsely claim gang affiliation. As a result, interactions between members of different gangs involve a process of observing, interpreting, and evaluating the actions and claims of other self-defined gang members.

Chapter 4 fully develops the paradox of legitimacy by recognizing the inevitable problem that arises when peers question each other's gang status during social interactions. Although gang members often label their peers as wannabe gang members, they are also at risk of being similarly labeled. Therefore, all self-defined gang members are eventually confronted with the problem of gaining and maintaining legitimacy. This is especially problematic when no agreed-upon standards exist to clearly differentiate real gang members from so-called fake gang members. In Indianapolis, the intergang environment lacks such agreed-upon standards, so the environment is characterized by innumerable self-serving understandings of gang. Therefore, a field boundary is created individually and is largely subjective. Consequently, any gang member can be labeled as fake at any time, and all gang members continuously struggle to gain or maintain legitimacy in the intergang environment.

Chapters 5, 6, and 7 describe how gang members negotiate the paradox of legitimacy and examine the consequences of the struggle for legitimacy in the intergang environment. Chapter 5 argues that although the intergang field lacks clear standards for establishing legitimacy, gang members do embrace a common expectation that legitimate gang members should be willing and able to use violence. A single violent act typically does not effectively communicate one's status to a broad audience, however, and gang members must continuously work to establish a widely accepted reputation for violence. To overcome the paradox of legitimacy, gang members must be widely known in the streets for their willingness and ability to use violence.

Chapter 6 argues that one's reputation is not simply the by-product of periodic violent events. Gang members develop their reputations when they gather with peers and talk about their social environment. In these social settings, gang members gain new information about their social environment, negatively gossip about peers, and develop self-characterizations that are congruent with the environmental expectation of violence. The resulting flow of information is a vital component of the intergang environment, and it is closely linked to the origins of intergang conflict. The information that circulates during routine peer interactions eventually disseminates throughout the intergang environment. During routine conversations, gang members ridicule other gangs, and other gang members. They sometimes suggest that these other gang members are not real gang members; they are wannabes. These comments are often disseminated into the intergang environment and become known to the dismissed gangs or gang members. Such gossip fuels hostility and increases the probability of conflict.

Chapter 7 examines the street beef, or the prolonged intergang conflict. Intergang conflicts are grounded in concerns of legitimacy, as groups observe and ultimately dismiss each other. Intergang conflicts gain momentum as gang members feverishly gossip and disseminate negative portrayals of their counterparts into the intergang environment. Consequently, intergang interactions become increasingly hostile, and everyone involved in the petty street beef gradually becomes immersed in a series of escalating threats that can quickly turn to violence.

Chapter 8 concludes the book by discussing the prospects of intervention. I describe my efforts to intervene in the lives of Shawn, Layboy, and TJ, and I contemplate the inherent challenges that confront the boys. The chapter also discusses the potential for and difficulties associated with change. It then ends with a harsh reminder of what gang life entails, and how the prospects of change can dissipate quickly.

CHAPTER 1

Gangs and Their Environments

AT FIRST GLANCE, the busy intersection of Keystone Avenue and Thirty-eighth Street in northeast Indianapolis seems relatively mundane. Various fast-food restaurants, stores, and financial service businesses line the streets that lead to this junction. Vehicles passing through are notably varied, indicating that people of different economic classes use these roads to traverse the city. The mostly small, run-down houses that line these intersecting streets suggest that this area is poorer than others, but they do not signify to outsiders that it is a ghetto. Visitors may know from experience, reputation, or media reports that the surrounding area includes some of the most violence-prone communities in Indianapolis, but such information is not readily apparent when driving through. An astute observer may notice a heavy police presence or a group of youths loitering in front of a strip mall during evening hours, yet there are few overt signs of criminal activity. Even at night, these streets are not lined with signs of vice, as prostitutes and drug dealers rarely position themselves along the streets. For most travelers, there is little reason to leave the confines of their vehicles when passing through. When stops are warranted, many outsiders do not seem fearful, as customers at local filling stations or fast-food restaurants appear both racially and economically diverse.

People more intimately connected to the surrounding community view it with a degree of ambivalence unique to poor urban areas. Far from seeing it as a stereotypical ghetto wasteland, many residents hold favorable opinions of the area. Some residents perceive a strong sense of community, exemplified by vibrant religious institutions and numerous benevolent organizations. Other people have large networks of friends and family that provide support in good and bad times. Residents also recognize, however, that severe problems plague this area. Most notably,

people living in the communities near this intersection deal with a ubiquitous threat of violence. During 2008, sixteen homicides occurred
within a one-mile radius of the Thirty-eighth Street and Keystone intersection.[1] These neighborhoods, though home to just under 2 percent of
the city's population, witnessed 14 percent of the city's homicides in
2008. For the researcher, such statistics are a reminder of how violence
is concentrated in relatively small geographical areas within cities (Braga
2005; Sherman, Gartin, and Bueger 1989). For residents of these neighborhoods, violence is devastatingly personal, too often forcing them to
bury their children, grandchildren, or friends.

In community meetings, violence symposiums, or private discussion,
concerned citizens often voice their frustrations and point to a myriad of
problems that cause this violence. Drugs, guns, unacceptably high school
dropout rates, apathetic parenting, and poverty are on the short list of
factors used to explain the problem. Invested community members are
especially exasperated with the large numbers of youths who become
gang members. This frustration is, unfortunately, based in the realities of
the street. Gangs are scattered about the neighborhoods surrounding this
intersection, and while violence is a multifaceted problem in Indianapolis,
street gangs are a major contributor.

There are reasons that street gangs are so common here. Even
though gangs have spread into small towns and relatively rural communities, the heart of the gang problem still lies in the inner city. Adverse
socioeconomic conditions in these areas provide a prime habitat for the
formation and proliferation of street gangs, and the concerns about gangs
expressed by northeast-side residents are not uncommon in other low-
income urban communities.[2] Indianapolis appears prosperous when
compared to other mid-west cities, but sections of the city still display
high levels of poverty. Indeed, when contrasted to the relatively wealthy
and peaceful neighborhoods just a few miles farther north, those neighborhoods near the Thirty-eighth and Keystone intersection are notably
poorer and more violent. Within these communities, various street gangs
share limited social space, so that each gang is immersed in a complex but
powerful intergang environment. This study focuses on how interactions
within this environment dramatically shape gang member behavior and
contends that intergang relationships are driven by a continuous need to
legitimize one's self or group to other gangs.

NORTHEAST INDIANAPOLIS: THE GANG'S SOCIOECONOMIC ENVIRONMENT

Indianapolis is located in the middle of America's rust belt, a section of the country that over the last fifty years has witnessed significant economic changes and the erosion of its once thriving industrial base (Bernard 1990). This type of change has had a transformative affect on the social organization of many northern cities. As industry in this region began to fade, the loss of high-paying blue-collar jobs caused many urban residents to migrate away from city centers for the comforts of suburban life. This outmigration in the latter half of the twentieth century led to dramatic population decreases in previously vibrant cities. Between 1970 and 2006, for example, the populations of Detroit, St. Louis, Cleveland, and Buffalo all decreased by over 40 percent. Minority populations that depended on industrial jobs within these cities for economic stability experienced the harshest consequences of deindustrialization (Wilson 1987 and 1996). Many residents who could leave did, and those who stayed faced increasingly grim job prospects. Most available jobs were in the low-paying service industries (Wilson 1987 and 1996). This transformation led to an increase in urban poverty and, perhaps more importantly, a growth in the concentration of that poverty (Wilson 1987 and 1996). In the United States between 1970 and 1990 the number of extreme poverty areas, or those areas that display poverty levels over 40 percent, doubled (Harding 2010; Jargowsky 1997), and a growing number of residents found themselves living in modern-day ghettos. Decades later, well into the twenty-first century, many northern cities exhibit concentrated areas of extreme poverty, and the physical environs in these areas are so neglected that they aptly fit the imagery of the rust belt.

Relative to neighboring cities, Indianapolis has been somewhat resistant to the social and economic consequences of deindustrialization.[3] Comparing the overall economic status of Indianapolis to Columbus, Chicago, Cincinnati, St. Louis, and Detroit reveals that the city's situation is better than all but Columbus's, which is similar. Detroit provides the most startling contrast. Whereas the median household income in Indianapolis is just over $43,000 per year, households in Detroit earn less than $30,000 per year.[4] The poverty rate in Detroit is almost double the rate in Indianapolis. Poverty in Detroit is also more concentrated,

as 107 census tracts, or 22 percent of the city's tracts, display poverty
rates above 40 percent, while only 13 census tracts in Indianapolis, or
6 percent of the city, exhibit extreme levels of poverty (poverty rate over
40 percent).[5] Indianapolis also has only one census tract with a poverty
rate over 60 percent, but that area is primarily home to university students. By contrast, Detroit has twenty-three census tracts that display
poverty rates over 60 percent, and some show levels as high as 90 percent. Cincinnati and St. Louis also display poverty levels much higher
than those of Indianapolis. Residents in both cities earn about $10,000
less each year than Indianapolis residents, and they are more likely to live
in a community marked by extreme poverty. Furthermore, Chicago
has more severe levels of concentrated poverty, as twenty-nine census
tracts reveal poverty rates over 60 percent, and, as in Detroit, some show
levels over 90 percent. Although Columbus is economically similar to
Indianapolis, it also contains a larger proportion of extreme poverty
areas, suggesting that poverty is more concentrated in Columbus.

The concentration of poverty in urban areas is also not evenly
distributed across racial groups, and blacks often disproportionately
reside in extreme poverty areas. Some scholars, like William Julius
Wilson (1996), persuasively argue that the loss of industry has affected
urban black communities more than other communities. Simply stated,
black industrial workers were less likely to find well-paying jobs when
factories closed and were therefore more likely to remain in the city
without viable incomes. Scholars also argue that years of racist housing
policies have segregated large portions of the black population into
sections of cities that were then decimated by the loss of good jobs
(Massey and Denton 1993). The housing industry in Indianapolis for
most of the twentieth century used formal and informal practices to seg-
regate black residents into three areas of the city, and one of these areas
was located just south of the Thirty-eighth Street and Keystone Avenue
intersection (Pierce 2005). For example, in 1926, the city passed an
ordinance that created sanctions against any black resident wishing to
purchase a house in a white neighborhood unless he or she obtained
written consent from the majority of his or her prospective white neighbors (ibid.). The ordinance was later deemed unconstitutional, but
for at least fifty years real estate agents and moneylenders informally
reinforced racial segregation in the city (ibid.). Consequently, sections of

Indianapolis remain predominantly black, and many of these areas remain relatively poor.

The degree to which black residents in Indianapolis live in extreme poverty areas is somewhat relative. In contrast to most neighboring cities, the black population in Indianapolis represents a smaller percentage of the total population, and, as such, accounts for a smaller percentage of residents living in concentrated poverty. However, black residents live in extreme poverty areas at a higher rate than their white counterparts. Although black residents account for 27 percent of the city's population, they represent 42 percent of all people living in extreme poverty areas, meaning that the black population resides in extreme poverty areas at a rate 56 percent higher than their overall representation in the city. Such disparity is not uncommon: Columbus, Cincinnati, and St. Louis all show a similar degree of disparity, though poverty areas in the latter two cities are filled with a greater percentage of black residents. By contrast, Chicago reveals the largest degree of disparity, as black residents account for 79 percent of the population living in extreme poverty areas, but they only represent 35 percent of Chicago's total population. The black population in Chicago, therefore, resides in extreme poverty areas at a rate that is 126 percent higher than its overall representation in the city. Interestingly, Detroit is the only other city in the region with comparable poverty levels: 78 percent of residents in the city are black and 80 percent of residents living in extreme poverty areas are black. Noting these two exceptions, Indianapolis's black residents are disproportionally represented in extreme poverty areas to a degree similar to that of other cities. Yet, because the total population of black residents in Indianapolis is lower than in other cities and because the economic status of the city is more stable, the level of concentrated poverty in the black community is lower in Indianapolis than in other cities.

The consequences of economic transformation and racial segregation are, however, still apparent in Indianapolis, and the city remains socially and economically disparate. The trend has not been as severe in Indianapolis as in neighboring cities, but Indianapolis has experienced the migration of central city residents to the periphery of the city (Barrows 1990). Therefore, some communities struggle with concentrated poverty while other communities remain quite affluent. The northeast side of Indianapolis, for example, is a diverse area marked by

TABLE 1.1

Economic and Racial Comparison of Neighboring Cities

	Indianapolis	Columbus	Chicago	Cincinnati	St. Louis	Detroit
Population						
2006 population	785,597	733,203	2,833,221	332,252	348,189	871,121
1970 population	744,624	539,677	3,369,359	452,524	622,236	1,514,063
Percentage change	5	26	−16	−27	−44	−42
Economic composition						
Median household income	43,351	43,569	48,761	33,855	34,227	29,447
Poverty percentage	17	20	21	25	24	33
Percentage of census tracts with poverty rates greater than 40%	6	13	15	13	19	22
Percentage of census tracts with poverty rates greater than 60%	.5	4	3	3	3.5	5
Racial composition						
Percentage white	68	68	43	55	48	16
Percentage black	27	27	35	43	50	78
Percentage of poverty-area residents who are black	42	44	79	67	79	80
Crime rate						
Average homicide rate (2000–2009)	13.8	11.8	18.5	19.9	36.7	41.5

SOURCES: United States Census Bureau 2010b; Federal Bureau of Investigation 2010.

both wealth and poverty, opportunity and disadvantage, peace and violence. Although neighborhoods marked by wealth, peace, and opportunity are typically insulated from neighborhoods more commonly associated with poverty, disadvantage, and violence, the poorest areas are not entirely isolated from the rest of the city. Residents in these communities are exposed to and must negotiate different cultural systems (see Harding 2010). Street gangs, which are common in these communities, are among these systems, and they are diverse in size, scope, and orientation. Residents, and, more specifically, gang members, struggle to define and understand the cultural significance of gangs in their communities.

The Keystone Corridor: Cutting Through the City

A trip down Keystone Avenue provides an ideal description of the socioeconomic organization of Indianapolis. The communities located at the edge of the city are relatively wealthy, while those located near the downtown loop are quite poor. Keystone Avenue begins in a wealthy northern suburb, enters the northern edge of Indianapolis in a relatively wealthy community, and proceeds south through upper-middle-income, middle-income, and then low-income areas. Located approximately two miles east of the city's center, Keystone encounters the poorest regions on the near northeast side and remains in these communities as it proceeds south into the city's east side. A trip down Keystone Avenue offers a startling contrast between the affluent northern communities and their poor neighbors to the south.

Keystone Avenue intersects Eighty-sixth Street on the city's north end in a distinctly upper-middle-income and predominantly white community. Census data indicate that the median annual household income for the neighborhoods surrounding this intersection is slightly below $73,000, and 96 percent of the population is white. Driving on the side streets allows one to discover large homes that are situated around small ponds, moderately sized but well maintained homes, and nicely kept condominiums. Perhaps best known for its shopping, the Eighty-sixth Street and Keystone Avenue intersection boasts a fashion mall filled with upscale stores, like Saks Fifth Avenue, Louis Vuitton, and Williams-Sonoma. There is little evidence of serious crime in this area, and in 2008 there were no murders within these surrounding communities.

For more maps, please visit www.TRIPinfo.com

1. Map of Indianapolis

Continuing south along Keystone, houses become much smaller, but most are well maintained. With median incomes of just over $50,000 per year, households in these communities make less money than their northern neighbors, but they are still financially viable. The area remains racially homogenous: about 95 percent of the residents are white. Violence is relatively rare here, but in 2008, two murders did occur in these communities, and there is a sense of uncomfortable closeness to the violence a few miles south. The intersection of Keystone and Sixty-second Street offers another shopping option. Even though a modest but nicely maintained mall was recently torn down, the area remains vibrant, with stores like Lowes, Staples, and Target as viable shopping options. A large secondhand store located across the street serves consumers throughout the area, but it is a favorite spot for some poorer residents. The area is within easy driving distance of the more southerly black communities, and patrons in the stores and restaurants are racially mixed. These businesses also have desirable jobs for local black youths and one commonly witnesses young black men and women at kiosks filling out applications. They are undoubtedly encouraged by the large number of black youths employed at these stores.

The area immediately south of Sixty-second Street begins a transition from middle-class to poor communities. Here, Keystone Avenue enters a primarily commercial area, as small retail stores, car dealers, and fast-food restaurants provide the scenery for a few miles. Businesses at the Forty-sixth Street intersection seem to denote a changing economic scene: the northwest corner boasts a newer and well-maintained CVS pharmacy, while the southwest corner of the intersection is abandoned. Indeed, Forty-sixth Street marks a clear transition between middle-class and poor neighborhoods. Accounting for the census tracts extending one mile west and two miles east of Keystone Avenue, households in the area six miles north of Forty-sixth Street boast a median income of $55,863 per year, and only 8 percent live in poverty. Residents living in an area six miles south of Forty-sixth Street have a median income of $27,099 per year, and 33 percent of the population lives in poverty. No community north of Forty-sixth Street is considered a poverty area, while twenty-three of the twenty-nine census tracts south of Forty-sixth Street are considered poverty areas.[6] Moreover, ten of those census tracts are extreme poverty areas with rates exceeding 40 percent. The communities south of Forty-sixth Street are also more racially diverse, as only 44 percent of the residents are white. However, 95 percent of the residents living within two miles of Forty-sixth Street are racial minorities, providing a clear reminder of the racial divide common to many cities.

By the Thirty-eighth Street intersection, Keystone has fully entered the poorer areas of the city. Businesses located along Thirty-eighth Street reflect the limited financial options of local residents. A popular and inexpensive fried chicken restaurant is located on one corner of the Thirty-eighth Street and Keystone Avenue intersection, while another fast-food restaurant serves sliders across the street. A nearby check advancement business symbolizes the financial desperation that some community residents face on a week-to-week basis. Physical structures in this area are visibly less cared for than their counterparts farther north. Franchised stores and restaurants have not been updated to meet the latest trends, and locally owned businesses, from gas stations to mechanics' garages, appear slightly rundown, as owners struggle to keep up with building maintenance.

The houses in these communities include tightly packed postwar ranch-style and older two-story homes. When driving through these communities, one appreciates the varied attention properties receive. Some houses are well maintained, with carefully landscaped yards boasting vibrant flower gardens. The insides of these houses, whose owners are often elderly, have older décor, but the homes remain quite functional and even comfortable. Other houses appear to be livable, but signs of physical dilapidation are apparent through unmaintained roofs, windows, siding, and landscaping. Inside, these houses need repair; some may only have cement floors, plumbing that is not entirely functional, and portions that are falling apart. Yet these houses remain inhabitable and lived in. Scattered about these communities are abandoned homes that are virtually unlivable. Some of these houses may be obvious from the street, as they display boarded-up windows, caved-in roofs, and grass four feet high. Other abandoned houses might only be viewed as hopeless upon entrance, as they reveal holes in the floor, crumbling walls, and kitchens or bathrooms in disrepair.

Perhaps there is no better reminder of the plight of the inner city than the threat of violence that permeates social interactions (Anderson

1999). Research suggests that criminal activity within cities is not evenly distributed across the geographical landscape. Instead, crime, and violence more specifically, often cluster in small geographical areas. Researchers consider these locations to be hotspots for crime and violence since such activities occur more frequently in these areas than in other parts of the city (Braga 2005; Braga et al. 1999; Sherman, Gartin, and Bueger 1989; Sherman and Rogan 1995; Wiesburd and Green 1995). By Forty-sixth Street, the relatively peaceful upper-middle-income neighborhoods are a distant memory, traded for neighborhoods too commonly riddled with violence. In 2008 the area north of Forty-sixth Street experienced four murders, while the area south of Forty-sixth Street witnessed forty murders, evidence of a continuum of violence that is common to many urban areas (see Anderson 1999). The farther one travels from the comforts of Indianapolis's northern edge, the closer one gets to those areas that experience the most concentrated violence. And with sixteen murders occurring within a one-mile radius of the Keystone Avenue and Thirty-eighth Street intersection, the area just south of Forty-sixth Street proves to be one of the deadliest in the city.

The East Thirty-eighth Street Area: A Gang's Natural Environment

The intersection of Keystone Avenue and Thirty-eighth Street serves as a geographical anchor for this study. Amid the single-family homes and low-income apartments that line the nearby side roads, local youths form social groups that they define as street gangs. During eighteen months of data collection, I followed gang members beyond those neighborhoods immediately adjacent to the intersection. Their disruptive home lives forced them to transition between multiple living situations. As a result, I spent time in different neighborhoods along East Thirty-eighth Street and talked to an array of people who were involved with gang life. The East Thirty-Eighth area begins about one-half mile west of the Thirty-eighth and Keystone intersection and extends eight miles east to the outer edges of the city. It also extends one mile north of Thirty-eighth Street to Forty-sixth Street and one mile south to Thirtieth Street. Like so many other urban communities where gangs are present, the East Thirty-eighth Street area is poor, has a large number of minority residents, and is home to high levels of violence.

The East Thirty-eighth Street area is, indeed, one of the most violent in the city of Indianapolis. In 2008, these sixteen square miles accounted for 30 of the city's 114 murders. The murder rate for this area was approximately 60 per 100,000 persons, which was significantly higher the than the city's rate of 17 per 100,000 persons.[7] Murders were also not evenly distributed. Three of the census tracts had homicide rates as high as 102, 127, and 216, per 100,000, while five census tracts had no murders. As previously noted, murders were concentrated near the Thirty-eighth and Keystone intersection but remained scattered throughout the eastern portion of the area. Some census tracts a few miles east of Thirty-eighth and Keystone had homicide rates of 78 and 97 per 100,000. Located near the eastern edge of the research site, Post Road has a well-deserved reputation for violence, and 2008 was no exception: five people were murdered along Post Road, most in and around apartments located near Forty-second Street.

Data from thirteen census tracts covering the area suggest that 82 percent of the residents living in these sixteen-square miles are racial minorities, and a relatively high number of them live in poverty. The median household income for this area is $28,309, and overall, nearly 26 percent of families live in poverty. These numbers suggest that the area is generally poorer than most of Indianapolis, which has a median annual household income of $43,351 and a 17 percent poverty rate. Nine of the fifteen census tracts in the research site are poverty areas, with at least 20 percent of households living in poverty. One census tract is an extreme poverty area, with more than 55 percent of households living in poverty. Of the remaining census tracts, only one area has less than 10 percent of families living in poverty.

One would be remiss to provide a monolithic depiction of local residents, although they are relatively poor. Pockets of relative affluence can be found near obvious signs of poverty. Although eight tracts have median family incomes below $30,000 a year, the median income of three census tracts is above $40,000 a year. The poorest tracts are located near the Keystone Avenue and Thirty-eighth Street intersection. Traveling east from that intersection, poverty areas are intermixed with more prosperous areas. Even within these specific tracts financial situations vary, as symbols of economic status can change considerably block by block. Sections of rundown or abandoned homes are sometimes

TABLE 1.2

Census Tract Description of Primary Research Area

Census tract	% minority	% below poverty	Poverty area	Population	Murders	Murder rate per 100,000
3226	86	27	Yes	3,026	2	66
3227	99	17	No	1,547	0	0
3308.01	86	39	Yes	7,181	4	56
3308.02	63	26	Yes	5,733	2	35
3309	90	30	Yes	5,222	2	38
3310	94	25	Yes	4,046	0	0
3505	96	26	Yes	1,966	2	102
3506	96	19	No	5,503	7	127
3507	85	8	No	1,897	0	0
3508	98	55	Yes/ extreme	2,774	6	216
3601.02	81	30	Yes	2,570	2	78
3602.01	47	23	Yes	3,103	3	97
3602.02	58	19	No	3,680	0	0

SOURCES: United State Census Bureau 2010b; *Indianapolis Star,* Marion County Homicide Map, 2008.

positioned next to a group of well-maintained houses. In some places, low-income apartment complexes are located within a few blocks of large middle-class homes. Even in the poorest neighborhoods, residents living in abject poverty are often living among people with enough income to maintain their homes and drive newer cars.

The East Thirty-eighth Street area is actually more economically secure than some communities found in neighboring cities. For example, significantly higher levels of poverty plague the Over the Rhine community on Cincinnati's near north side. Data from fifteen census tracts covering much of that community reveal approximately 51 percent of residents living in poverty. Some census tracts display poverty levels as high as 79 percent (see census tract 0017). The median family income for that area is slightly over 16,749 dollars annually, and some census tracts reveal shocking levels of poverty with median incomes under 8,000 dollars per year (see census tract 0009). The poverty levels in Cincinnati,

though exceedingly high, can also be found in other cities close to
Indianapolis. A quick examination of Chicago and Detroit reveals census tracts that display poverty levels close to or above 90 percent.[8] One
also need not search extensively to find enclaves of concentrated poverty
in St. Louis, where poverty rates exceed 40 percent more frequently than
they do in Indianapolis. The contrast between poor neighborhoods in
Indianapolis and those in neighboring cities is another reminder that the
city has remained relatively resistant to the social consequences of recent
economic changes. The poor are not as numerous or as concentrated in
Indianapolis as they are in other cities.

Such variation influences the social and cultural dynamics in
communities, and the degree and distribution of poverty in the East
Thirty-eighth Street area likely produces a unique social setting. The
distribution of poverty can influence interaction patterns between city
residents. William Julius Wilson (1987 and 1996), for example, argues
that African Americans living in areas of concentrated poverty are
socially isolated from both conventional institutions and culture. As
high-paying, low-skill industrial jobs leave urban areas and members of
the middle class migrate away from city centers, become unemployed, or
settle for low-paying jobs in service industries, fewer individuals living
in these areas have meaningful ties with mainstream persons or institutions. This trend can have a transformative affect on community culture.
Residents in these communities may decreasingly see the tangible rewards
of mainstream values such as hard work and education, and they become
therefore, less willing to pursue such endeavors. Moreover, the shared
experience of living in concentrated poverty produces a number of
cultural adaptations, which leads to what Wilson calls ghetto-related
behavior. Street gangs represent one such adaptation, as youths spurn
traditional avenues of success for an alternative pathway that helps them
resolve both practical and momentary problems. Given that ghetto-
related adaptations are directly related to concentrated poverty and
social isolation, their prevalence and intensity should vary across cities.
The pervasiveness and concentration of gangs in cities should also vary,
leading to unique intergang environments.

In Indianapolis, the intergang environment does seem to reflect
the broader social milieu of the city. For example, most residents living
in the East Thirty-eighth Street community do not seem to be socially

isolated, perhaps because the area is not generally characterized by extreme poverty. They live among and interact with people of varying economic levels who embrace divergent cultural models. It is not uncommon to encounter a college-educated person in the same social setting as someone who dropped out of high school. Streetwise ex-cons interact with local business people, active gang members socialize with college students, and honest pastors with advanced degrees mingle with street criminals. The area displays a remarkable level of what David Harding calls cultural heterogeneity, or "the presence of a diverse array of competing and conflicting cultural models" (2010, 143). Street gangs merely represent one cultural model that has a strong, but not ubiquitous, presence in the East Thirty-eighth Street area. Given this dynamic, gang members are also not socially isolated or confined to small geographic locations. They often interact with youths from different neighborhoods, freely move about the city, and contribute to a diverse intergang environment.

Defined here as "any durable, street oriented youth group whose involvement in illegal activity is part of its group identity" (Klein 2005, 136), the gangs of this community, and Indianapolis in general, are varied. Fluid and overlapping labels, different types of affiliations, and dissimilarities in commitment to gang life characterize the intergang environment. Some gang members pledge affiliations to national gangs based in Chicago, like the Black Gangster Disciples or the Conservative Vice Lords, and many older members remain invested in the more formal aspects of these gangs (see Knox and Papachristos 2002; Knox 2006). The degree to which these affiliates are actually connected to their organized counterparts in Chicago is somewhat ambiguous. I encountered a few older gang members who claimed to be directly connected to Chicago gangs through their position within a national leadership structure. For example, one older gang member said that he attended an annual meeting of gang leaders and had a distinct oversight role in the city of Indianapolis. Moreover, he indicated that the gang was organized and extensively involved in dealing drugs. Other gang members supported his claims, and he did display an ability to move through different neighborhoods counseling younger gang members, but such statements were generally difficult to validate.[9] Many others in this study also claimed to be high-ranking, four-star generals in national gangs. Such labels seemed to be used freely in the city and, at times, arbitrarily by anyone trying to sound important. Teenage gang members also claimed affiliation with these well-known gangs, but their connection to an organized national gang structure was, again, questionable. When speaking about their gang, some mentioned rules, internal discipline, a hierarchy, gang literature, and other elements common to more organized gangs, but such accounts were inconsistent and confused.

Although many of the younger generation of gang members claim affiliation to Chicago-based gangs, they are more likely to orient their gang activity around hoods and smaller clique structures. Even when they do claim affiliation to a national gang, their commitment to a clique or a hood is often more salient in their daily lives. Hoods can represent broader communities such as Haughville on the city's west side, more specific neighborhoods like Post Road on the far east side, or specific apartment complexes like "the Balt" located near Keystone and Thirtieth Street. Gang members representing these geographical areas may or may not be affiliated with smaller cliques, which are typically made up of twenty to seventy-five friends and family members who give themselves a name and adopt a gang identity. The East Thirty-eighth Street area is host to a number of cliques, hoods, and groups that use the names of national gangs. For example, many youths use the city's east–west roads as an indication of clique or hood affiliations. Although a number of hood gangs, such as Twenty-first Street or Tenth Street, can be found in the poor east-side neighborhoods located just south of the Thirty-eighth Street corridor, few claim territory north of Forty-sixth Street. Within the Thirty-eighth Street corridor, however, nearly every major east–west road (Thirtieth Street, Thirty-fourth Street, and Forty-second Street) is affiliated with a hood gang.

These hood gangs and cliques generally resemble the unorganized gangs located in other emergent gang cities, or those cities with a limited history of gang activity (see Klein 1995; Miller 2001; Decker and Van Winkle 1996; Decker, Bynum, and Weisel 1998). They lack stable leadership, established rules, and a system of internal discipline. Members' endeavors are not particularly focused, and groups do not specialize in a specific criminal activity. Gang members commonly deal drugs, but they typically operate autonomously. They are responsible for gaining access to drugs, and they keep all of the profits. Some gang members, in fact, vehemently reject the wisdom and utility of being a part of a more organized system that fronts them drugs and forces them to pay dues. They do not want to share their profits or lose their autonomy by acquiring debt. More generally, the criminal activities of these gangs are sporadic, as members opportunistically but inconsistently engage in different criminal endeavors. As will be noted throughout this book, gang members fight, rob people, and break into houses, yet most of their time is spent just hanging out. During these uneventful times gang members are very similar to non-gang-member youths in the community.

Primarily located within the East Thirty-eighth Street area, the Down for Whatever Boyz (DFW Boyz) exemplify such a group. The DFW Boyz was formed a few years before I began my research by a group of teenagers who lived in the same apartment complex. Shawn and Layboy, who were central figures in this study, were vital to this process. The boys had been in the streets since they were small children, and they often fondly recounted the days when their activities included stealing bikes and dogs. Their street-oriented activities escalated during their teenage years. Positioned in the middle of a large extended family, Shawn and Layboy had both older relatives invested in the streets and younger siblings who mimicked their way of life. Connections to older and more influential street figures provided them insight into gangs and street life. Shawn and Layboy were strong, attractive, intelligent, articulate teenagers who naturally drew a following of peers. When these attributes were combined with their position in a large local family, they had access to a pool of impressionable kids who were loyal and willing to learn. Together they formed the DFW Boyz.

Affiliation with the DFW Boyz was not mutually exclusive with other hood or national gang affiliations. For example, Layboy and Shawn lived in the East Thirty-eighth Street area and identified themselves as DFW Boyz, but, because they had lived on the west side of Indianapolis as children, they also claimed affiliation with the west-side hood of Haughville. Moreover, Layboy claimed to be a member of the Insane Vice Lords, while Shawn pledged allegiance to the Gangster Disciples. Their fellow DFW Boyz also had affiliations with other gangs or hoods. Some DFW Boyz claimed Forty-second Street, while others claimed Thirty-fourth Street. Some DFW Boyz claimed the far east side hood of Post Road, while others claimed the Balt. Within the group, Gangster

Disciples intermixed with Vice Lords, Bloods, and individuals who claimed no affiliation to national gangs. A year prior to the start of this research, the group even "cliqued up," or joined forces with a few other groups to form an informal conglomerate under a new name. The DFW Boyz collectively distanced themselves from this new name only after the conglomeration was publically associated with a string of burglaries in the city. Despite various hood and national gang affiliations, members of the clique were united around the idea of being part of the DFW Boyz, which was their primary loyalty.

Since its inception, the gang had maintained durability for a few years, but more recent movement had dispersed its members. The group's activities were originally concentrated in and around an apartment complex on the city's far east side, but intense police pressure and member movement caused the group to become fragmented. At the time of my research, Layboy and Shawn lived about five miles from the location that birthed the DFW Boyz. The gang therefore lacked cohesion but still thrived, as members relied on informal subgroups that were positioned throughout the city. Shawn and Layboy were connected to multiple groups in different areas of the city, but they mostly operated in a few East Thirty-eighth Street neighborhoods. They were, therefore, able to travel throughout most the city without negative consequences. Their travels extended well beyond a single neighborhood or even the Thirty-eighth Street community. I accompanied them to locations on the south, west, near north, and far east sides of the city. They also interacted with people who were variably involved in gang life. Still, Shawn and Layboy's daily interactions were typically confined to a select group of peers. Although they infrequently interacted with most DFW Boyz, Layboy and Shawn were very close to members who either lived close to them or were family members. These individuals were also central figures in this study.

In addition to being durable, the group displayed the other defining elements of a street gang. The group's activities were oriented toward the streets, as members routinely met at parties or while hanging out in parks, malls, and street corners. Nearly every member of the DFW Boyz was younger than twenty, and the group's identity focused on criminal activity. The moniker Down for Whatever represented their understanding of the group's defining trait. Members had to be down for whatever or they misrepresented the group. Members understood that the DFW Boyz opportunistically, and somewhat haphazardly, pursued criminal activities that provided them with meager sums of money. Some gang members sold drugs, but this was not a defining element of the gang's identity. More often they robbed people, broke into houses, or stole merchandise. A more prominent part of the gang's identity involved a willingness and ability to fight whenever needed.

The informal nature of the DFW Boyz is a microcosm of gang life in Indianapolis. Mixed, overlapping, and, at times, fluid affiliations create a complex and confusing intergang environment. The general heterogeneity in the community, marked by mixed interactions, creates widespread exposure to gang life so that the boundaries of gang affiliation become blurred. Youth come into the area, either to live or to visit, and interact with gang members. Gang affiliations are then variably embraced and sporadically employed by youths who may or may not have actual connections to gangs. Moreover, in the continuous cycle of movement and maturation, new groups form and seek to stake their claim in the streets. Amid such an environment, self-defined gang members struggle to establish a clear and widely embraced understanding of what it actually means to be in a gang. The intergang environment in Indianapolis is, therefore, characterized by uncertainty, a dynamic that dramatically influences intergang interactions.

A FIELD OF GANGS: BOUNDING A GANG'S SOCIAL ENVIRONMENT

Gangs are not isolated in the streets of Indianapolis; their social environment is characterized by mutual interaction. These interactions are a focal concern to gang members, who, in a manner consistent with their adolescence, spend an inordinate amount of energy assessing the characteristics and actions of others. Individuals who are active and invested in the streets typically operate with impressively in-depth understandings of the gangs in both their surrounding community and the city in general. In Indianapolis, gang members living and operating on the city's far east side are familiar with the various cliques and gangs in other parts of the city. Their working knowledge includes elaborate impressions of different gangs and gang members. Conversations between friends or fellow gang members often represent a collective effort to label other groups.

In time, one comes to understand that a specific gang operating near Thirtieth Street and Central Avenue "don't play around" and should not be messed with. Or, the gang located in the apartments along East Twenty-first Street is weak and talks too much. Although some of this focus is the inevitable byproduct of the dangers that stem from intergang conflict, much of it reflects large numbers of teenagers and young adults belonging to an extended network of similar groups. Being in a gang is meaningful, and the characteristics and actions of other so-called gangs provide a frame of reference that can either be admired or mocked.

For the average gang member, other gangs become known through direct contact or street gossip. Contact between members of different gangs occurs fairly regularly, as they attend the same schools, go to the same parties or clubs, share jail time with each other, and at times even live in the same apartment complexes. Some members of the DFW Boyz, for example, had been kicked out of so many schools that they established contacts with gangs on each side of Indianapolis. Frequent, and often hostile, banter on networking Web sites signifies another avenue for interactions between members of different gangs. Even if an individual does not have direct contact with another gang, he or she is likely to hear about it. Conversations routinely focus on which cliques or hoods were represented at the latest party or the current status of an ongoing street beef (conflict). Although no single gang is fully knowledgeable about the happenings of the street, each gang actively observes and evaluates other similar groups.

Thus each gang is embedded in a complex environment characterized by mutual awareness and interaction. Conceptualizing such an environment requires a theoretical construct that can adequately account for large numbers of similar groups. Organizational theorists have created and utilized various theoretical concepts to represent aggregations of similar collectivities (Benson 1975; DiMaggio and Powell 1991; Fligstein 2001; Kenis and Knoke 2002; Scott and Meyer 1991; Warren 1967). An organizational field, for example, is a social construct that represents "those organizations that, in aggregate, constitute a recognized area of social life" (DiMaggio and Powell, 1991, 64). By grouping similar organizations, researchers have been able to study the formation and maturation of a field, its relationship with other social arenas, interogazational influences within that field, and those in-field pressures placed on a focal organization or members of that organization (for examples see Brint and Karabel 1991; DiMaggio 1991; Fligstein 1991; Lune and Martinez 1999). By applying the notion of a field to the intergang environment, researchers can better frame an array of important empirical and theoretical issues. This study, for example, is concerned with how pressures within the intergang environment, particularly in relation to the construction of field boundaries, influences gang member behavior.

Although most gangs cannot be accurately described as organizations (Klein 1995; Klein and Maxson 2006), street gangs when combined do represent a distinct area of social life. Scholars have largely neglected to develop theoretical ideas about the collection of gangs in a given area. More importantly, studies have undertheorized the content of intergang interactions. Studies that do examine such interactions focus only on the existence and consequences of conflict between gangs (Decker 1996; Decker and Van Winkle 1996; Klein 1971; Short and Strodtbeck 1974). The complexity of intergang interactions encompasses more than conflict, as gang members continually observe, interpret, and evaluate the actions of individuals representing other gangs. However, before this process can be examined, three basic characteristics of the intergang field must be clarified.

Establishing Field Boundaries

Given that a field represents a collection of similar groups, individuals invested in the concept must decide which groups do and do not belong in the field. Often researchers attempt to objectively establish such a boundary through a systematic selection process. For example, to ensure cross-study consistency, gang researchers have openly debated the definition of a gang (Ball and Curry 1995; Bjerregaard 2002; Esbensen et al. 2001; Klein 1995; Klein 2005; Winfree et al. 1992). When attempting to define the boundary of an intergang field, a researcher can use a widely accepted definition of "gang" to appropriately identify which groups belong in the intergang field. Meticulous application of this generally agreed-upon definition reduces the possibility of false labeling. For the sake of research, the parameters of that field are further limited to a geographical area (all gangs in Indianapolis) or empirically derived through network analysis. Thus when one uses a widely accepted method to distinguish gang members from non–gang members, the boundaries of the intergang field are clearly defined, and one can be certain that all groups are appropriately labeled.

Fields can be defined externally, but they are not just artificial constructs created for research. They are meaningful to participants, and researchers must examine how groups come to define their social environment (DiMaggio 1991; Fligstein 2001). Detached from academic discussions of gang definitions or concerns about cross-research consistency, gang members are fixated on what a gang is and what it means to be a gang member. Each member forms an individualized understanding of the requirements needed not only for inclusion into his or her focal gang but also for the greater gang environment. Some groups are labeled as real gangs, while other groups do not meet the established standards. In many fields that are unrelated to street gangs, such individualized understanding about the location of a field boundary does not lead to widespread disagreement. Through mutual interaction, participants in a field often establish agreed-upon standards to determine the outer limits of the field boundary. Those groups that belong to and are accepted as viable members of a field share similar goals, functions, output, and appearance/structures, or meet a formalized standard that may come from practices like accreditation (DiMaggio and Powell 1991; Scott and Meyer 1991). Agreement produces environmental certainty, as it assures a focal group that inclusion into the field will be met with unanimous acceptance.

If objective standards create general agreement about field boundaries, the opposite can also be true. In the absence of objective standards, a field will be characterized by widespread disagreement and general uncertainty about which groups do and do not belong. This dynamic is more representative of the intergang environment in Indianapolis. Without agreed-upon standards, individualized understandings of gangs are fairly inconsistent between gangs and gang members. Each member subjectively forms his or her understanding of "gang" through personal experience, so there are as many definitions of the term "street gang" as there are definers. This profoundly impacts the field, as each invested gang or gang member has a different understanding of who is and who is not a part of the general gang environment. The resulting uncertainty impacts the everyday actions and concerns of gang members.

Intergroup Interactions

Another essential characteristic of the intergang field involves the multifaceted social connections between different street gangs. Researchers have understandably focused on the role of threat or conflict in the context of these interactions. Conflict between gangs or gang members is associated with the formation of gangs, group cohesion, and contagious violence (Decker 1996; Klein 1971; Papachristos 2009; Thrasher 1967). Driven by systematic efforts to thwart gang violence, scholars have also begun to trace the existence or absence of conflict between known gangs in a given city (Kennedy, Braga, and Piehl 2001; McGloin 2005; Tita, Riley, and Greenwood 2001). Yet focusing only on the presence or absence of intergang conflict oversimplifies the content of such ties. It also does not provide much insight into the interactive process that leads to intergang conflict. Rarely do members of different gangs engage each other violently without a history predicated on patterned interactions. Expanding theoretical conceptions of intergang ties beyond conflict or threat can actually lead to new insights that may help explain intergang conflict.

The concept of an intergang field provides a basic framework for examining another powerful dynamic common to intergang interactions. Since the notion of "gang" is meaningful to gang members, and they are invested in establishing a field boundary, intergang interactions are often characterized by an interpretive process whereby all involved assess others' right to belong. Inconsistent understandings about the meaning of "street gang" and "gang member" lead to a general lack of agreement about the boundary of the field. So while gang members perceive themselves to be a viable part of the intergang field, others may disagree. Such external assessments are indeed prevalent in the intergang environment and are vital to understanding gang interactions. Intergang interactions can, at times, be dominated by overt dismissals in which one's gang affiliation is openly mocked. More often, gang members are aware that peers evaluate them, and they are therefore motivated to demonstrate their place within the field boundary. Both aspects of intergang interactions precede, and can induce, conflict.

Legitimacy

The gang and gang member must be studied as elements within an intergang field. Lacking agreed-upon standards that clearly establish a boundary, the intergang field in and around Indianapolis is characterized by widespread disagreement and uncertainty. This uncertainty fundamentally shapes intergang interactions, as gang members use individualized understandings about the meaning of "gang" and "gang membership" to accept or reject peers who claim to be a part of the intergang field. This process becomes most problematic when an outsider claims that a self-defined gang or gang member is being inauthentic. When disagreements arise about the authenticity of a gang or gang member, all invested parties are confronted with a problem of legitimacy. According to Mark Suchman, "Legitimacy is a generalized perception or assumption that the actions of an entity are desirable, proper, or appropriate within some socially constructed system of norms, values, beliefs, and definitions" (1995, 574). Interactions within the intergang environment are the avenues through which assessments of legitimacy are made. They are also the medium that creates the norms, values, beliefs, and definitions used to make such evaluations. Establishing legitimacy is simple when everyone involved in a given social milieu reaches a general understanding about the requirements needed for acceptance; an individual or group simply needs to meet those standards. When agreement does not exist, however, and involved parties are still making evaluations about legitimacy, the process of establishing legitimacy becomes problematic. This is the case in the intergang environment.

The gang members in this study are caught in a constant struggle for legitimacy, which is gained not from conventional society but from the assessments of other gangs or the intergang environment. Self-defined gang members strongly believe that their group is a gang and that they are gang members. Yet the intergang environment is skeptical of those claims, as too many youths falsely assert gang affiliation or embrace a weakened version of a gang. Accordingly, these individuals are not considered to be real gang members. They are perceived to be positioned outside the intergang field and are treated accordingly. Thus each gang member struggles to validate his or her claim of gang membership to the broader gang environment. Without fieldwide agreement about the norms, values, beliefs, and definitions needed to establish legitimacy, each claimant is left without a clear method to attain legitimacy. This is the paradox of legitimacy. A dubious intergang environment forces gang members to seek out legitimacy, but it does not provide any objective criteria for establishing legitimacy.

CONCLUSION

The intergang environment is not a concept specific to the city of Indianapolis. Street gangs reside in most, if not all, cities, and gang members interact frequently enough to establish mutual awareness. Moreover, the construction of the intergang field, through the establishment of environmental boundaries, is also a general process that can, and should, be examined in other cities. This process is, however, influenced by variations in social networks that guide social interaction. To the degree that a community or group of people is socially isolated, their social interactions will be limited to a relatively small number of people and will produce similar cultural ideas. In an isolated community where mutual interaction is high, the establishment of a field boundary should be clear and disagreements should be minimal. When social isolation is not evident, interactions are mixed and divergent ideas emerge. In impoverished urban communities that do not exemplify high levels of social isolation, street gangs still emerge and are an option for many youth. Yet diversity in interactions creates numerous ideas about the boundaries of the intergang environment. Not everyone in Indianapolis agrees about the meaning of "gang," and this produces both high levels of uncertainty in the intergang environment and a constant struggle for legitimacy. Such a dynamic may not be perfectly reflected in other cities. Fluctuations in concentrated poverty may influence the degree of social isolation in cities, and this may influence the level of uncertainty within intergang environments. With the possible exception of prisons, however, communities are rarely fully isolated, and within these communities different ideas about the parameters of the intergang environment coexist. The struggle for legitimacy in the intergang environment probably exists in most cities, though the nature of the struggle varies.

This pursuit of legitimacy reflects a continuous and enduring cultural process whereby gang members create and negotiate various cultural artifacts that provide meaning to daily life. The idea of being a real gang member is one such artifact that is meaningful, yet subject to the subtleties of social interactions. Gang members, often through routine conversation, discuss what "gang" means. Moreover, they contrast real gang members with supposedly fake gang members, which allows them to develop a set of behavioral expectations for real gang members. These culturally proscribed expectations then shape their interpretations of situations and cause them to "do gang," or act in a manner that real gang members are supposed to act, so that they are not labeled fake. They also embrace and contribute to broader cultural narratives that both contribute to the uncertainty in Indianapolis's intergang environment and reinforce the need to gain and maintain legitimacy in that environment.

Considerations of field boundaries and legitimacy arise only after one joins a gang and embraces a gang identity. Understanding the precursors of membership provides insight into the reasons why some gang members remain heavily invested in the idea of being a gang member. Moreover, examining the origins of gang membership reveals a fundamental contradiction that is common to gang life. For many youth, the street gang serves as a stabilizing force in the midst of relative chaos. But gang membership is also accompanied by entrance into the intergang environment, and subsequent intergang interactions are fraught with uncertainly, angst, and even violence.

CHAPTER 2

Joining a Gang

As was often the case in the course of my research, I was ending a day by driving a few members of the DFW Boyz to their desired locations. Accompanying me were brothers Layboy and Shawn, and their cousin TJ. The boys defined certain settings as turf, but their movement through Indianapolis was not defined by geography. The original members of the gang knew each other from hanging out in a far-east-side neighborhood, but few resided there anymore. Layboy and Shawn, for example, had created so many problems in their far-east-side recent apartment complex that their mother was again forced to move. They had also been kicked out of multiple high schools in the city and were attending a school far from home. This movement allowed them to expand their social connections, so that they asked to be dropped off in many different locations.

Layboy and Shawn's neighborhood and school situations were rather fluid, and their living situation was even less specific. Their mother, grandmother, and aunt all lived in different locations along Thirty-eighth Street, and, at various times during the course of my research, each location seemed to be the boys' primary place of residence. For a while, they were even living with a community leader, until he kicked them out for their gang activities. In the past, their mother had ignored petty criminal behavior, but with her sons getting older she had become worrisome and hounded them about their activities. Her concerns were undoubtedly reasonable, as Shawn and Layboy's entire family seemed involved in gang activity. To the boys her fears were an unnecessary annoyance. They found more freedom at TJ's apartment, and their aunt, TJ's mother, seemed to function as their primary caregiver. On this day, however, sixteen-year-old Layboy told me that he would be living with another brother, Aaron, age twenty, who had recently rented an apartment on the city's far east side.

Heading east on Thirty-eighth Street, I relinquished control of the radio as Layboy turned up the local hip-hop station. Although music often monopolized the trips I made as the boys' driver, these drives proved to be invaluable for understanding the concerns of teenagers. When the car was full, the guys would openly converse about what was going on in the streets. They would also talk about topics ranging from girls, to parties, to specific boys who were rapping (talking negatively) about the gang. Sometimes the drives provided opportunities to ask questions. On rare occasions, the boys candidly talked about the more intimate and difficult aspects of their lives. Without displaying an awareness that comes with maturity, they, in passing, mentioned lifelong struggles with anger, poverty, or family members. On this day, however, music dominated as we traveled without much conversation.

Turning my vehicle into a far-east-side apartment complex, I was reminded that many of the low-rent apartments scattered about Thirty-eighth Street appeared relatively well maintained. Even the most notorious apartment complexes did not initially appear poorly kept, and one had to look closely to find evidence of physical disrepair. This particular apartment complex was quite ordinary. It resembled some of the complexes that my fellow graduate students were living in at that time in Bloomington, Indiana. There were no signs of vice in or around the apartments, and, with the exception of unmarked police cars that were routinely staked out in the complex, I rarely saw signs of vice all summer. The most prominent characteristic of the small one-bedroom apartment was its emptiness. The living room, dining room, and kitchen were completely bare. The only thing in the apartment was an air mattress that was being used as a bed. The apartment also did not seem to contain any food. In fact, throughout that summer, I would often arrive at the apartment to find a few hungry teenagers hoping that I would buy them food at a local fast-food restaurant. This was hardly an attractive place to live, especially when contrasted with the larger and better-furbished apartment that Layboy's aunt lived in.

Layboy's desire and ability to live with his brother in this empty one-bedroom apartment reflected his rather chaotic life. Despite multiple adults taking some role in raising Layboy, no one was willing or able to limit the time he spent in the apartment. Although he was only sixteen years old, Layboy was generally unsupervised, and he would run the streets late into the night. At times during the summer when I would come by the apartment late in the morning, it would reek of marijuana, and a few girls would be lounging about. More frequently, Layboy would inform me about a fight, party, or robbery that he had participated in since we last talked. Even Shawn usually chose not to stay at the apartment because "too much stuff" was going on there. His aunt's apartment provided Shawn unlimited access to the streets, but it also provided a respite if needed. Layboy, however, found the constant activity of Aaron's apartment too enticing to leave behind.

The instability in Layboy's life was not just a temporary state associated with his current living situation. It had been consistent throughout his entire life. There are many possible indices of instability, and Layboy and his brothers experienced poverty, a troubled family life, numerous moves, and exposure to drugs, gangs, and violence at an early age. They also had complete access to the streets during their preadolescent years. Although no singular pathway leads to gang membership (Thornberry et al. 2003), the individuals in this study often had a story similar to Layboy's. For most gang members, gang life represented either a possible solution to an unresolved problem or an option embraced after repeated contacts with friends or family. For some members, a street gang provided an attractive substitute for a disagreeable home life, or it provided friendship and protection when needed most. Other members viewed gang life as a chance to increase illicit moneymaking opportunities made attractive by overt poverty. Or, they perceived gang life to be a quick avenue for gaining respect in the streets, and they were also attracted to a lifestyle of unrestrained hedonism. For all gang members, the gang provided a reliable network of peers who were invested in both a unified identity and the preservation of self and close associates. The relationships formed within the gang were often tight, and gang members viewed their close associates as being part of the family rather than just members of the same group. They became "my boys," "my bros," or "my niggas." As such, in the midst of instability and chaotic life circumstances, the gang provided the illusion of stability.

BECOMING A GANG MEMBER

Most youths do not join gangs. National data indicate that about 5 percent of youths have been in a gang, and 2 percent are currently in a gang (Klein and Maxson 2006). Even in at-risk communities, 70 to 80 percent of youths do not join gangs (ibid.). For those invested in gang life, membership is merely a significant turning point in the course of a complicated and often troubled life. Rarely are youths arbitrarily targeted by gangs and coerced to join. Rather, gang membership is the result of a series of life conditions that make gang life appear attractive or necessary. Although there is no single combination of circumstances and events that deterministically leads to gang membership (Thornberry et al. 2003), there are factors associated with gang membership. When compared to their non-gang peers, for example, gang members are more likely to experience negative life events, be unsupervised by adults, display nondelinquent problem behaviors, and associate with friends who participate in delinquent activities and/or exhibit pro-gang attitudes (Craig et al. 2002; Eitle, Gunkel, and Van Gundy 2004; Esbensen and Deschenes 1998; Esbensen and Weerman 2005; Gatti et al. 2005; Hill et al. 1999; Klein and Maxson 2006; Maxson, Whitlock, and Klein 1998; Thornberry et al. 2003). Moreover, the transition into gang membership is enhanced by other factors that motivate an individual to pursue gang membership. Scott Decker and Barrik Van Winkle (1996) report that some prospective gang members are pulled into gang life by attractive opportunities to make fast money or gain status in the streets. Other prospective gang members are pushed into gang life by family/peer influence, or because they need protection in a threatening environment.

When recounting the events and circumstances that eventually led to gang activity, individuals in this study often told stories fraught with generalized instability and chaos. They recalled how troubled households either forced them to find refuge in gang life or gave them the opportunity to run the streets at an early age. Confronted with the reality of street life, they found protection, status, opportunities to make money, and a sense of belonging in gang life. They often viewed joining a gang as a resolution to an array of difficult life circumstances.

Family Life and Street Participation

A common theme in research is that gang membership represents an attractive alternative to a deficient and troublesome home life (Eitle, Gunkel, and Van Gundy 2004). Multiple researchers note the presence of abuse, disruption, and hostility in the homes of gang members (Fleisher 1998; Miller 2001; Moore 1978 and 1991; Vigil 1991), causing some researchers to view gangs as surrogate families (Moore 1978 and 1991; Vigil 1991). Broader and more representative studies typically agree that gang members are more likely than non-gang peers to have dysfunctional home lives, but the exact reasons for such dysfunction remain somewhat unclear (Craig et al. 2002). Although research generally concludes that low levels of parental supervision are associated with gang membership, findings are less supportive for single-parent family structures and low parent/child attachment (for a good review see Klein and Maxson 2006). Furthermore, studies examining levels of family deviance and family hostility exhibit mixed findings (ibid.). The gang members in this study consistently identified family problems as being a reason for their gang activity, but such problems typically did not directly lead to gang membership. Instead, family life caused prospective gang members to enter the streets at an early age, and conditions in the streets eventually produced the motivation to join a street gang.

In the East Thirty-eighth Street area of Indianapolis, home life must be understood within the context of neighborhood environments. Each family is positioned in close proximity to the seductive lure of the streets. Organized around illicit markets and an underground economy, the streets are a ghetto institution regulated by extralegal and often violent activities. The streets socialize impressionable youths on the ways of adulthood by reinforcing the importance of toughness, street smarts, virility, and autonomy, while also teaching youths that violence is an appropriate response to disagreements or personal affronts (Anderson 1999; Oliver 1994 and 2006). For youths, there are strong attractions to street life. Teenagers uninterested in deferred gratification can find the promise of fast cash, material possessions, drugs, status, wanton sexual activity, and unfettered freedoms in the streets. Consequently, parenting in proximity to the streets is accompanied by unique challenges. And while the negative consequences of family instability, generalized dysfunction, and child maltreatment are universal, children in the inner city simply have different options than their rural and suburban counterparts.[1] They often turn to the streets.

Unrestrained participation in street activity during pre- and early adolescence typically precedes gang membership, and such access to the streets is largely controlled by family environment. Most households within the Thirty-eighth Street community embrace cultural ideas that directly oppose alternative ideas found in the streets, and parents seek to limit their children's access to street life. Therefore, many youths experience intense conflict between home life and street life, which typically reduces their desire and/or ability to routinely participate in street life. Devon, a college student who grew up in the East Thirty-eighth Street area but did not become invested in the streets, remembered how his mother constantly monitored his activities:

> Oh, she was very strict, and I think that that's one of the reasons why I stayed out of trouble. That's the biggest reason right there. When the lights came on, we had to be in the house. She didn't play about that. Like I said, she was in the church, so she would always make us go on Friday nights. It's funny how all the old people used to do it because on Friday and Saturday night we always going to church. We like, "Why we got to go to church on Friday and Saturday night?" But those were the nights where most people do their stuff. I'm realizing that they did that because they wanted us to keep us out of trouble. We always used to go to choir rehearsal. We always had to do Bible study. We had to do those kinds of things. At night she knew where we as at. She was so strict that by the time I got to high school she didn't have to give me a curfew because she conditioned me so much to be in the house. So I would come home straight from school, because we would literally get our butts beat if we didn't come straight home from school first and tell where we was at.

The existence of a conflict between home life and street life decreases one's probability of being exposed to the streets at an early age. Such conflict is often conceptualized as a contrast in cultural orientations; many families in the urban poor areas reject street life (see Anderson 1999; Hannerz 1969). Youths from non-street or "decent" households pursue conventional endeavors like stable employment and education, while those from street-oriented households focus more on street activities. Although such variation is important, households that reject street life must also successfully limit the opportunities children have to participate freely in street activities. Some households that reject street life allow access to the streets by failing to adequately monitor relatively young children. Despite routine exposure to a conflicting cultural model, youths given the opportunity to participate freely in street activities are likely to do so.

In Indianapolis, I found that three non-mutually exclusive home types provided youths access to the streets at an early age. The first involved street-oriented families who were engaged in criminal activities, drugs, and gangs, while they also deemphasized conventional avenues for success, like school performance and steady employment (Anderson 1999; Hannerz 1969). Some of these families directly influenced gang membership by reinforcing pro-gang mentalities. For example, a large number of Layboy and Shawn's extended family were active in the streets. The boys had uncles and older brothers who were heavily invested in gangs, violence, and dealing drugs. Many of Shawn and Layboy's close contacts in the DFW Boyz were also younger brothers, stepbrothers, or cousins. Their sisters and female cousins were also part of the gang as DFW Girlz. Consequently, there was little conflict between family life and street life, and most family members transitioned into gang activities at a young age.

There was also an absence of conflict between family life and street life in families who lacked a strong gang tradition but had a history of engaging in illicit street activities. A parent's participation in illicit street activities often reduced one's desire and ability to monitor his or her child's activities, and it reinforced street life within the family. Gang members often recounted how their guardian's illicit activities both exposed them to street activities and gave them the motivation and opportunity to participate in street life. For example, some gang members noted how their parent's incarceration created uncertain living situations, frustration, insecurity, and allowed them to run the streets unsupervised. When asked about the events that led him to join a gang, Michael, a nineteen-year-old gang member, referenced his childhood living situation: "My family, man. My living situation. My momma's been to prison. My daddy's been to prison. We done live with like four or five different people. Since they been locked up, we had to move from house to house. There wasn't really nobody there you know. So we stayed out in the street." Ronnie, another teenage gang member, discussed how troubled familial relationships and his father's incarceration caused instability in his home life:

> At first I was living on the west side. I lived with my mom for a while, her and my dad got into it. She threw me out of the house, 'cause she wanted to be spiteful toward my dad. I lived with him for a minute. He stayed in trouble with the law, so I had to move back in with my mom. We didn't click well, so I moved in with my grandmother. Everything was cool for a minute, and I guess I moved back in with my mom. Stuff started to get bad. We moved into the projects, and I got introduced to fighting all the time, gang banging, this, that, and the other. That's when I met all my friends basically. Everybody I with now I met at that point in my life.

Youth from street-oriented families experienced little conflict between their street life and their home life. Street culture was often transmitted between generations, and youth in these households were also exposed to an unsettled pace of life. Incarceration, drug addiction, and/or routine late nights diminished parent's desire and ability to monitor their children's activities. With little direct supervision, these children had access to the streets at an early age, and they were more likely than their peers to become involved in street activity.

The second type of home was characterized by apathy, in that parents did not prioritize their children's development or monitor their children's activities. Although some of these families were invested in street life, others were not. For example, Bryan, a former gang member, recounted his childhood by lamenting that his parents' lack of involvement produced not only resentment but also the motivation and opportunity to run the streets:

> From the time I left school, until maybe 10:00 at night I was out. Weekends and summers I was gone all day long. As I got a little older and was into females, I would be out gone even longer. I actually hated the environment that I was in. I would go to friends' houses, and it was completely different. Mom and Dad would play the role of family just like on TV. The house would be clean. I wouldn't see any bugs. So it gave me an outlook that when

I had company over to my house I was ashamed to have people over, especially girls. I never wanted to be home, and mom was always working. She was an LPN, she was always working, and when she got off of work she went to bingo. So she was rarely home to monitor any situation. Pops worked hard and when he came home he went bowling. So when they came home I was just getting in. They didn't really monitor what I was doing. I saw my mom struggle. I can look at it now and see that she mismanaged her money. Pops mismanaged his money. We'd wash our clothes once a month. What the hell am I going to wear to school tomorrow? There's a pair of socks, some old drawers, and some pants that I didn't wear this week. I got old car parts in there 'cause Pops is a car freak, but it's in my room. Sometimes I wouldn't eat so my mom could eat and she was trying to do the same thing. She wouldn't eat so I could eat. Food was scarce. A lot of bad decisions.

Some households that embraced a more conventional lifestyle might not have approved of children engaging in street activity, but they did little to prevent it. Parents might have been unaware that their sons or daughters sold drugs, carried a gun, or were heavily involved with gang activity. Thus youth with apathetic parents or guardians might have experienced some conflict between home life and street activities, but they were not prevented from running the streets.

The third type of home was characterized more by neglect and abuse than by apathy. Killa-Con, a member of the DFW Boyz, recalled how, at the age of thirteen, his mother kicked him out of the house and forced him to fend for himself on the streets:

Like me, I grew up by myself. I moved out here when I was thirteen. As soon as I moved out here my momma put me out. So all I knew was the streets. I grew up on the streets by myself, trying to find somewhere to live, somewhere to sleep, somewhere to try to get something to eat. Try to get some money or whatever. So me growing up like that, ain't nothing else to care about but the streets, that's all I know. I got in because I moved from the west side of Indianapolis and came out east. I started getting cool with everybody out here. I'm already a Vice Lord or whatever. I came out here I met Layboy, one of the DFW Boyz. I met Layboy, they was like, "Shit, you be on the same shit we be on. You be down for whatever too. So why don't you get down with us?" So I got down.

Other prospective gang members sought refuge in the streets after suffering through years of mental and physical abuse.[2] Children who lived in an abusive household might or might not have experienced conflict between home life and street life. If conflict did exist, their desire to escape the home overpowered any attempts by guardians to limit their access to the street. For children who lived in abusive or negligent households, the world outside of their front door was more appealing, and it could offer more hope than the environment behind it.

Conflict, Protection, and Respect

Whether for one day or an extended period of time, leaving home to run the streets places an individual at risk for violent encounters. There is no shortage of reasons why someone might find himself or herself in a threatening situation. While in the process of learning to sell drugs, one may mistakenly conduct business on another person's turf, or mismanage his or her funds and short a drug supplier. Perhaps the individual unknowingly disrespects someone, or insults a peer in an attempt to build up his or her reputation. A sexual partner may make up stories to stir jealousies and induce anger from other interested parties. Or the individual is victimized by a group of local youth that enjoys harassing and beating up easy targets. Given that most gang members report being invested in the streets by the age of thirteen, their actions are initially guided more by naïveté and inexperience than genuine street smarts. The choice to join a gang must, therefore, be understood through the lens of someone in his or her early adolescent years attempting to negotiate a dangerous and violent environment. Lacking information and foresight, many youth view a street gang as a source of protection.

For some gang members in Indianapolis, this need for protection was the direct result of an ongoing conflict or problem that could be potentially resolved by acquiring allies within a street gang. Reggie, an inactive gang member, explained how routine confrontations with gang members in a new neighborhood provided motivation to join a different gang:

> My first involvement in gangs came 'cause the neighborhood I grew up in. Once we moved over there, I have two brothers and a sister, there were three new boys in the neighborhood, and we did not belong to a gang. So the boys in the neighborhood began to jump on us every day, bully us, pressure us, and beat us up. They wanted to fight us just because we were the new guys. Then they wanted to recruit us to be in their gang. But, of course, by us being attacked by them on a regular basis we had no desire to be with that gang. We actually wanted to get even with them. So at some point in time, with us fighting them on a regular basis, one of my cousins came over one weekend and we began to fight as usual. My cousin jumped in. Well, my cousin at that time, we didn't know it, was in another gang. The gang that was jumping us was considered BGD or Disciples. My cousin, at the time, happened to be a member of the Vice Lord gang. So after he got jumped the following week, he was like, "I'm going to get my boys and we'll be back and we'll deal with this. We'll help." He went to get his Vice Lord friends or gang members to help fight the gang that lived in the apartment complex, who were Black Gangster Disciples. They told us they would come over and help us whenever we needed help in exchange for us hanging with them and being apart of their gang. Being affiliated, because they weren't in it just to provide protection to anybody. So if we wanted to get help from other gangs we had to be in a gang. So what initially caused me or led me to join a gang was getting tired of getting jumped by these guys, and here are some guys that's willing to help me. And they happen to be a gang too. So that's about the time when my gang involvement starts.

Gang membership was accompanied by an expectation of mutual support during interpersonal conflicts. Unless a member was viewed as being completely unreasonable, problems with one member usually meant problems with the gang. For the adolescent tired of being beaten up, gang life offered safety in numbers.

This benefit also extended into the day-to-day activities of the street. In addition to providing support during conflicts, established gangs were thought to garner immediate respect for their members. Four DFW Boyz talked about the practical benefits of membership by noting that outsiders understood the consequences of messing with one of their own:

Young-G: They don't respect you when you're really nobody, but when you become somebody they know you get that respect.

Killa-Con: When you by yourself they will whoop your ass. If you walking down the street at two or three in the morning with about thirty-five DFW Boyz, all got on black long sleeve shirts, black shoes, black jeans. Boy rolls by talking about, "Come here." Rest of your clique like, "Nigga what's up, what's happening?" See, they ain't going to let you walk up to this nigga's car by yourself, and you don't know what this nigga is on. They going to be right behind you like, "What's up, if you got something to say you got something to say to all of us."

Shawn: You say it to one of us, you say it to all.

Layboy: Like the situation with him [Young-G], dude pulled up or whatever and tried to holler at him. I said, "Nah, it ain't going to be you holler at him. You holler at him you holler at all of us. You holler at him when all of us right there, you know what I'm saying." We had the gun. Dude just thought he was hard. He was rapping, I was like, "What you want? What's up?"

Ignoring the obvious consequence that mutual obligation actually placed the gang member in the middle of more conflicts, the power of such backing was somewhat intoxicating. For the previously outnumbered individual, this newly acquired reinforcement created a false sense of certainty in an otherwise chaotic environment.

Money and the Gang Lifestyle

Although a threatening environment often compelled an individual to join a gang, others were attracted to gang life by perceived monetary benefits associated with some gangs. In East Thirty-eighth Street neighborhoods, youth were immersed in an environment that pressured them to find illicit means to get money. For some, the source of this pressure came from the immediate consequences of overt poverty. Some children lived in homes that either could not or did not provide basic needs, such as consistent food and adequate clothing. Other children permanently left home at a relatively young age and were forced to survive without parental support. For these youth, who were typically not old enough to enter the legal job market, the opportunity to make quick money through illicit activities was tempting. As Kenny, a sixteen-year-old gang member, recounted:

> I mean you grow up with roaches and rats and all that. Do you know what I mean? Some people working two or three jobs just to take care of their kids. When they still come home, they come home to a shack. I mean clothes and stuff everywhere, holes in the roof, roaches all over the wall. It's crazy—mice running around. They've been living like this forever, man. That's why people sell drugs. People think that we sell drugs because it's cute or something. You got to do what you got to do in order to come up. You don't want to be broke your whole life, you feel me? . . . To be honest I had to sell drugs at a young age, at ten years old, 'cause my little sister and my little brother was starving, you know what I mean? We had nothing to eat, you feel me? My momma tried to work but you can't do fast food restaurants your whole life.

When given the opportunity to run the streets, children living in poverty easily justified illegal activities as being necessary to acquire basic needs. Putting in some work selling drugs could yield enough money to buy food or clothing. Such activities may have also provided preadolescent youth access to meager luxuries, such as junk food, cool clothing, additional cell phone minutes, or the latest CD/music download. These desires were modest, but in the context of overt poverty, motivation was strong.

Although the desire to make money originated from the immediate consequences of overt poverty, youths were quickly immersed in a culture that emphasized conspicuous living (Wright and Decker 1997). In the streets, many youths were attracted to, and experienced, albeit very briefly, a lifestyle of self-indulgence characterized by desperate partying and superficial displays of independence (Jacobs and Wright 1999; Shover and Honaker 1992; Wright, Brookman, and Bennett 2006; Wright and Decker 1997). For example, Nikki, an eighteen-year-old inactive gang member, remembered the days when she was dating a temporarily successful drug-dealing gang member:

> The money. The flashiness. The lifestyle. I was sixteen, going to the club and drinking expensive stuff. And it was like, "Shit, my momma don't even drink this expensive champagne." I'm getting money from my boyfriend, and he's got his Chevy on 24's [tire or rim size]. It's the lifestyle that attracts the females to them. But they got to know in the long run they going to leave them. But you don't think that way when you in it. When you in the situation, you riding in the Chevy, he bought you an outfit, hell he might even bought you a car. But you don't think about it until, shit, he go to jail, you get pregnant, and he leaves you. That's what I think attracts a lot of people. That's what I think attracted me, the lifestyle. I enjoyed being around and kicking it, just hanging out.

Such extravagance is the exception and not the rule, but displays of financial solvency often provide the impression that the streets are lucrative. The reality of street life is much more modest; most people invested in illicit moneymaking endeavors earn just enough to support their party and/or drug habits (Bourgois 1999; Fleisher 1998; Jacobs 1999; Jacobs and Wright, 1999; Levitt and Venkatesh 2000; Wright and Decker 1997). The allure of fast cash is always present in the streets, however, and despite being positioned in the poorest urban communities, there are ample opportunities to make money. The underground economy is nearly synonymous with street life, and there are wide-ranging hustles that allow people to make money and access the rewards of street life (Venkatesh 2006). Youths are exposed to an array of options, from drug dealing to prostitution to armed robbery, that can potentially lead to fast cash.

One does not need to join a gang to fully participate in such moneymaking endeavors, but some prospective members perceive gang life as being lucrative. This perception is somewhat rational: the gang can, for some, potentially increase a member's ability to negotiate a competitive market that is common to the underground drug economy (Fleisher 1998; Sanchez-Jankowski 1991). It provides social contacts, learning opportunities, and a pool of loyal friends to resolve the chaotic and often dangerous situations that inevitably occur when money changes hands in the streets (see Venkatesh 2006). In contrast to conventional wisdom, most gang members do not just rely on organized drug dealing as a source of fast money. More accurately, they participate in what Malcolm Klein (1995) calls cafeteria-style crime, picking and choosing their criminal activities as opportunities arise. Gang members sell drugs, participate in robberies, break into houses, and engage in other illegal money-generating activities. Such activities are made easier by the social support found within gangs. In a sense, the strength in numbers provided by gang membership allows individuals to take better advantage of illicit moneymaking opportunities.

Even though the DFW Boyz were generally not, as a collective body, entrepreneurially involved in street activities, there were informal monetary benefits to joining the gang. Some members of the DFW Boyz explained that they joined the gang to make money:

YOUNG-G: Why? Shit, like I said, I ain't been out long [due to being incarcerated] so I needed some money. I needed something. I was hurting bad. He [Killa-Con] was just talking. I didn't even know they was going to put me in. They like, "You want to be in?"

"Yeah, got to get this money."

"Go get the money."

I'm down for the money. I'm down for whatever.

As I continued to ask questions about why membership in the DFW Boyz was a financially attractive option, he and other members explained:

TL: So how does being in the clique help you guys get money?

KILLA-CON: Say it like this, if I get an ounce of weed, and if I'm like the only one out of all the people in the group, I'm going to wait until I get my money up. Then I'll be able to put this person up. Then when he do that, he do the same thing, and we can go around. By next summer we all be riding on something good. If we get to the point where we can't get money and we needed it at that point.

Although establishing a network of peers to aid in dealing drugs was one possible benefit of being in the DFW Boyz, this response seemed more like wishful thinking than an actual plan. Some DFW Boyz did sell marijuana, but it wasn't a prevalent activity in the group. As we continued to talk, the boys began to discuss a more common approach to making money that was greatly enhanced by membership in the gang:

YOUNG-G: We'll rob a motherfucker.

KILLA-CON: If we really need it, we'll go out there and catch somebody slipping. Go get it—the whole definition of being down for whatever.

They continued to describe a recent night in which some DFW Boyz collectively ran the streets actively looking for an opportunity to break into houses or rob vulnerable individuals:

KILLA-CON: This one night we didn't have no money, and you know me, trying to get some money and shit. We was walking on Thirty-eighth Street coming from the gas station and shit. I'm behind, I'm lingering. I'm high, fucked up and shit. Then Layboy like, "This nigga got a chain." I see the chain and I want it. So I'm following the nigga all the way back to Forty-second Street. He gets in front of me.
They like, "Go get him, go get him."
I said, "Go get him?"
They like "Yeah." I said, "Hey nigga I want your chain." Ran up on him, like, "Don't run nigga.'" He took off. I'm like, I'm not about to run. Bop, bop, start shooting at him [Killa-Con is laughing].
They like, "Nigga you shot at him."
I'm like, "Bro,' think he dead" [he is still laughing]. I was like, "Fuck it."

LAYBOY: That same night ran into some girls. We was on the same thing they was on. We was in black, there was a couple of girls. They had bats.
We was like, "What's up?"
They said, "We about to whoop this nigga's ass. My baby daddy ain't take care of my baby."

KILLA-CON: Hold on, before I saw they had bats I was about to rob their ass.

LAYBOY: They took us to his house or whatever, dude got flat screens, PlayStation.

KILLA-CON: PlayStation, no money, no guns, he got dope.

YOUNG-G: I'm high so I'm like, "It's whatever." I knock on the door three times, I heard him come to the door the first time. So I said fuck it, kicked that bitch open. He was like "Ok, ok, the police on their way." We didn't even run off, we walked off and I shot in the air "DFW Boyz." So we go cross the street.

KILLA-CON: We had to kick this gate in to get to the other side of the city and shit. We catch this dude in his truck, so we like, let's go get him, he about to go in the house. So I run up to his truck and put my gun in his face and say, "Give me your money." He's like, "I ain't got no money."

YOUNG-G: He said, "I ain't got no money."

LAYBOY: It was an old dude. He had false teeth that fell out and everything.

KILLA-CON: I'm patting him down like, "Where your money at?" He looked back at the house and told whoever was back at the house to get the pistol.

LAYBOY: He said, "Go get the gun." He started beeping the horn.

KILLA-CON: He slammed the door on my fucking leg.

LAYBOY: We just start running. He's beeping the horn. He's on the horn for like five minutes.

On this night the boys' criminal efforts were unsuccessful, but being affiliated with a group of peers who were also willing to pursue money through violent means had its advantages. Having the group's backing increased their willingness and opportunity to commit such acts, and the probability of success increased with the number of attempts. On this night they were just unlucky. If the first victim had not run or the second victim had not called the police or the third victim had been carrying cash, the boys would have profited from their crime spree.

Social Relationships

A street gang represents a collection of individuals bound not only by group affiliation but also by meaningful routine interactions. For most gang members, the relational ties found within the group provide an underlying motivation for joining the gang. The attraction of such relationships builds over time, as most youths join gangs after establishing a pattern of hanging out with a group of gang members. These relationships, however, contain different meanings for different people. Some members view the gang as a surrogate family that takes care of their

needs during difficult times. Other members view the gang as an accepting peer group that helps them build self-confidence and negotiate street
life. For some members, the gang is simply a collection of peers that
shares mutual interests. Regardless of the exact role these relationships
play in the lives of members, gang youth perceive these social ties as
being positive elements in their lives.

Perhaps the strongest attraction to gang life is the sense of belonging
that an individual gains from joining a gang. This sense of belonging,
however, is positioned inside an exchange system whereby the gang
conditionally accepts all members. Most gang members understand that
their peers accept them because they are useful to the gang. Yet this
utility is bidirectional, and gang members get a sense of purpose and satisfaction from their ability to contribute to the gang. Such contributions
do not typically come from scripted, formal roles in the gang; rather,
they arise over time as youths demonstrate their place within the group.

Most DFW Boyz, for example, enjoyed talking about their role in
the group. One member described himself as the crazy one, and another
member embraced the label of a hot boy, or someone willing to shoot a
gun during a conflict. Both individuals proved to be quite useful to the
gang, and both took pride in those roles. Having noticed this, I had
developed a habit of asking new study participants about their individual
identity within the group. For example, during one conversation, a
few DFW Boyz introduced me to Big-D and then described his role in
the gang:

TL: Who are you in the clique?

SHAWN: We call him the bodyguard. He the big man.

BIG-D: I am like the bodyguard, but I do as much as they do.

SHAWN: He put in work just like we do. He like, the biggest one.

BIG-D: If someone is trying to fight someone, I'll probably be the first
one to run up and help.

SHAWN: He the biggest one most of the time. They send somebody big
anyways. They going to get intimidated. So we throw Big-D at
them.

LAYBOY: He can take hits too. Ah, yeah. He can take a punch, still be
funny at the same time.

BIG-D: I be sitting back and laughing at the niggas' trying to hit me.

Most of the DFW Boyz were not very big. Although Layboy and Shawn liked to show off their well-sculpted bodies, both were under six feet tall and did not lift weights frequently enough to expand their muscle mass. Many of the younger gang members were skinny boys and could not have weighed more than 150 pounds. Big-D, however, stood at or just over six feet tall and had a thick body that was neither obese nor muscular. He must have weighed 230 to 240 pounds. Almost by default, he embraced the bodyguard role, but, despite his size, Big-D was not naturally aggressive. According to Shawn, Big-D had been an unconfident and weak child before becoming affiliated with the DFW Boyz. His ascension to being the group's intimidator was the result of a process in which members of the DFW Boyz noticed his size and then taught him to be tough. The methods used for such a goal were simple:

SHAWN: We used to make him stand there while we punched him up. He'd stand against the wall and we'd beat him up. He take the punches.

BIG-D: They showed up at a bad time for me.

SHAWN: We like family. We all fight, ain't no one-on-one fight. That's how that works. Keep everybody on their feet, that's what's up.

Although the DFW Boyz interest in Big-D was largely self-serving, their efforts, according to Big-D, were very helpful. The gang gained another person with a big body who gradually became accustomed to fighting, and Big-D gained the acceptance of peers who seemed invested in his so-called personal development. He gained a sense of purpose as he developed an appreciation for his role in the group. He was no longer an unconfident social outcast. The exchange, it seemed, went both ways. The gang supposedly helped members stay on their feet, while the members made important contributions to gang.

Relationships guided individuals into gang membership and often continued to reinforce the value of being in the gang. When facing a dangerous street environment, or when struggling to make money on the streets, relationships found within the gang provided immediate relief. Relationships were also a source of esteem, as early adolescent youth gained a sense of identity and purpose from their role in the group. For those members capable of benefiting the group, gang life offered a network of peers committed to helping them in various situations. The gang, for some members, became like a family.

THREE LIFE STORIES

Although the factors that lead to gang membership provide valuable insight, they lose descriptive power when removed from the context of everyday life. Each story told here uniquely interweaves the aforementioned factors into personal life histories to explain gang participation. With the exception of some subtle editing to help make the stories more readable, they are presented directly from the individuals themselves. The first comes from nineteen-year-old Tyrese, who at the time of the interviews did not consider himself actively involved in gangs. This inactivity was largely due to recent armed robbery convictions. His friends and coconspirators went to prison, while Tyrese did not. The second story focuses on Jon, a thirty-five-year-old inactive gang member who had spent the majority of his adult life in prison. He had recently been released from prison after serving a lengthy sentence for murdering someone during a botched drug deal. By all accounts, he had been a very influential member of an organized gang. The final story focuses on Shauna, a twenty-five-year-old inactive gang member who spent a large portion of her teenage years in juvenile facilities. Thanks to a caring family friend and some help from a community organization, she departed from gang life, and at the time of the interviews was attending a local university. The chaos in the lives of these three individuals is unmistakable, and although each uniquely describes his or her attraction to the gang, they all present a common theme: the gang provided some semblance of certainty amid unstable life circumstances.

Tyrese's Story

I grew up on East Thirty-fourth Street until I was about seven or eight, and then lived on Thirtieth Street for a while. I now stay out farther east. I had a rough childhood, but I don't complain, because I feel like everything I have been through has made me stronger. My mother's white, my daddy's black, and we lived pretty rough because they were both drug addicts. I don't know how we lived or what money we lived off of, but they eventually chose drugs over their kids. I have two sisters and a brother. I have never met one of my sisters, but I am close with my brother and my other sister. We lived from motel to motel, from shelter to shelter. We stayed with my grandma off and on. My father finally left and my mother finally gave us up to Child Protective Services. We lived in a guardian home for about two years; I was finally adopted when I was nine.

The woman who adopted me was a churchgoing woman, and she taught me a lot of Christian principles about morals and stuff. But I still had the mentality that I saw all my life. All my cousins were gangbangers, and they taught me the wrong stuff. At that time it did not seem like the wrong stuff, because it was just what they knew. It was what their friends and parents taught them. I was real young at the time so I really didn't understand it, but their motto was "money over bitches." If you don't have money you can't do anything. So that was the number one thing they taught. They were going to get money any way they could. So they did that.

When I got adopted I still kept in contact with my real family. I wasn't supposed to, but I did anyway. We all got into a lot of trouble with social services for doing that, but we didn't really care. I just wanted to please my cousins so bad. I wanted them to accept me. I felt like they only accepted me because I was their family. I was quiet, not wild like they were. I didn't like to make a scene like they did. I liked to be undercover and keep to myself. I wasn't really like them. But when it came to money, I felt like our mentalities were on the same level. They were all in the drug game, and I was introduced to that early at age thirteen.

Two of my cousins were Vice Lords. They taught me a lot of the stuff, but I never wanted to be in their gang. I did everything with them. I did the same stuff they did, but I wasn't officially a part of the gang. I never got jumped in or anything, because that just wasn't for me. They were too wild. They were reckless and would do things without thinking. It could be a Monday morning, and they could just wake up, get drunk, decide to go outside, and start shooting their guns in the air. They would pick people out who were walking down the street and beat them up just because they felt like it. They would commit robberies for no reason at all. That was too reckless. They drew too much attention. But even if they were wrong, I was always in their corner. When they had problems with other people, I was always there for them.

We used to rob dope houses when I was about thirteen years old, and I thought that was the tightest [coolest] thing in the world. That was my little fun. One night we were robbing dope houses, and we hit one right there right off of Thirty-second Street. But we ran up in there on a dice game. They were having a dice game, so it could have been a good lick [score] that night, but so many people had guns. We were not expecting that many people. There were only two of us. We ran in there and went through the whole procedure. Everyone was down for a while, and then I started hearing shots. Next thing I know he was murdered. He was gone. He was out the game. I didn't know him real well. My cousin put me in contact with him to do this, and he brought the guns. He got shot up. I didn't because I was gone. I was a track star. I was outa' there. I will never hesitate to run. I don't care. Call me a punk or call me whatever. I will run because you can't stop a bullet. So yeah, that turned out real bad. That was too much for me. I wasn't a violent person. I just had the love of money, same as they did.

But then I got introduced to the Gangster Disciples. They weren't Gangster Disciples at first. They called themselves something else. But basically their color was blue, their side was right, and I joined their gang. They were more discreet and sensible than my cousins. They just didn't get hot when somebody violated or came on their set. We were not really about the sets, neighborhoods, and streets. We were just about the family unity. I got initiated, and that's why I got the tattoo loyalty on my hand, because that's the most important thing. You have to be loyal because it is a family. They looked out for each other. It wasn't like we were out shooting people or robbing and doing crazy stuff. We were looking out for each other. When I was younger, they made sure that I would get my homework done. They made sure I stayed on top of my schoolwork. I would go there if I didn't have any food, and they would feed us. They would clothe me. They kept money in my pockets. They protected me. I stayed in their cribs. That's why I felt obligated to do whatever they asked. They wanted loyalty. If something go down and we get caught, just keep my mouth shut. That's all they were asking.

My best friend was actually in the opposite gang. His colors were red. Mine were blue. We became best friends because we had the same type of mind. We both wanted money so that's what we pursued. We made a lot of mistakes, and we did a lot of stuff that we never got caught for. We started doing the robberies, and everyone wanted to make it gang affiliated, but it really wasn't. We were just in desperate need of money. I didn't want to sell drugs, because it carried too much time. All my family had been to prison, so I knew what could happen if I sold drugs. It was hard, but it was fun. I took heat for a lot of people, and I got beat up for a lot of people. But when you know you had all your boys looking out for you, you feel invincible. If you feel you haven't ever been touched, then you feel like you can't be touched.

Jon's Story

I didn't know my real father, because my mother said I wasn't his and told him to leave us alone. My stepfather treated my little brother and me differently. He was mentally abusive and sometimes physically abusive. So there was not a lot of love at home. I spent a lot of time with my godmother and grandmother until eighth grade. In sixth grade my grandmother died. In eighth grade my godmother died. I was by myself from that point on. My parents made good money, but people couldn't tell when they looked at me. I looked like I came from the mission. I used to have to explain to people why my brother was dressed real nice, and I was dressed real bad. Everybody around me treated us that way. When outsiders saw me, just like reading the cover of a book, they would treat me like I looked. They would cater to my baby brother because they knew he was my father's favorite, and then they would mistreat me if they thought it would please my father.

My mother and stepfather were churchgoing people so I was raised in church. Apartments surrounded my neighborhood, so I had to learn how to live in the streets. I grew up in the church, but when I went outside I knew I had to live another way. It was hard to be raised not to fight and be peaceful, and then have someone hitting me upside the head when I went out to buy candy. I had a baby brother who was always with me so I had to protect him. I started running the streets when I was twelve. One day my mother came home, and I was sitting in the house watching TV. She was like, "You spend too much time in the house, get out." I said, "Where I'm going to go?" She said, "I don't care, just get out." So I got out and started hanging with a good friend of mine.

I began to get certain freedoms, and I got peace from being away from home. I was just tortured at home. My home life was horrible for me. As the years went by, I did whatever it took to stay away from the house. When I was young I didn't know how to fight. But I learned that if I could beat someone up, I could get a name for myself. I just didn't know how to fight, so I would lose. My baby brother had a loud mouth, so when somebody messed with him he'd say, "I'll get my brother and he'll whoop you." So to win I would come up with a plan. If there was a person that jumped on me every day, I would set traps. If he jumped me in a certain spot I could run five feet where I had a brick hidden. Most people just want to fight, and I learned that if I go to the next step it would bring a positive outcome for me. I was willing to grab a brick and run up between someone and their grandma, aunt, or mom and dad, and bust their head wide open. Most people were not willing to do that. But if I do that, people would know that I would do anything. The thing is, if you didn't bother me, you never had that coming. So that's how I kept people off of me.

I liked getting high and drinking. I liked smoking a nice joint and getting alcohol in me so any pain I had went away. When I got sober it came back, so I would get some more. I chased girls, got high, and stayed okay in school. I was a party guy. I always made sure I was the one who brought the drugs and alcohol. I always made sure I was the guy who knew where to find it. I hung with a gang three years before I joined. When we was just hanging out it was like, "You cool, you down but you ain't part of us." I wasn't really obligated, but I also didn't have any of the perks that came along with being in it. I just figured I had been with them so long, and I was going to keep hanging out with them that it might was well be official. When I joined I was family. I had all the perks and all the privileges that came along with it. I was trustworthy because I had things governing over my life that made me trustworthy.

What really made me be in the gang was they were like family to me. They would die for me. If I was hungry they would feed me. If I needed clothes they would clothe me. They made me feel like they wanted me to be around. That's my family. They gave me a new name. I needed a coat one year because it was cold. When I got out of the joint, they gave me a black leather jacket. It was nice. I was so high I didn't really want to go home, and I didn't want to hear from my parents. They hid me out in their mother's house. We had an ultimate goal. We were trying to get somewhere. We wanted to buy property. We wanted to get businesses going. I ran my high school. If we went to high school and I said to you, "Man your best bet is to never step foot in here again," and you did, you was going to the hospital. Might die, might not. That's a lot of power. That's power I eventually gained.

When my parents found out what I was they couldn't believe it. My momma's jaw hit the ground. She couldn't believe it. The principal at my school knew my family personally. When she found out I was running the gang in her high school, she called my parents and asked them, "Do you know your son is in a gang?"

My mom said, "Yeah we knew."

"You mean that you knew he was in a gang and didn't do nothing?"

"Well, we didn't think he had what it takes to be in a gang. We figured eventually they would beat him up and put him out."

So she was like, "Tell your mother what you is around here."

I said, "I'm chief violator."

She was like, "Tell your mother what you is."

So I was like, "I'm a five-star general."

My mom said, "What that mean?"

I said, "I run everything around here, don't nothing happen unless I know about it."

Your kids are more than what you think they are. And if you don't do anything for them, the streets will. Whatever you don't teach and show them, the streets will be more than happy to. The outcome might not be what you expect. I'm thirty-five years old, and for all my adult years I have been incarcerated in some form or another. I have never been able to run as a free man. The way a free man should. The best way to keep a child out of the gang is to stay involved in the child's life. Be your child's gang leader. A lot of people don't have enough time to invest in their children. They always have something else to do. I wanted my dad to kick my behind and take me to my gang leaders and say, "This is not your gang member, this is my son." He never did that. So I figured, if they don't care, why should I?

Shauna's Story

Around the age of twelve I became very rebellious, because I experienced a lot of domestic violence at home. My dad was an abusive alcoholic, and my parents always fought. As a young child I saw so much violence at home. It never really stopped. The summer when I was eighteen, I lived at home for a while, and my parents still fought to the point where my father and I would get really physical. Guns would occasionally get pulled out. He would pull a gun out on me, and I would try to find a gun to pull on him. It got real bad. People don't understand that domestic violence gets worse over time. The only way it gets better is if the parents separate. But my mom was raising five kids, and some parts of the situation were good. We had our own rooms, our own stuff. You know, we had our own crib.

When we were big enough, we would physically pull him off of her. My oldest brother is thirty-one and he's doing 116 years in prison. My other brother is twenty-seven. My sister's twenty-nine, I'm twenty-five, and my little brother is twenty-three. At some point the oldest one's stepped up to confront my father so the rest of us would step up with them. So as I was older, he had to deal with his kids. When he had four or five kids jumping on him, he got the mentality of, "I brought you in and I'll take you out." He decided not to let his kids get the best of him. As teenagers, we were protecting our momma. We had a mentality that we would kill him to protect her. And we kept that mentality. My father kicked all of us out when we turned eighteen years old. The police escorted me out of the house. My baby brother was arrested on a trespass warrant for coming on my daddy's property. My sister got pregnant in order to get out of the house and away from my father.

My home life gave me an excuse to behave the same way in other situations. At the age of twelve, I saw my mom and dad fight all the time, so it was easy to go to school and want to fight my teachers. My real authority figures were not holding themselves accountable and being good role models. So what do you expect? When I got to sixth grade I went nuts. I fought all the time. I've always been the leader of anything that I do. So, if I said that I wanted to start a fight, I would have ten people willing to go with me. But I was the one who did all of the damage. I was the class clown, and nobody could tell me what to do—no teacher, no security, and no principal. I had so much anger built up inside of me that I refused to obey. Time and time again teachers used to say, "Oh, you know she's just such a bright student. She's very smart." But I refused to let the good come out, because everything going on at home was so bad. My feelings about my parents defeated any of the good. What's the purpose of making straight As when your mom and dad is fighting like cats and dogs? In sixth grade I also joined a gang. I considered myself to be a Gangster Disciple. It was a way for me to express myself.

I was also in the streets at a young age. I would follow around my older brother and try to do what he was doing. I was a tomboy and didn't do anything girly. When the boys fought or wrestled I would be in the back wrestling with them, and they would slam me around. Eventually, I started running the streets with them. When they started smoking weed so did I. There used to be ten or twelve dudes, and I was always following. My brother would tell me to go home, but his buddies would say, "Come on, you cool, you can hang." I got into the mix because a few of my brother's friends took me up under their wing. So when my brother didn't want me around, those guys would smoke weed with me and tell me everything I needed to know. If they were on their way to a certain neighborhood, I'd walk with them. If they didn't like certain dudes in the neighborhood, neither did I. That's kind of how it rotated with me.

I got street cred' immediately because of who my brothers were. So, when I started behaving like them, it wasn't a front. It was sincere. Imagine a skinny little twelve-year-old girl who has ten dudes treating her like a sister. I eventually had the same attitude they had, and I had the same amount love they had for me. So when there were five guys on the east side that they didn't like, I was riding with them. If the most I could do was hold their hoodies while they take their shirts off to fight, then that's what I did. I was a part of the gang. If the most I could do is say, "Here come the police," that's what I did. Because this is my clique, and these are my buddies. If one of them is getting ready to go to jail or they had a warrant, I would spend the quality time with him. He couldn't hang in the streets, so we would hang out in the crack house and just kick it. I have to stress that sex was never a thing. I was a tomboy and sex was not what we thought about. To run with all those boys, they know you're not easy. They know you don't want to sleep with them.

By the time I was twelve, I was in the streets one hundred percent. I was in the back of the clubs owned by guys who are now in the federal penitentiary. I was in their cars, which were bought with drug money, rolling up blunts. Some of these guys were twenty-nine years old, and

I was eleven or twelve. I ain't old enough to get in the club, but I could sit in the car behind it and smoke weed. So I felt that the big dogs blessed me in. They were the first ones that gave me my nickname. I knew that I was a part of the clique, because they gave me that nickname. They were like, "This little bitty skinny thing hangs with us and rolls blunts really good." I did roll them really good. I knew all the lyrics to the music they listened to, and I could keep up with their conversations. They would ask, "What you know about gangsters? What make you gangster?" I could sit for a whole hour and have a conversation, cuss, and tell them what I knew. That's part of my initiation right there. When I could sit and have a conversation with someone who's facing thirty years to life, somebody who already killed someone, somebody who's dealing kilos of coke, and they tell me, "You got some fire, you hip. We are going to give you a nickname." What more did I need?

In middle school, I hooked up with some friends who lived on Thirty-fourth Street where there was a lot of heroin being sold and a lot of crack houses. My buddy was already a Vice Lord, and she wanted to set me up with her baby daddy's twin brother. I was into boys at that time so one day I didn't go home after school so I could meet him. We were into getting the best possible drug dealers, and I knew he had money. She took me home, and as soon as I walked in his mother was like, "Yeah, she's real pretty." I remember her saying, "That's going to be my daughter-in-law." She used to sell drugs back in the day, and she was like a queen pin. She got her sons involved in dealing drugs. He came out of the bathroom, and I knew he was grown because he had all this chest hair. I was just a skinny little girl, and I knew he was older than me. I was fourteen or fifteen years old, and he was nineteen or twenty years old. I always lied about my age. I never told my real age until I was eighteen. He came out, saw me, and we hugged. After that I didn't go home any more. I didn't go home because I liked him. From that night on, I was riding with them.

I also left home because of the physical confrontations with my dad. He was an abusive alcoholic, so it was always physical. We also didn't have friends. We were not allowed to bring kids in the house. I really couldn't talk on the phone with my friends, so how could I have fun with them? Maybe puberty was also getting in the way. I was going through phases of trying to learn who I was. What were my likes and dislikes? Am I beautiful or am I not beautiful? So when I got attention from older boys, it made me want to experiment a little more with relationships. Not sexually, but just to have a boy liking me. Before this, I used to run away for shorter periods of time. I wouldn't come home from school because once I was home I could not get out of the house. So I would not get on the school bus. Instead, I would go over to my friend's house when I knew her mom and dad were not going to send me home. Of course, they didn't know my situation, because I didn't want anyone else to know.

After I left home, I used to hang in the crack house with my boyfriend's gang and sell drugs. They taught me the ins and outs of it, and that's what I used to do. Since I was a runaway, I sold crack to get new clothes and shoes. To be honest, I was really good at it, which made me do it even more. I was young and a runaway, making seventy to eighty dollars in one day. It's against the law, but I was making money. Actually, the ring I have on was given to me in exchange for crack. I remember the guy didn't have any money, so he gave me this ring for some crack. I also used to fight all the time. If any girls came through and they didn't represent Vice Lords or GD, they were going to get beat up. And because I am so skinny I felt like I had something to prove. So I used to fight big girls. I also used to go to school and clip people for their rings. I used to pick on the white kids, or the kids that I knew were good kids. I would be like, "Let me see that ring." Then I would put it on my finger and cut out because I knew they weren't going to fight me back. That's how bad of a bully I was.

I almost got raped twice while I was staying there, and I was assaulted many times. I was so young and spent most nights in a crack house. Twice when the guy I dated was passed out on drugs, his uncles tried to rape me in my sleep. I was quietly in a room fighting off these overgrown men. There were two or three men over top of me trying to snatch my clothes off. I was so young and dumb that I was worried about my boyfriend's reaction, so all I could think of is fight them quietly. I didn't want him to think that I was like the other girls that come over all the time to have sex. I was fighting these three men, trying to get them off of me. If I am only 105 pounds now, I couldn't have been much more than 90 pounds back then. But there was so much anger in me that I fought three grown men, and they had to get off of me. But who could

I tell the next day? I could not go home and tell momma. So it just makes me even angrier. It made me want to sell more dope, beat up somebody else, and if I ever got the opportunity to shoot or stab one of them I would have done it.

My dad knew I was over there, because he rode the bus, and he would see me at the crack house. He used to come over and try to get me. But I would hide in the house, and all the guys in there ain't going to let my daddy come in. They'd cuss my father out and tell him I wasn't there. He'd threaten to call the police. The police came for me many times, but I would be gone. It was a crack house. We'd be in and out. We would go on the next street and wait until it cleared up. I never went home, because I knew my father was going to beat me down. Once I was runaway, I was scared to go home. I felt like it didn't matter if I had been gone for three hours or two days, I going to get the same treatment. I knew I was going to a guardian home, and I did not want to go to a guardian home. So I was gone for as long as I could be gone. I knew if I went home, my momma and daddy wouldn't trust me anymore. I knew it was just over for us, so I stayed gone as long as I could. The only reason I left is because a friend's mother and my former boyfriend came looking for me. They caught me sleeping in the house at nine in the morning. That's the only reason I got out. I probably still would be out there. I probably wouldn't be where I am now. Just the fear of going back home was enough to keep me there. But my friend's mother took me in and let me live with her. She accepted who I was and what I had done. She didn't try to beat me down and be like, "You ain't no good, you ain't no good, you ain't no good." My mommy and daddy weren't ready to be that easy on me.

If all these people keep jumping on me [treating me poorly], I am definitely going to run to the streets. The streets don't treat you like that. The streets know you messed up. The streets know you come from a messed up home. The streets know you got issues. The streets know you want to fit in. And they are going to embrace you. Instead of saying, "You ugly, you dumb, don't no boys like you," they going to hook you up with your first boyfriend. Instead of saying you don't know how to drink or smoke, they're going to introduce you to your first blunt, your first drink. Instead of saying you're a punk or you're a fag, they going to show you how to fight. Instead of saying you broke, you ugly, you ain't got no shoes, you ain't got no food, they going to show you how to steal a bag of chips. They are going to teach you how to steal your first pair of tennis shoes. And you feel like I finally got some friends. My brothers and sisters are always picking on me. My sister won't do my hair. My mom won't pay for me to get some decent shoes. My family, my gang, is going to give me their hand-me-downs, they going to let me wear the expensive tennis shoes. A girl that's in the gang will do your hair. She'll do your hair in an expensive hairstyle instead of you having to beg your mom and dad for it. She'll give you your first lipstick, whatever the case may be. That's what it was for me. It wasn't about continually being bad. It was about being embraced by people who I felt loved me and cared about me.

CONCLUSION

For youth exposed to street life at a young age, gang membership can be an attractive solution to problems. Gang membership can give some youth a sense of protection in a threatening environment, or it can them access new illicit opportunities to make money. The gang can offer refuge from a disagreeable home life and give impressionable adolescents a sense of purpose and belonging that they do not get anywhere else. Yet the benefits of gang membership experienced by many gang members are easily outnumbered by the direct negative consequences of gang membership. The rest of this book examines one such problem that dramatically influences gang members' lives.

The process of joining a gang, as described in this chapter, also indicated that most gang members were not innately different from their peers. They did not seem, as some researchers have argued, more likely to suffer from low self-control or a psychological illness (see Fleisher 1995; Yablonsky 1959 and 1967). Their pathway into the gang was not, as some researchers have suggested, fostered by a proclivity for violence and an inability to socialize with peers (see Hirschi 2006; Yablonsky 1959 and 1967). Some gang members participated in criminal activity before they joined a gang. Shawn and Layboy, for example, committed petty theft before they became gang members. Joe admitted to fighting in the streets and using drugs before he joined a gang. Shauna was experienced with marijuana before she became a gang member. Killa-Con gravitated to the DFW Boyz because his behavior was already consistent with the gang's collective behavior. Yet for most gang members, serious delinquent behavior increased dramatically after they became gang members. Something about gang life enhanced or facilitated criminal activity among members.

This observation is consistent with the current state of gang research. Scholars in multiple locations have provided convincing evidence that gang members are more likely than their peers to engage in serious delinquent behavior. Moreover, there is strong evidence that this behavior substantially increases after membership begins (Gatti et al. 2005, Gordon et al. 2004; Lacourse et al. 2003; Thornberry et al. 1993 and 2003). Researchers are left with the challenge of explaining why gang membership has such a significant impact on the lives of youth. The following chapters provide new insights into the question. Most notably, intergang interactions and the struggle for legitimacy in the intergang environment produce strong pressures for gang members to cultivate violent reputations, and this can induce violent behavior and intergang conflict.

CHAPTER 3

The Dilution Narrative

An Understanding That Some Gang Members Are Not "Real"

ALTHOUGH GANG MEMBERSHIP may be caused by an individual's response to his or her chaotic social, familial, or economic environment, it is not a particularly successful avenue for solving one's problems. Gangs may provide real friendship, and even a secondary family in which widespread loyalty mandates that members look out and care for other members. They can offer an escape for a distasteful home life, school experience, or peer environment. For some, gang life offers a short-term solution to abject poverty. Despite these benefits, gang membership has short- and long-term negative consequences. Most notably, individuals often join gangs for protection, only to become more at risk of criminal victimization (Decker and Van Winkle 1996; Melde, Taylor, and Esbensen 2009; Taylor 2007; Taylor, Feng et al. 2008; Taylor, Peterson et al. 2008). They are more likely to participate in serious criminal behavior, have repeated contact with the criminal justice system, and drop out of school (Thornberry et al. 2003). For many individuals, entrance into a gang marks a transition into a long-term pattern of chaos and disruption.

Gang membership, then, is a logical but dysfunctional adaptation to adverse life circumstances. Gangs provide a reprieve from some life circumstances, but they create new, more severe problems. This chapter focuses on one such problem. Self-defined gang members are confident about their status as "real" gang members, but they must negotiate a skeptical peer environment that routinely questions their claims of legitimacy.

A Gang's Internal Certainty

A common byproduct of the interactions between members of the same street gang is a collective identity that defines the core values of the group.[1] The DFW Boyz, for example, are unified around the idea of being down for whatever, and they emphasize behavior that is consistent with this ethic. Members are informally encouraged to maintain the DFW Boyz reputation by intimidating, fighting, and opportunistically participating in a wide range of criminal activities. Gang members often reinforced this central identity during group conversations by providing vivid, even idealistic, self-characterizations that were consistent with the group's ideals. Moreover, they told stories about how the gang was, indeed, down for whatever. They also reinterpreted past events to emphasize the group's most valued characteristics, and they openly communicated those traits to peers.

In Indianapolis not all gang identities were alike.[2] Some groups, like the DFW Boyz, openly valued a willingness to engage in violence or other criminal activities. Other gang members claimed affiliation to larger gangs, like the Conservative Vice Lords or Black Gangster Disciples, and viewed themselves as belonging to a highly developed street organization that was entrepreneurially invested in the drug markets. Unlike the DFW Boyz, the most salient trait of these gangs was making money, and they stressed this pursuit over maintaining the group's reputation. Other individuals were more involved in hood gangs and therefore emphasized turf or neighborhood respect more than making money. Despite these differences, there was an important yet simple similarity between groups. They all had a fundamental understanding that their group was decidedly a gang.[3]

Being known as a gang member can be advantageous in the streets. The generic label of "gang" or "gang member" efficiently communicates a series of attributes that causes most people to engage the labeled group or individual cautiously. The gang label evokes ideas of violence and reciprocation in the face of conflict or disrespect. If, in the course of a potentially hostile interaction, an individual claims gang membership, the opposing party must consider the possible negative ramifications of angering a loyal and potentially violent street gang. Moreover, the label of "gang" or "gang member" is intimately attached to characteristics generally embraced in the streets. Gangs are considered to be tough, and some are considered to be prosperous. Gang members often host parties or control gatherings at nightclubs, which can make gang membership socially desirable. If claims of membership are taken seriously, there is a degree of respect granted to the gang member that is difficult to match in the streets.

Interactions between members of the same gang produce an internal certainty about the status of the group and, by extension, the members themselves. In fact, it would be rather odd to hear self-defined gang members diminish the group's status or offer a self-description that stressed deficiencies. Instead, the messages articulated within the group ubiquitously reinforce not only its status as a gang but also its status as a group that plays a significant role in the streets. For example, routine conversations between members of the DFW Boyz often reflected hyperbolic efforts to position the group at the pinnacle of street life. Shawn once reinforced the status of the DFW Boyz by noting both the group's standing in the streets and its popularity among local youth: "We probably one of the most known cliques that everybody want to get with. Everybody trying to get down with us. We hear people all the time trying to get with us and clique up. We just tell them, 'Nah, we cool.'" A later conversation between Shawn, Layboy, and another member of the DFW Boyz demonstrated the level of confidence that gang members had in their status within the urban landscape:

LAYBOY: We got stronger, we known, we been known. We got the DFW Boyz, we been known.

SHAWN: We been known since day one when we went to school.

LAYBOY: We made the name that night, the next day everybody knew us.

G-DOG: We take over. We take over like that.

SHAWN: We take over.

LAYBOY: We take over, especially out East. The police had a stack on us that high [motioning with his hands]. Used to get chased by police everyday. They knew where we stay at.

"Being known" referred to the degree to which peers recognized the DFW Boyz as a viable gang worthy of respect. There was little doubt among the DFW Boyz that the gang and its individual members had become widely recognized in the streets of Indianapolis. They assumed that outsiders should have also accepted the collective identity embraced by members of the group. The DFW Boyz was a gang, and the group was recognized as such in the streets.

EXAMINING THE DILUTION NARRATIVE

The certainty afforded by a relatively small number of close associates is not always reflective of the broader gang environment. More accurately, the intergang environment can exhibit widespread disagreement, skepticism, and uncertainty about which groups and which individuals should be considered legitimate gangs/gang members. Just because members of a particular collectivity identify their group as a gang, and themselves as gang members, does not mean that others in their social environment will share a similar evaluation. More likely, peers will question that evaluation or even dismiss the group as not being a real street gang. One's certainty about his or her membership is, therefore, matched by external doubt.

This doubt is produced by a general belief that the notion of gang has been diluted, so that nearly any willing individual can claim membership. Dilution occurs when a pure substance is combined with other elements that weaken the original composition. Relative to gangs, a common narrative suggests that as large numbers of urban youths have embraced gang life, they become increasingly detached from pure gang forms. The word "gang" is applied inaccurately so that it includes a range of collectivities that are clearly different from the pure, ideal, or intended conceptualization of "gang." Many groups claim to be a gang, but they are weakened imitations. Many individuals claim to be gang members, but they are perpetrating a fraud. For example, Sidney, a forty-five-year-old ex-convict, was often skeptical of gang members in Indianapolis:

> Basically you have a lot of wannabes or drug dealers who just want to lay with their set. They're basically just drug dealers that have united and decided to give themselves a name. They are not real bangers. They ain't holdin' no turf. They ain't holdin' no fifteen city blocks. You know what I mean? Like you go to some cities where for a fifteen-, twenty-block or two-mile radius you better not get caught with your hat cocked to the right or left side or in a blue shirt or red shirt, or something like that. That's why I said there's a lot

perpetration in Indianapolis, because they don't know. If there was a gang in the Meadows [a low-income housing complex] there should only be one gang. Meadows is not that big. It don't cover that much territory to cover two or three different colors walkin' around up in there. That's why I say you got more misguided youth than anything that want to imitate a gang. And they don't understand it. . . . Over the years it became a fad. Like I say, you go in one corner and you got a group of guys claiming to be Vice Lords. And you go two blocks over and another group of individuals claim to Vice Lords and they don't know each other and don't know nothing about each other. That's where it has manifested to now.

Dilution is a story. It is a common interpretation of local gang life that allows street participants to better understand their world. The following discussion does not seek to evaluate the accuracy of that story but instead attempts to better understand the ideas of dilution that permeate street life. The narrative involves both an attempt to construct a boundary that differentiates real gangs from lesser groups and an explanation for how the pure gang form has become diluted.

The dilution narrative reflects a collective, though fragmented, attempt by those invested in street life and street gangs to ascribe meaning to the various collectivities that inhabit their surroundings. Surveying the social landscape of Indianapolis leads one to identify countless multifaceted and often overlapping groups. Some formal groups, like youth choirs, drum lines, or athletic teams, are clear in their purpose, appearance, and membership. Other groups are more ambiguous. In the communities along East Thirty-eighth Street, youths form informal groups, routinely hanging out or interacting with the same people on a day-to-day basis. Although most of these groups are simply nondescript networks of friends, many embrace a collective gang identity. The gang label is not taken lightly; those invested in the concept implicitly understand that a gang should be fundamentally different from other groups. Although there are many formal and informal social groups within the East Thirty-eighth Street area, only some can rightfully be classified as street gangs.

Proper classification can only occur through the establishment of a field boundary that separates gangs from alternative social groups. In the streets of Indianapolis, the criteria used for establishing this boundary are widely varied. Many older gang members, who are loosely affiliated with Chicago-based street organizations or prison gangs, establish a field boundary according to formal standards. In doing so, they dismiss many youths as being fake gang members. Those self-defined gang members who are dismissed by the older generation remain certain of their gang status, but they also disseminate the dilution narrative by applying it to a broader understanding of the intergang environment. All self-defined gang members are actively involved in establishing the intergang field boundary, as they all perceive peers as being either real or fake.

Original Gangstas and Tales of Standards

Even though many self-defined gangs in Indianapolis could be objectively defined as loosely affiliated, disorganized groups, many older gang members, or Original Gangstas (OGs), relied on ideas of organizational sophistication to differentiate real from fake gangs. Groups could not just claim to be gangs. They had to meet certain standards to establish legitimacy. This belief was most likely the byproduct of both experience and a tendency to romanticize or reify the gangs of their youth. Many OGs grew up in a time when major Chicago street gangs such as the Vice Lords, Black Gangster Disciples, and El Rukns evolved into well-organized street organizations (Knox 2006; Knox and Papachristos 2002). Some claimed to have been in contact with these Chicago gangs during the 1970s, and they modeled Indianapolis gangs according to similar organizational ideals. Although I was never able to independently verify the existence of these gangs in Indianapolis, numerous trustworthy OGs claimed that some gangs remained organizationally sophisticated in the city. In addition, since many OGs spent a substantial amount of time in state and federal prison, they were exposed to a different level of gang participation. After leaving prison, they defined real gangs according to what they had experienced in prison. Street gangs were not as sophisticated as prison gangs, so they were not real gangs.

OGs often disagreed about how real gangs should be organized, but they did agree that real gangs should employ stringent standards for becoming and remaining a member. Some major gangs had lengthy manifestos that clearly articulated a formal leadership structure, rules, and doctrine (see Knox 2006; Knox and Papachristos 2002). Real members were supposed to memorize large portions of this literature and recall it at will. Such displays were quite impressive, as relatively uneducated gang members could "spit," or recite, their rather lengthy literature with relative ease. Original Gangstas generally noted that most of the younger gang members in Indianapolis were not following stringent standards of membership and could not be considered real gang members. One OG expressed to me how gangs operated back in the 1980s. By all accounts, Jon, who was quoted at length in the preceding chapter, was a high-ranking Vice Lord within the city. He was recently released from prison where he had been incarcerated for second-degree homicide for stabbing someone during a botched drug deal:

> Back when I was coming up you had to prove yourself worthy to be a Lord or a Disciple. You couldn't just say, "Ah, I'm folks or I'm almighty." You couldn't say that. First of all you had to be branded. You could say, "Ah, well I'm almighty." I would say, "Alright show me, let me see your branding." If you couldn't produce, that you would get whooped. I'm not just talking about getting beat up or black eye. No, you got whooped and sent to the hospital behind that. It was serious back then. We was trying to kill each other back then. We weren't no friends. Like right now you got the Vice Lords and the Disciples. Ain't no standing across the street. There was rules. This was their spot. This was our spot. Didn't no Disciple walk down the street in Lord neighborhood with his hat turned to the right. But on the other side you didn't go walking down no Disciple neighborhood with your hat cocked to the left. 'Cause you knew and you wore your hat straight. You move through there real swift like, try to get where you had to go.
>
> Vice Lords is we got rules and by-laws. You got to learn the rules and by-laws. We got prayers. We got ways you got to carry yourself. Older Lords got to look out for younger Lords. They made us go to school. You don't go to school you getting violated, you getting jumped on. Just go, we ain't trippin' if you do good but just go to school. These things they don't do, know what I'm saying? You never leave a man down in the streets. If you got to stand there and die with them you got to stand there and dies with them . . . now, if you talk about active gang members? Nah, they're not following the principles.

The structure within his gang provided a degree of verifiability when an individual claimed gang membership. One could not simply claim to be a Lord or Disciple without a realistic threat of someone questioning that claim and using severe punishments for incidents of false claiming.

Despite these ideals, many OGs argued that individuals who claimed to be gang members did not know their literature, and many gangs had neglected standards for verifying membership. Thus the meaning of "gang" had become diluted. The process of becoming a gang member had become arbitrary, so that self-defined gang members were detached from the ideals of real gangs. Some OGs suggested that this trend had grown to the point where anyone could claim membership without fear of punishment. Knowledge, standards, and rules were no longer a part of many gang members' lives. Noting this trend, Delron, an active drug dealer who had recently been released from prison where he had served time for two counts of second-degree murder, observed, "You just can't walk around and say, "Ah, I'm Vice Lords or I'm GD," or this and that. Ok, what makes you Vice Lord? Have you been through what you need to be a part of this gang? Do you know all the literature behind this gang? That's just like me. I can go out 'I'm Vice Lord, what's up peeps,' and ain't nobody going to say nothing about it. See what I'm saying? I'm really not Vice Lord. That's how they acting out here." If gangs did not utilize or embrace standards for membership, and if they did not establish requirements for gang members, there were no limitations on who could claim membership. Many youths claimed membership but were not real members. They were perpetrating a fraud and were summarily dismissed by those with insight into the nature of real gangs.

Another OG, Trey, made this point quite clear, as he suggested that the pointless behavior common to many so-called gangs was an indication that they were not real:

TL: So you talk about a real gangster, what's not real?

TREY: Doing stupid stuff.

TL: What's stupid stuff?

TREY: Robberies, killing for no reason. Instead of taking out a whole organization you taking out a few. Killing kids is no, women no. They not gangstas.

TL: Do you see a lot of that stuff in Indianapolis today?

TREY: I'm seeing that stuff today like I never seen it in my life.

TL: The stupid stuff?

TREY: Stupid stuff. Real men fought. Might get your head busted. Might get stabbed, but now they blowing your face off. Running into your house like cowards. Disrespecting your momma's, your aunts. They ain't got nothing to do with life that you claim. See? You a man. Act like a man. Stand up. Put your dukes up and get knocked out like your daddy used to do it. That's real. Cowardly is this [gestures shooting a gun]. I never had to use one in my life, and when I did have it, it's because you have one. I ain't going to trip on it. Mess with blood, blood going to ride nationwide.

Real gangs had standards of conduct that members followed. Senseless acts were simply not tolerated. The presence of large numbers of gang members acting without consideration for these codes of conduct was, according to Trey, evidence of dilution. Consequently, these gang members were not real, as they represented a weakened and insufficient version of gang. They were perpetrating a fraud.

Dilution and Younger Gang Members

The older generation of gang members did not have a monopoly on establishing the boundaries of "real." Younger gang members, who were likely to be dismissed by the older generation, attached different meanings to the notion of "gang" and continued to propagate the dilution narrative. Their conceptualization of the intergang environment included more than just well-organized gangs, as they considered various hoods and loosely organized cliques as being worthy ganglike affiliations. Even with this broader understanding of their environment, younger gang members still believed that the notion of what a gang was had become diluted.

This realization first became apparent during a routine conversation with Shawn, Layboy, and two other younger gang members. The conversation began as I was hanging out with Shawn and Layboy in front of their aunt's apartment. Relative to other low-income complexes located on or near Thirty-eighth Street, this recently built apartment complex was well maintained and attractive. The external structure boasted a mix of brick and vinyl siding, and the roof was varied in height and slope, giving the appearance of distinct though connected condominiums. A new playground sat across from the building. The surrounding parking lots were generally busy, as teenagers hung out in the open space and younger kids rode their bikes or played on the pavement, but the lot in front of this specific apartment building lacked activity. A few teenagers walked by as they were going to the nearby bus stop, and a few younger children rode their bikes around the circular drive in front of the building. Based on the scenery, an unsuspecting person would probably not have assumed that the complex had problems similar to more notorious complexes located only a short walk down the road. Yet only a few weeks before, someone had been murdered during the early evening hours in a store parking lot visible from where we stood. That summer, a few other shootings occurred in or in front of those apartments. Violence, it seemed, was always abstract and impersonal, yet close.

It was still early in the afternoon and tolerably warm, and we leaned on my car and talked about the streets. The boys told me that the apartments at the other end of the complex were rife with drug activity, but their end was relatively quiet. Indeed, marked police cars were often parked at the other end of the complex, and while I always expected my presence to raise suspicion, officers never seemed to notice me. Given that members of the DFW Boyz were scattered about the city and only sporadically involved in drug dealing, the police could not have targeted one location for such activities. Moreover, Shawn and Layboy did not sell drugs, and the police would not have known about this location. Their aunt's apartment was merely one place among many for gang members to congregate, and while they were often left unsupervised, they typically reserved street activities for other locations. Instead, this location served as a comfortable and relatively quiet place to hang out.

Cars occasionally rolled by, which caused us to abandon our conversation to glance at passersby. Passengers in the cars would do the same, at times giving us a quick nod as they drove by. Shawn and Layboy seemed comfortable in this setting, never pensive about passing cars. Each time a car passed by, I could not help but wonder what people were thinking when they noticed a rather conspicuous six-foot-four-inch young white man casually talking to local teenagers. This thought was heightened on days like this when I held a tape recorder. Over time, I learned that most youths and adults accepted my role in their environment, tape recorder included, if Layboy and Shawn said I was cool. They boys turned out to be invaluable resources for establishing credibility.

As we talked, two teenage boys approached. I recognized them from the time I had spent in a local youth center, but I had not seen them for months. After a quick introduction that included the formality of having them sign consent forms, we began an informal discussion. Joe, the older of the two, looked down at the tape recorder and said, telling me his hood affiliation, "My name is Joe. I'm from the Balt."

Taking his usual role in such conversations, Shawn assured him that talking to me was safe by saying, "Tell him about the Balt."

Joe replied questioningly, "Tell him what we're doing in the hood? Everything, what regular gang bangers do?"

"What's going on in the Balt?" replied Shawn, almost taking over as the researcher.

I added, "Yeah, I went through there two or three years ago with some church people, and there were five or six guys your age following us around that didn't want us to be there. So what's going on in those apartments?"

Joe replied, "See, in the Balt there's stuff going on out there. I ain't trying to be racist or nothing, but a white boy like you walking into the Balt like that, they going to think something's up with you. We ain't used to having white people coming around. So you come in there and walk around and you look suspicious."

His younger brother Jordan chimed in, "They going to jump you, no doubt."

"They going to jump you." Joe continued, "I don't know if you going to make it out."

"I did, fortunately."

"That's good," said Joe. This caused Shawn to laugh at the notion that Joe needed to validate the fact that I had not been beaten as being a good thing. He repeated what Joe said to relive the humor.

I had been through the Baltimore apartments a few years before with a small church group that was attempting to reduce crime in Indianapolis. They were modeling some of the approaches made famous by Boston's TenPoint Coalition (see Kennedy, Braga, and Piehl 2001). Many of the churches in Indianapolis's high-crime areas had organized to help community residents. In addition to providing programs that helped struggling residents and placing political pressure on local politicians, they formed multiple small groups every Friday night and walked the streets in high-crime areas. The night we went into the Baltimore apartments was one of the few times that I was concerned for my safety. One of the church members tried to approach a group of teenage boys, who, without talking, all turned their backs to us and dispersed. The boys followed us through the apartment complex. As the light began to fade, I became increasingly uncomfortable, but no one else in my group seemed to notice. We eventually left without incident, but I gained the impression that even though these church members were local residents, they were somewhat naive. Over time, I learned that the apartment complex, indeed, had a bad reputation, as it was a haven for drugs and gangs.

Joe's reaction was, however, a bit overstated. As a general rule, I operated under the assumption that the probability of violent victimization was low, even in the most high crime communities. I would often say to others, my wife included, that driving to the research site was more dangerous than actually being in the research site. Most people who lived in the Balt were probably law abiding, and those involved in criminal activity would not have benefited from my victimization. Gang members, especially those selling drugs in low-income apartment complexes, were aware of the consequences that followed when outsiders were injured or threatened. Unwanted attention often followed a high-profile incident, and gang members generally exercised restraint unless they were directly threatened. Years before this research began, a major gang in this area was dismantled by criminal justice agencies after a young girl was murdered during a shooting (McGarrell and Chermak 2003). People still occasionally talked about the event, and such attention was avoided if possible.

Up to this point in the research process, I had heard many OGs employ the dilution narrative to dismiss their younger counterparts. Such claims, I thought, were indicative of a generational rejection of newer trends coupled with nostalgic and skewed recollections of times past. As such, I easily overlooked or ignored these accounts, and I did not think that such ideas heavily influenced younger and more active gang members. As we continued to talk, the boys began to reveal how they also embraced similar ideas. The dilution narrative largely shaped their negotiation of the intergang environment, as they seemed concerned with distinguishing real gang members from individuals who merely imitated gang members. When compared with their older counterparts, however, the boys clung to vague notions of standards but embraced a more fluid conception of their environment.

False Flagging and Fake Gang Members

Making distinctions between real and fake gangs could be a confusing endeavor. In an attempt to establish a field boundary, younger gang members did not just rely on the formal standards used by their predecessors. In fact, the reality of the Indianapolis streets was that most self-defined gangs did not abide by stringent, formal standards. So, if such standards did indeed distinguish real gang members from fake gang members, the OGs use of the dilution narrative would have been accurate. Regardless of how they were perceived by the older generation, youthful gang members remained convinced that they were real gang members, while some of their peers were not. As a result, they were involved in a continuous process of defining their environment, but they did so without the convenience of explicit standards.

Jordan continued to talk about life in the streets by identifying his gang affiliation, "Everybody in the hood Vice Lords but we ain't no Vice Lords. We G's, I'm a G."

"So everybody in Baltimore is Vice Lords and you're G's?" I asked for further clarification.

He replied, "Some of them Vice Lords out there."

Still trying to understand the relationship between the Gangster Disciples and Vice Lords, I asked, "Is that a problem for you out there?"

"No," Jordan responded, "We ain't got no problems out there. We hood, we all together."

Thirtieth Street is a well-known clique, or hood gang, located in and around the Baltimore apartments, so I asked, "Are you guys in a clique?"

"We ain't got no clique, we just a hood," Jordan responded. "Been there since we was little. So we just the hood."

Joe added, "I had a chance to be with folks [GD's alliance], but I chose not to, though. Go through all that, the training get my ranks,

I was going to do that, but I decided not to do it." He was now referring to the more formal aspects of the Gangster Disciples. Again, more formal gangs did seem to exist in Indianapolis, but they were not as dominant as the more loosely affiliated cliques that beset communities.

"Why GDs and not Vice Lords?"

Joe tried somewhat unsuccessfully to clarify, "Nah, nah, you see everybody can't be GDs or Vice Lords. . . . I know mostly Vice Lords. But I know a lot of GDs folk. I know a lot about gang banging, but it's just that I don't use it against nobody 'cause I don't feel like anybody need it."

"We ain't got no problems," agreed Jordan.

Joe quickly added, "But if somebody come up trying to say something about the gang that's just false, I can handle it for real because you're false claiming."

Although Jordan claimed affiliation with the Gangster Disciples, his connection to the hood was more integral to his sense of belonging. Some street-oriented individuals who lived in the Baltimore apartments were unified more by place of residence than by gang affiliation. Yet the fluidity of these affiliations could be confusing. Youths who lived in the Baltimore apartments grew up around gangs. They knew gang members and were familiar with gang symbols and rituals. This familiarity may have caused some youths to inconsistently claim affiliation. It seemed to provide Joe with an option to claim gang membership if needed, but he did not see himself as an integral part of the GDs, only the hood. This option was not uncommon. Gang affiliation by convenience was a possibility for some individuals but unacceptable for others, and few gang members acknowledged the contradiction.

Gang members considered the issue of false claiming to be a significant problem. At times, youths falsely claimed membership to build up their reputations, fit in, or convince others not to mess with them. Other youths genuinely believed that they were affiliated, but they really did not understand gang life or the streets. As a cultural entity, the street gang had become so familiar that many youths could superficially appear to be gang members. Their understanding of the boundary between real and fake was constantly being challenged.

The belief that large numbers of youths falsely embraced gang life was central to the dilution narrative. Shawn, Layboy, and other associates often focused on these so-called fake gang members or "false flaggers." Although Gangster Disciples and Vice Lords dominated this conversation, the distinction between real and fake was not just directed toward people claiming affiliation with those specific groups. Unlike the OGs, younger gang members embraced a conception of "gang" that was more inclusive, but they maintained that their peers were also prone to falsely claim affiliation with the various cliques or hoods throughout the city. Layboy and Shawn, for example, occasionally encountered an unfamiliar person who claimed membership in the DFW Boyz. This often occurred because another DFW Boy invited that person to join the gang without first getting the approval of Shawn and Layboy. Sometimes the individual was just using the name of the group to build up his or her reputation. In either situation, the boys expressed a concern that the group was expanding too quickly and was losing its potency. Too many weak or soft individuals had begun to claim membership in the DFW Boyz. That was a problem.

Similar issues occurred with hood affiliations. For example, many youths with limited access to the Baltimore apartments claimed that hood. Jordan and Joe occasionally expressed frustration with boys who lived in other areas but came to the apartments to visit friends or family. Spending a few nights in the apartments did not make someone a part of the hood, and yet many visitors left and claimed the Balt. Youths in the streets also evaluated the various Indianapolis hoods. Only specific communities were considered to be legitimate gang hoods. If someone had grown up or resided in those areas, his or her ability to handle the streets was not immediately questioned. Youths from other parts of the city, however, were immediately perceived as being weak, or soft. Claiming Thirtieth Street, Tenth Street, or Forty-second Street might have initially given someone street credibility. However, claiming Eighty-sixth Street did not give someone credibility, as communities that far north were generally middle class, and residents were labeled soft.

Referencing this, Jordan explained, "There's a lot of people that come into the hood thinking they're hard from different hoods. Yeah, they think they hard."

"If you claiming Gangster Disciples, but you can't spit your lick, then what's with you? [4] See what I'm saying?" Said Joe, redirecting the conversation to the GDs and Vice Lords.

A lick is a formal element used by larger gangs like the Gangster Disciples and the Vice Lords to validate membership. The older original gangstas identified the importance of such information but said that there were rules about when such signifiers could be used. For example, signifiers should only be used within the gang, and an outsider could not request that a member reveal his or her lick, or gang-specific signifier. As such, a lick would not be a useful tool for someone who was not affiliated with that specific gang. Aware of these issues, I asked, "How do you know if somebody is false claiming?"

Jordan responded predictably by saying, "Me personally, there's plenty of ways. Like, take for example, another GD, two GDs. All right, you claiming GD right? And you say, 'Spit your lick,' and you saying something that's in the Bible . . ."

With this comment the group erupted with laughter. Although the idea that someone would respond with a lick that came from the Bible was indeed ridiculous, it was not uncommon for the boys to encounter people who claimed membership in the GDs or VLs but who did not understand the concept of a lick.

Joe continued, "Sir, you don't know what you're doing. You not really in this clique, sorry to say. You not with the gang banging. Now a GD can't ask a Vice Lord 'spit your lick.' They're not supposed to. We not supposed to ask a Vice Lord, 'Spit your lick.' If you do, you're violated [punished], you're violated bro.' That's violated right there."

The boy's discussion of false flagging represented a common belief among gang youth. Many local youths claimed to be gang members, but few actually were. Instead, they embraced gang life and superficially represented gangs without having any connection to real gangs, or having an understanding of what gang life was all about. Unlike their older counterparts, youths considered hoods and cliques to be under the auspices of gang life, so they assumed that the same principles applied to these less sophisticated gang forms.

Improper Channels of Membership

As we continued to talk, I began to wonder where one's under-standing of gang membership came from. Although it was possible that some youths embraced an identity that was not reinforced by others, I thought it quite improbable. More likely, individuals came to embrace their gang status through repeated interactions with a group that claimed to be a gang. The dilution narrative assumed not only that large numbers of youths falsely represented gang membership, but also that they learned to do so through improper channels. Again, this notion was contingent on an assumption that there were a limited number of ways to form or join a gang, and those employing the narrative had unique insight into such processes.

A few months earlier, I had spoken to Naaz, an older and inactive Gangster Disciple, who was originally from Chicago but had moved to Indianapolis after spending ten years in prison. He was adamant that most Indianapolis youths who claimed to be Gangster Disciples or Vice Lords were not really affiliated with those groups. Such claims were instead based on a series of relationships that convinced impressionable youths that they were gang members and that their groups were gangs. Naaz emphasized that the processes that led individuals to falsely represent gang membership were wide-ranging, and he used a hypothetical scenario to describe how spontaneously formed relationships in correctional facilities commonly led to such errors:

> You know my cousin was Folk, so now when I go over there I am Folk. Three years later, never actively involved or never did anything, don't know anything about it, I go into Marion county jail. It rough as fuck, and now I am Folks. There might be two or three guys from my cousin's neighborhood that knew me three years ago and:
>
> "Ah, what's up Jeff?"
> "Ah what's up, what's happening GD? All right."
>
> And now it just goes on, and it's like as you meet more and more individuals,
>
> "Ah this is so and so he's folks from so and so."
>
> You go on to a penal institution, and I always used to say: you know in the Army they say, "Be all that you can be," in prison it's, "Be whoever you want to be." 'Cause everyone has a story to tell, and nobody knows if you are telling the truth or not.

Past associations gave someone enough exposure to street gangs so that he or she could look or act like a gang member in certain contexts. This was made easier by an intergang environment that undervalued, as many

OGs suggested, the use of stringent standards for membership. In effect, a person could claim membership to the GDs or VLs because everyone else who claimed membership lacked the knowledge about gang codes, manifestos, and rituals that would be required to challenge a membership claim. When a person claimed gang affiliation, and peers unquestioningly accepted his or her membership, the temporary identity, which was embraced to negotiate a difficult environment, became more permanent. To Naaz, these individuals were not real gang members.

As my conversation with Layboy, Shawn, Joe, and Jordan continued, the boys also displayed a belief that large numbers of youths were using inappropriate means to gain access to gangs. Instead of focusing on social relationships, however, the boys discussed how the Internet allowed youths to access information about gangs. Given their access to supposedly secret gang knowledge, many youths boldly represented those gangs.

Layboy, still amused by the Bible verse comment made earlier, laughed again and said, "Spit your Bible verse."

"Where did you learn your lick?" I asked.

Jordan replied, "Where did I learn my lick from? I learned it from a lot of places. You can get it from the Internet."

"Yeah," added Layboy, "you can get it from the Internet."

Shawn ended his unusually long period silence by clarifying, "Call them Internet gangstas," as if there was a distinction between an Internet gangsta and a real gangsta.

"Yeah, call them Internet gangstas," agreed Layboy.

"You can see the heart," continued Jordan. "You can see all that stuff [showing me gang signs], you can see them all. It's all on there."

"They show you all the gang signs," agreed Layboy.

Although they superficially displayed gang membership through gang symbols, speech patterns, or body language, and may have demonstrated knowledge about some of the formal aspects of gang life, so-called Internet gangsters were not real. They gained insight into the formal rules of larger, more established gangs through online resources. Anyone, after all, could easily access information about well-known gangs through Internet searches that quickly locate formerly privileged information regarding codes, rules, literature, and manifestos of major gangs like the Black Gangster Disciples or Conservative Vice Lords (see Knox 2006; Knox and Papachristos 2002). Networking sites like

MySpace also provided youths with virtual access to so-called gang members who freely exhibited gang secrets. Such access gave some youths enough knowledge to appear like gang members, but, according to the boys, they were only perpetrating a fraud.

The individuals involved with this study, both young and old, strongly believed that large numbers of youths were using improper avenues to become affiliated with gangs. Although the older generation of gang members spoke of strict standards to distinguish real from fake, the younger generation used a broader understanding of the intergang environment that was not bound by explicit standards. Notions of real, fake, and false pathways to membership related not only to affiliations like the Gangster Disciples and Vice Lords but also to cliques and hoods scattered throughout the city. Incidents of perceived false representation of cliques and hoods were a problem. There was also a general understanding among gang youths that entire groups falsely claimed gang or clique affiliation. Given the popularity of gang life in some East Thirty-eighth Street neighborhoods, youths routinely formed groups, created a name, and adopted ganglike symbols. Through social contacts or Internet access, they might have modeled well-known gangs like the Gangster Disciples and Vice Lords, or they might have formed an independent clique. To individuals in the street, just because a group thought it was a gang and modeled the appearance of a gang did not mean it actually was a gang. Shawn and Layboy even admitted that as children they formed a group named after a cartoon series. They laughed at their younger selves and their earlier assumptions that such a group was a real gang. In retrospect, it was not a real gang, and it did not last long. They were just children trying to imitate the real gangs they saw in the streets. Many youths in the streets formed similar groups that tried to act like a gang, but according to Shawn, Layboy, and other gang members, they were perpetrating a fraud.

Interpreting "Real"

Another central assumption made by individuals who embraced the dilution narrative was that they were able to accurately discern who was and who was not a real gang member. Issues of false flagging typically arose and became problematic when one's understanding of real gang membership was inconsistent with peer's understand of real gang membership. Some youths might have intentionally misrepresented themselves for personal gain, but more often those individuals accused of false representation genuinely believed that they were part of a gang. The boy or girl that represented a given hood, clique, or gang was not knowingly violating a peer's expectations for gang membership. Only through interactions with peers would he or she even become aware of this evaluation.

Intergang interactions involved an interpretive process whereby invested parties assessed their counterpart's right to belong. Whereas previous encounters or group reputations informed most intergang interactions, gang members did encounter unfamiliar individuals or groups. Both parties often clarified gang affiliation during these encounters (for a more nuanced discussion of these encounters see Garot 2010). The manner by which individuals clarified their gang affiliation was not guided by formal process in which both parties followed a patterned and rehearsed introduction. Rather, it evolved informally, as parties used different gang signifiers to announce their affiliation. Nearly all gangs, hoods, or cliques in Indianapolis embraced these signifiers, and members relied on codes, gestures, speech patterns, and colors to communicate gang membership. Being accepted as a real gang member during an initial encounter should ideally be contingent on these signifiers.

Throughout my research, gang members confidently broadcasted their abilities to discern real gang members from fake gang members. At times, their judgments were grounded in an innate ability to sense emotions in another person. For example, some gang members confidently proclaimed that they could tell if someone was fake moments after meeting that person. Such clarity was not produced by the use of secret gang rituals but by an innate ability to sense fear in that person. It was good that they were not able to perceive skepticism emanating from me. More often, gang members mentioned that they relied heavily on various gang signifiers to discern real from fake. Such clarity was, however, unconvincing.

As our conversation continued, I asked Shawn, Layboy, Joe, and Jordan, "How do you tell an Internet gangster from a real one?"

"The way they're dressed," replied Jordan. "They'll have on all red or all blue. If you're cripping [representing the Crips] it you'll have on all blue. If you a Blood you going to have on all that red." It was an odd response, given that colors were probably the best-known gang symbol and were perhaps the easiest to fabricate.

"You can tell," Layboy added with an air of certainty. "You can tell when somebody lying, man."

"It's easy to tell if somebody's lying," agreed Joe.

Layboy explained, "Like, for instance, everybody used to say 'on the G' even if they Vice Lord, 'cause everybody used to say 'on the G.' They really didn't know."

"Gangster Disciple," clarified Shawn. "On the G" was supposed to be a phrase used by Gangster Disciples, but it became popular with many youths who claimed affiliations to other gangs.

Admitting that he, too, used this terminology without an understanding of the real meaning, Layboy said, "'Cause I used to say when I was really little, 'On the G, on the G,' but I didn't really know what it mean. I didn't really know what it mean. 'Til I got older. People used to ask me, 'Why do you say 'on the G?'"

"But mostly 'on the G' was a word, it was a word," added Joe, implying that the phrase had lost its meaning. "But if you say 'on the six' or something like that."

Layboy included, "That's how you know most people, they really don't say anybody 'on the six' or 'on the five.'"

"They don't say 'on the five' or 'on the six,'" agreed Jordan.

Both responses were somewhat surprising, as the boys implied that Internet gangsters would not know about these phrases. I had heard otherwise. One Gangster Disciple from Chicago told me that Indianapolis youths often recited patterns of numbers that were meaningful to the GDs, but they really did not know what the numbers meant. "On the six" was a much simpler phrase that could easily be transmitted through networks of youths who did not understand its meaning. It signified the Gangster Disciples, who represented themselves with a six-pointed star. By contrast, five-pointed star represented the Vice Lords, and so the phrase "on the five" signified Vice Lord affiliation. A simple Internet search of "on the five, on the six" leads to such insights. It also reveals inflammatory phrases like "six poppin' and five droppin'," which implies that the GDs are shooting, and the VLs are being killed. These messages are often posted on MySpace pages and are not difficult to access.

Joe acknowledged this to be true, "'On the five' because I ain't going to lie, back in the day I ain't know what they mean when they say 'on the five.' I thought five was a line number [bus line], I didn't know what it meant, I didn't know none of it."

"On the seven, on the seven," chimed Jordan randomly.

Shawn clarified, "That's Brightwood Boyz." Brightwood was a hood just south of Thirtieth Street along Keystone Avenue. Cliques also seemed to adopt their own vernacular.

Layboy asked, "On the seven?"

This too was an odd response. Layboy was heavily invested in the various Indianapolis cliques, especially those on the northeast side of the city, and I was surprised that he was not familiar with this phrase. Perhaps the number of subtle symbols and linguistic devices used by a large number of different hoods, cliques, and gangs was just too complicated for the average gang member to keep up with. Ironically, youths lacking full insight into the range of gang signifiers also used their limited knowledge to dismiss and disparage others.

This last insight further verified what I was beginning to suspect. For those embracing the dilution narrative, there was a true and clear distinction between real and fake gang members. The boys ardently believed that there was a discernable boundary to an intergang field, and through interactions they could distinguish real and fake gang members. Some self-defined gang members belonged to the intergang field, but many did not. Yet with this last question, Layboy revealed a deficiency in his knowledge about a particular group. During the course of an interaction, would Layboy have summarily dismissed someone who was saying "on the seven" simply because he was unfamiliar with the phrase? My skepticism about the boys' ability to discern real from fake contrasted with their confidence. The subtleties involved in this interaction process were too complicated, I thought, and the standards for evaluation were too ambiguous for such certainty. The self-defined gang members who were dismissed by the DFW Boyz would have genuinely believed that they were part of the general gang environment, and they might have employed a different understanding of gang to dismiss their detractors. Were there groups or individuals in Indianapolis that would have labeled Layboy, Shawn, and DFW Boyz as being a fake gang?

I wanted to examine the consequences of these assessments, so I asked, "So what do you do with the fake guys, the guys you think are fake?" My skepticism had unintentionally surfaced in the end of the question.

"You can tell if they're fake or not," clarified Layboy in response to the last part of my question. Apparently, there was no ambiguity in this process.

Shawn responded, "Get them up out of here."

"Most people say 'on the five, on the five,'" included Layboy. "Try asking them a question, they don't know nothing. 'Spit your lick.' 'What?'"

"If you respond with 'what,' time for you get up out of here. Get them up out of here," agreed Shawn, as he implied that the person would be threatened and/or forced to leave if he or she did not respond appropriately.

"Is the lick your literature, or is it numbers?" Given that Layboy provided a secondary question used for validating membership, I wanted to verify the substance of a "lick." During earlier interviews with gang members not affiliated with the DFW Boyz,' I had been exposed to both styles of verification.

"Yeah, literature," responded Joe.

Jordan disagreed, "Numbers, numbers."

I noted the inconsistency; it could have been caused by confusion or an understanding that the numbers used for the lick originated in gang literature. It also could have reflected the different methods used by the GDs and VLs. Based on my earlier interactions with gang members, the Vice Lords recited literature at length, while the GDs used numbers.

Layboy further elaborated, "Some people just make up stuff. Like the dudes I used to hang around with, the high-ranking Vice Lords I used to hang around, they say 'on the five,' and spit their lick, 'on the five, something, something, something, something, something.' If you just copy them after hearing them say it—some people just copy it right off the street. Some people write it on paper, write their lick on paper."

Joe added, "They be drawing gang signs and everything. Five-point crown and all of that. They got a lot of stuff. There's this dude in my school wearing a five-point crown. But see what it is, dude in my school because he was about to get saying Insane [Vice Lords] lick and he was Almighty. He had the Insane lick on his body but he was Almighty, though. So Insane was going to jump him though, there's only three Insanes in my school. There's supposed to be three Almighty. The rest is just fake."

To the boys, this last example provided clear evidence that the notion of "gang" had become diluted. While interacting with individuals at school, they learned that many peers claimed affiliation to the Gangster Disciples or Vice Lords, but only a few could actually validate their claims. It was an idea embraced by nearly everyone in this study, regardless of their age or experience. Some gang members were real and some were not. All self-defined gang members, it seemed, believed in and established a boundary that clearly distinguished the two groups.

CONCLUSION

The confidence expressed by gang members related to both their self-assessments and their evaluations of other groups. Gang members were supremely confident in their gang's status, not only as a real gang but also as an elite gang. Moreover, members commonly embraced the dilution narrative and fervently alleged that many youths falsely claimed gang affiliation. Gang members confidently labeled other groups or individuals as being fraudulent without considering that they might have erred in their evaluations. Such confidence was, however, overshadowed by the harsh reality that the greater intergang environment did not match their internal certainty. Self-defined gang members who were willing to label other gangs as fraudulent were equally likely to be labeled as imitators of real gangs. The intergang environment was filled with contradicting evaluations and generalized uncertainty.

A central problem for gang members, therefore, involves the continuous need to reconcile their self-assessments with the dismissive appraisals of peers. One wonders if the street participant who is not affiliated with gang life experiences a similar sort of pressure. Does the active armed robber, the drug dealer, the pimp, the hustler, or the prostitute experience a clear disconnect between parts of his or her identity and the evaluations of relevant peers? These street roles are grounded in specific activities, so the boundary between real and fake is clear. If one robs, he or she is, by definition, a robber. Perhaps there is a difference between a person who defines him- or herself as an armed robber and a person who only sporadically commits an act of robbery. But such distinctions are not problematic for street participants. The gang member identity is, however, easily embraced and frequently questioned on the streets.

Scholars have identified a few other categories or identities that can create a similar pressure, but they are not mutually exclusive with gang life. For example, gang members and non-gang members alike "do gender," as they pursue ideal masculine and feminine roles in the streets (Anderson 1999; Campbell 1984 and 1987; Copes and Hochstetler 2003; Miller 1998; Miller and Brunson 2000; Miller and Decker 2001; Oliver 1994; Wilkinson 2001). Whereas females can use gender stereotypes to minimize or alter their participation in violent events (Miller 1998; Miller and Brunson 2000; Miller and Decker, 2001), males often strive to emulate the masculine ideals of toughness and physical, sexual, or mental prowess (Anderson 1999; Copes and Hochstetler 2003; Oliver 1994; Wilkinson 2001). Street-oriented males experience pressure to demonstrate to others that they are, in fact, real men. To some extent, the construction of masculinity is similar to the construction of gang identities. Just as a self-defined gang member can be labeled as a "wannabe," a male can be labeled as a "pussy" or a "bitch." In both cases the victim of the negative label has been cast outside of a socially constructed boundary. Yet male gang members are subjected to a unique need to demonstrate that they are both real men and real gang members. Although many street participants experience pressures that accompany the former identity, self-defined gang members uniquely experience the pressures attached to the latter identity.

This aspect of gang life reveals an important distinction between gang members and non-gang members, and it may partially explain why gang members are more heavily involved in criminal behavior. A gang member's need to reconcile any disagreement between his or her gang's collective identity and conflicting peer assessments forces the gang member to demonstrate authenticity according to his or her understanding of "real." At best, this need forces gang members to validate their identity by employing harmless signifiers of gang status (symbols or codes), but this method is often ineffective. At worst, this need causes gang members to behave in a manner that is consistent with their gang's collective identity. For example, the DFW Boyz define themselves as being down for whatever, and so they respond to a skeptical environment accordingly. Unfortunately, violence is a core element of that identity.

CHAPTER 4

The Paradox of Legitimacy

GIVEN THAT GANG MEMBERS are immersed in a social environment that is characterized by pervasive skepticism, their social routines are influenced by the mere possibility that a peer or peer group is observing and assessing their actions. Such concerns are heightened by the uncertainty that accompanies that skepticism. The dilution narrative is a commonly embraced story, but it is not accompanied by stable, predictable, and clear indices that allow for objective distinctions between real and fake gang members. One may be tempted to accept unquestioningly a single version of "real" offered by an OG or the members of a particular gang, but the impartiality guiding such perceived truth is questionable. A gang member's understanding of what a real gang is is largely self-serving and based on personal experience. The intergang environment, therefore, consists of innumerable self-serving definitions of "real," and disagreements abound. For example, not all other self-defined gang members in Indianapolis shared the dismissive sentiments of the DFW Boyz. Rejected peers were unlikely to agree with negative appraisals of the gang, and they may have even viewed the DFW Boyz as a collection of fraudulent gang members.

Gang members are caught in a troubling paradox. They face constant pressure to validate their claims to gang membership in the presence of skepticism and derision, and they are, therefore, centrally concerned with gaining and maintaining legitimacy in the intergang environment. Individuals who officially join a gang are thrust into an uncertain environment in which they repeatedly have to demonstrate to others that they are a genuine part of this new social environment. This is not so much about proving themselves within the group but rather about establishing legitimacy to outsiders, especially those who also claim gang affiliation. It is somewhat ironic, then, that individuals join gangs in response to troubling circumstances, only to be confronted with an enduring struggle for legitimacy. What is paradoxical about legitimacy in the intergang environment, however, is not only the presence of this struggle, but also the reality that the intergang environment lacks clear, agreed-upon standards for establishing and maintaining legitimacy. Gang members are immersed in a social environment that is heavily invested in assessments of real and not real, yet they are unable to demonstrate objectively to peers that they belong to the intergang field.

SOCIALLY CONSTRUCTED
FIELD BOUNDARIES

In the streets, the notion of a "real gang member" is a social construct created during routine social interactions between self-defined gang members who are struggling to establish the boundaries of the intergang field. The process of establishing a clear distinction between real and fake gang members is similar to what some scholars have termed "boundary work," which involves the collective and continuous efforts of relevant actors to distinguish that which belongs from that which does not in a given social forum (see Gieryn 1983). The notions of "real gang" or "real gang member," therefore, signify a symbolic boundary that conceptually distinguishes high-status groups or people from low-status groups or people (see Lamont and Molnar 2002). In the context of a gang member's day-to-day social setting, an array of labels can be used to either validate or marginalize another group or person. And, as noted in chapter 3, gang members are quite willing to marginalize their peers.

The construction of field boundaries is not unique to gang life; many collections of people struggle to define the parameters of their social arena. For example, scientists constantly work to establish the scope of their influence in response to competing unscientific perspectives. They must convince outsiders and policy makers that science has a monopoly on real knowledge for certain issues (Gieryn 1983 and 1999; Shackley and Wynne 1996). This struggle has been evident in the debate on climate change, as scientists collectively work to convince the public that the answers to the climate issue are found exclusively within the boundaries of science (Shackley and Wynne 1996; Zehr 2000). In the effort to expand their influence, or to resist external control efforts, organizations also work to establish field boundaries. During the 1980s, credit unions, for example, collectively formed a national federation that helped combat interference from the banking industry by defining the parameters of credit unions (Lune and Martinez 1999). The collective struggle to develop and use the notion of a boundary is common in many different social arenas.

Gang members, however, are not collectively etching out their place of influence in society; nor are they striving for political or economic viability. They are, instead, struggling to find meaning and gain dominance within an uncertain social environment. Instead of collectively struggling to define real in response to an external threat, gang members are focused on casting judgment on peers in the intergang environment. This process is complicated by both a lack of uniformity in that environment and the inability to establish a set of criteria that serve as boundary objects, or stable and reproducible ideas that create consensus between divergent social actors (see Shackley and Wynne 1996; Star and Griesemer 1989). Even within a limited area like Indianapolis, subtle variations between gangs create disagreements, and few standards exist to reconcile differing opinions.

Street gangs provide some natural impediments for establishing relatively stable criteria that properly distinguish groups that belong from groups that do not. For example, they vary by size, structure, and degree of organizational sophistication (Decker, Bynum, and Weisel 1998; Klein and Maxson 2006). Most gangs have no clear function, and they cannot be accurately described as having a rational output. Some gangs are entrepreneurially involved in drug sales, but most are not (Klein 1995; Klein and Maxson 2006). Although gang members embrace street culture, that cultural system also includes many individuals who do not claim gang membership. The impediments to establishing a clear boundary are so great that researchers have historically struggled over the definition of "gang." Only through rigorous debate and numerous public disagreements have researchers narrowed their understanding of the definition (see Ball and Curry 1995; Bjerregaard 2002; Esbensen et al. 2001; Klein 1995 and 2005; Winfree et al. 1992). Self-defined gang members who are personally invested in the establishment of a field boundary are not, however, actively engaged in a wide-ranging open debate about the placement of that boundary.

Gang members do undoubtedly embrace an array of cultural cues that are intended to communicate gang status. Although an outsider may mistakenly view these cues as objective signifiers of real gang membership, many street participants view the use of stereotypical gang symbols like colors, licks, tattoos, signs, or speech patterns as dubious attempts to act like a gang member. Indeed, a closer examination of these cues reveals that they have limited capacity to transcend the dilution narrative and serve as clarifiers in the streets. Too often they are vague or inconsistent; nearly all superficial signifiers of gang membership are easily falsifiable and are often viewed skeptically by others in the gang environment.

When asked to clarify how they distinguish between real and fake gang members, individuals not connected to the DFW Boyz, and therefore detached from my conversations with Layboy, Shawn, and their associates, also relied heavily on superficial and symbolic displays of gang membership. They commonly used colors, licks, tattoos, speech, or vague behavioral patterns as indicators of gang status. Yet their confidence was accompanied by admissions of doubt, as they admitted that many youths use these cultural cues to falsely represent gang membership:

TL: How do you know if somebody is a gang member?

KENNY: Down here—rags. Vice Lord—red. To be honest, I'm a folk. GD's folks to the fullest, know what I mean? My rag would be blue. Other gangs, getting tattoos, you see a tat. They show you a tat. They got their gang on there. I mean, that's where they're from. Gang signs, niggas throw up their hood and all of that. That's how you really know. How the way they talk. How the way they approach you. Like gangsters come up to you, "What's up, folk." That's how you really know. Niggas be trying to act though, hard. Like niggas try to act. You got to give them a test. You feel me? Like this nigga, you know what I'm saying, you got to give them a test. Niggas trying to be too much, trying to be what they can't be. I just tell them they be pushing it to the limit, a little too far, man.

TL: So you have GDs over here and GDs over there. How do you know that one group is not just twenty kids wearing the right colors?

KENNY: 'Cause you got a lick. "What's your lick? What's your number?" My lick's 74741234 [the last four numbers are fake substitutes].

If you don't know your lick you not a gangster. I mean that's in the G code. Hoover wrote that. The Vice Lords too. We don't know nothing about they lick. All the Gs got different licks. Like different colors of blue, but everybody's still folks. It comes from your general, it comes from your leader, it comes from the person that jumped you in folks. It all depends on where you come from. You got area codes too. I'm from downtown 12 now. My hood number went in there too with me, 12. 74741234. Thirty-four is the number of members that's a part of the gang and 7474 is when the GDs got started. 1974.

When I asked similar questions to Tyrese, he replied:

TYRESE: If they were really, really into, because a lot of people say they're a G, 'cause they say "on the 5" "on the 6" so people say it, but it don't really mean nothing. If you was really initiated and you was really gang banging then you would know it. You would have your colors on. You would be representing your colors. You would hear it in their slang. "What's up, cuz'?" They call you cuz', they GDs. If they say, "What up, blood?" or "What up?" Cuz' is GD, bloods is Vice Lords, and you would always hear that slang because it became part of your life. It was a part of your personality. It was what you was, what you lived for. So if you really was, you would know it, and you wouldn't be afraid to tell it. They be like, "What's your colors, homie?" or "What up?" or they'll look at you. You on their set and you wearing red. "What up, cuz'?" 'cause they know you ain't a cuz'. They going to say it because they letting you know that, "Hey you in the wrong territory." They letting you know that this is, "What up, cuz'?" They saying cuz' because they are letting you know that's their language. And they know if you really gang bang- ing you know. You know it all. So if I was coming and another G saw me or something and I was speaking to him, he'll shake up with you. You gotta know the hand shake. If you can't shake up there is no way you can be a part of it. 'Cause a lot of people claim it, a lot of people do but not even half the people are really out there living by the code. 'Cause you live by codes. You just know by the appear- ance by everything. If you can't tell if they are then they are not. They are not. A lot of people front and pretend. They just pretenders.

As indicators of authenticity, these symbols, gestures, and speech patterns, while stereotypical of gang life, were inherently problematic. Two significant deficiencies accompanied these symbols and diminished their ability to clearly differentiate real gang members from fake gang members.

First, the symbols used for verifying status were inconsistent, as members often differed in their opinions of which symbols validated gang membership. For example, a lick was often a source of confusion for gang members, and everyone in the streets did not accept the numerical sequence listed above. In fact, the numerical sequence of 74741234 might have been meaningful to one self-defined member of the Gangster Disciples, but it might have been meaningless to another. Without revealing the last four digits of the lick, I showed both younger and older Gangster Disciples the sequence of numbers, and most looked at it with confusion. Some gang members suggested that the significance of 74 did not come from the gang's date of origin, but it is a numerical code for GD. G is the seventh letter of the alphabet and D is the fourth letter of the alphabet, hence 74. Other gang members discussed how many so-called Gangster Disciples recited numerical sequences with little understanding of what the numbers meant. For some gang members, the lick was significant. For other gang members, it was not. Without unanimity, the lick could not be used to establish widespread legitimacy.

Second, where agreement did exist, the standards were susceptible to environmental skepticism. A central tenant of the dilution narrative was that youths gained insight into the more secretive aspects of gang life through illegitimate means, and the symbols used to validate gang membership were easily falsified. Youths could gain access to gang colors, speech patterns, literature, and licks through social contacts or Web sites. As noted in chapter 3, external evaluations of gang membership were often shaped by the belief that many self-defined gang members were fraudulently using these symbols. In effect, these symbols were too well known and embraced by youths outside of the field boundary. Therefore, someone saying, "What up, cuz'?" or flashing gang signs, displaying a tattoo, wearing colors, or even using coded numerical sequences, could be viewed skeptically by others in the gang environment. Moreover, descriptions of the clarification process were often accompanied by the caveat that many people used these symbols to claim gang affiliation falsely. Gang members acknowledged that the indicators used for establishing field boundaries were flawed, that many so-called wannabes mirrored the appearance of real gang members. Thus symbols could not be used accurately to differentiate real gang members from fake gang members.

Gang members lacked clear means to gain the approval of others in their environment. The symbols traditionally used for validation had become so common that self-defined gang members struggled to discern authentic gang members from peers who falsely represented gang affiliation. More problematically, some gang members were likely to receive contradicting appraisals from peers in their environment. These gang members might have gained acceptance from some peers, but this acceptance did not eliminate the threat of rejection. The child who was standing on the corner spouting numerical sequences and claiming membership in the Gangster Disciples would have appeared to be a legitimate gang member to some observers, but he or she would have looked like a fool to others. This problem only increased for smaller cliques that embraced a gang identity. If childhood associates simply embraced the idea of being a gang, adopted a name, and made up a few rudimentary symbols to demonstrate their gang status, were they in a gang? This question influences formal scholarly attempts to define and measure gang membership, but it profoundly influenced the day-to-day lives of gang members in Indianapolis.

At its core, this dilemma on the streets of Indianapolis is an issue of environmental uncertainty caused by natural variations between gangs. It was exaggerated because gang members generally lacked boundary objects, or clear indices of authenticity that created an acceptable level of consensus about the parameters of "real." Instead, gang members continuously participated in boundary work, but their efforts produced self-serving and subjective field boundaries. Since no collection of gangs had a monopoly on establishing the boundaries of "real" and "not real," and since there was no collective effort to establish objective boundaries, focal gang members drew from their experiences to establish an under-standing of "real" that included themselves and excluded others. Self-defined gang members who were dismissed by another gang attached a different meaning to the notion of "gang" and continued to propagate the dilution narrative. The gang labeled as fake also labeled other gangs as fake. The objectivity that accompanies widespread agreement was replaced by innumerable self-serving and individually derived definitions of real gangs and wannabe groups.[1]

Self-serving understandings of "real" were born out of current or past gang associations. Each definer of "gang" was included within his or her boundary of "real." This self-centeredness was quite apparent when talking to gang members. For example, Shauna, who was featured in chapter 2, used age to create a division between real and fake gangs. The point of division between the older, more legitimate gangs and the younger, reckless gangs also happened to be her age: twenty-five:

TL: How organized are gangs up here?

SHAUNA: Uh, I would have to break them up in age ranks. I would say this current generation, they don't care. There's no questions to be asked, there's no thought process, there's no loyalty . . . twenty-five and up I would consider more mafia status. Twenty-five and under its reckless gang banging. That's what it is. It's like taking the rules to how the gang is originally supposed to be, and you use it how you want to use it. There's no godfather of the gang, there's no ringleader in the gang. Each individual that's in the gang, they are the ring leader.

During a later interview, I asked her about the standards used by the younger generation of gang members. She suggested that many youths had rejected the organized components of gangs, and they operated with little regard for the standards or purposive action exhibited by real gangs:

TL: So this newer generation of gangs, what are their criteria for joining?

SHAUNA: Nothing. Nothing. That's the sad part about it. That's why I say they took what they hear and what they learn about gangs from the past, and they build their own. Their criteria is you gotta' steal, it ain't even about stealing. Take what's yours, get what you want. That's their criteria, to have some balls. Be grimey, don't show no weakness.

TL: No literature?

SHAUNA: No. They couldn't even tell you who the first kingpin was. It's about having a pistol and knowing how to shoot it. Being able to kill somebody, at least being able to wound somebody, 'cause it's nothing to having a gun if you've never really used it on somebody. You know that's their criteria. Have some money in their pocket. Get it the fastest, quickest way you can. And the more money you got you proved yourself, you somebody. Being able to have some type of transportation—don't care how you get it. Being able to sleep with as many girls as you want to and treat them as bad as you can. That's their criteria, I'm so serious. Nothing about respect and morals is involved in this younger generation's criteria. It's like how can you mix good with bad? But with the real gangs that's what it was about. It was about good and bad, you know because everybody in the gangs wasn't bad. A lot of people in the real gangs stood for something. To make you think about it's just like corporate America.

According to Shauna, gangs made up of individuals under the age of twenty-five represented deviations from pure or real gangs. She was not included in this group. Interestingly, however, the criteria she followed during her gang tenure were less than idyllic. For example, Shauna claimed to be a member of the Gangster Disciples, but she was in a relationship with an older male Vice Lord. Because of that relationship, she spent a significant amount of time as a teenager hanging out with Vice Lords. She sold drugs for them, fought with them, and was even involved in their shootings. Her close relationship with a female friend in the Vice Lords even caused Shauna to mark herself as a Vice Lord. Gangster Disciples wear blue and favor the right side of their bodies. Vice Lords wear red and favor the left side of their bodies. Each gang has signifiers that can be placed on the appropriate side of the body to claim membership. Often, gang members put a gold crown on an upper tooth located either in the right or left side of the mouth. Despite being a GD and favoring the right side, Shauna crowned a tooth on the left side of her mouth in honor of her Vice Lord friend. To many gang members, this act would have been a clear indication that Shauna was not a real gang member. To Shauna, the contradiction was a nonissue.

Ryan, a nineteen-year-old street participant, created a definition of real gangs based on his experience in another town. Born in St. Louis, he moved to Indianapolis when he was thirteen. He did not view the contrasts between St. Louis gangs and Indianapolis gangs to be subtle differences between the two cities. Instead, he viewed St. Louis gangs to be real and Indianapolis gangs to be fake:

> Gangs in St. Louis is like you grow up into it. Say like my uncle, he's GD or whatever. So my uncle is a GD, my brother is going to be a GD, and I'm going to be a GD. So if I cross that line, I'm going to get a taste. So like in St. Louis you raised in it. It's like a whole family is from one set. Down here it's like if you was born on Forty-sixth, so you going to claim Forty-sixth. You can move, whatever. It's fake down here. It's not like a real gang. Everybody is just talking about what street they're from. . . . . Fake, somebody can claim it, "Ah I'm a G, I'm a G." Somebody could like try to call them out, and they don't know what they talking about. If you real you ain't got to talk, you just be who you are.

Ryan's interpretation of his experiences in two cities provided a clear depiction of a self-serving definition of "real." Gang members in Indianapolis did not look or act like gang members in St. Louis. When challenged, Indianapolis gang members could not provide an adequate justification for their claims of membership; their knowledge was not consistent with Ryan's understanding of "real." At no point did Ryan consider that the opposite might have been true.

This tendency to form a self-serving understanding of "real" could be applied to most gangs and gang members in Indianapolis. Individually derived understandings of gang were embraced and used to dismiss others within the social environment. Minor differences were the reason for overt dismissals, as few gang members considered that natural variations between gangs led to a diversified environment. Although each gang member assessed the validity of other environmental participants' claims to gang membership, each gang member also negotiated a skeptical environment. Certainty within a given group did not determine acceptance by others in the environment. When generalized, this generated a dynamic in which large numbers of self-defined gangs were free to dismiss each other.

Legitimacy

Despite the confidence of a given set of gang members and the immediate perception that symbols or codes can signify real gang membership, the intergang environment is marred by uncertainty. Gang members must face the possibility that their faultless self-evaluations are incongruent with the assessments of others in the intergang environment. When that environment consists of confident, self-defined gang members who also embrace and enact the dilution narrative, inconsistent evaluations are inevitable. This produces a persistent need among self-defined gang members to prove to outsiders that they are indeed real gang members. Therefore, they are constantly pursuing legitimacy in the intergang environment.

The notion of legitimacy has been well developed by organizational theorists. At its most basic level, the pursuit of legitimacy occurs when a group seeks to justify its right to exist to other relevant actors (Dowling and Pfeffer 1975). Such justification only occurs when a group's actions are congruent with the expectations of relevant peers within a given field (Deephouse 1996; Galaskiewicz 1985; Kostova and Zaheer 1999; Pfeffer and Salancik 1978).[2] When contradicting appraisals exist, the dismissed group can only gain legitimacy by resolving the inconsistency. It must prove its place in the field by meeting the expectations of relevant field participants. When this occurs, members of the field come to view the group as legitimate. A group that has been labeled as illegitimate must, therefore, prove to established field participants that it belongs either by changing or by demonstrating that an error has been made.

Legitimacy is more complicated than just proving oneself to field participants, however. Two qualifying elements create a more detailed understanding of the relationship between groups, the intergroup environment or field, and the notion of legitimacy.

First, although legitimacy can be negotiated in the context of an overt challenge, more commonly it is continuously gained, maintained, or lost through routine interactions with field participants. Once established, legitimacy is resistant to isolated challenges, but it is still dependent on prior events (Suchman 1995). A group gains approval by establishing a pattern of behavior that matches the expectations of other field participants. Improper behavior before the establishment of legitimacy can lead to a general rejection of the group. An approved group can lose legitimacy but is afforded some margin of error. Inappropriate behavior in a few situations, or the inability of a group member to meet field standards, will not immediately reflect poorly on the group.

Although a legitimate entity can suffer some embarrassing events without being rejected, there is a threshold that can put it at risk for losing past gains. Thus the pursuit of legitimacy must be understood as a continuous process, whereby the illegitimate can become accepted, and the legitimate can be rejected. For gang members, concerns about legitimacy create a constant pressure, acutely felt through overt dismissals but experienced in all social settings.

Second, legitimacy is largely contingent on generally agreed upon norms that are used to distinguish legitimate groups from illegitimate groups. Through mutual interaction, field participants continuously create, define, and reinforce the tenets of appropriateness used to establish a field boundary (DiMaggio and Powell 1991; Scott and Meyer 1991). This process, though imperfect, typically leads to a general agreement about the required norms or standards for gaining acceptance into a given field. In organizational studies, for example, boundary lines are drawn according to an organization's function, form or appearance, output or product, or normative qualifications (DiMaggio and Powell 1991; Scott and Meyer 1991). When field participants agree on the requirements for inclusion, the process of gaining legitimacy is clear. A focal group must simply meet the expectations for field participation, and fieldwide acceptance will follow accordingly. Thus, certainty in the legitimizing process is directly related to the establishment of clear standards that are accepted by nearly all field participants. If such standards do not exist, ubiquitous acceptance is problematic, and the process of gaining and maintaining legitimacy is characterized by uncertainty. Universal acceptance may not be possible.

Intergang interactions create an enduring need to prove one's rightful place within the intergang environment. Pursuing legitimacy is a continuous process that is heavily dependent on established, clear, agreed-upon norms. For Shawn, Layboy, the DFW Boyz, and other Indianapolis gang members, claims of legitimacy must be impervious to the dilution narrative. The boys must be able to demonstrate to relevant field participants that their gang affiliation is not the byproduct of false avenues, such as dubious social relationships or the Internet. The boys must establish that they are not just a collection of children trying to act like a gang. They must rely on agreed-upon norms or standards to absolve doubt and prove that they belong within the boundaries of the intergang field. If they cannot meet these standards, or if such standards do not exist, pursuing legitimacy becomes a tenuous endeavor.

THE PROBLEM OF CONTRADICTING APPRAISALS AND THE PARADOX OF LEGITIMACY

On a hot day in mid-June, the problematic nature of gaining and maintaining legitimacy in the intergang environment became readily apparent, as I again accompanied Layboy and Shawn during their daily activities. A few weeks had passed since my conversation with Layboy, Shawn, Jordan, and Joe. By that point in the research, frequent interactions allowed me to establish strong bonds with Shawn, Layboy, their older brother Aaron, cousin TJ, and another member of the gang, Lonnie. I was also friendly with, but not especially close to, a broader group of DFW Boyz and their associates. The drive to Indianapolis from Bloomington, like many other aspects of the research, had become taxing. I spent approximately ten hours each week (two to three hours each day) driving to and from the research site and many more hours in my car with the boys, as they liked to drive around the city. The hours of boredom that accompanied my time at the research site were perhaps more arduous. The activities of the gang members in this study revealed an odd contradiction. Because they participated in significantly more serious criminal behavior than their peers, and because they periodically committed troubling acts of violence, they were an interesting topic of research. Yet most of their activities were mundane, and they spent a large amount of time loafing around their apartments. Perhaps if the DFW Boyz were heavily invested in selling drugs, their days would have been more interesting. But on the few occasions that I witnessed drug deals, the act was understated, informal, and ignored by everyone else present at the time.

The boys seemed affected by the dullness of their life. They took advantage of any opportunity to keep busy during the day, and my willingness to escort them around the city seemed to alleviate their daily tedium. I often stopped by whatever apartment they had stayed at the night before, hung out for a while, and then drove them around the city. Some days they wanted to look for jobs, while other days they wanted to hang out with clique members who lived in the area. Almost every day they wanted to get something to eat. At the end of each day I returned to my normal life of transcribing, taking and organizing notes, and teaching college classes, but the monotony of their days endured. Their nights and evenings were somewhat more active, as they occasionally went to parties and underage dance clubs, smoked weed, drank alcoholic beverages, had sex with girls, and sporadically got into fights, broke into homes, or robbed people. All of these activities occurred more frequently when they stayed at their brother Aaron's apartment on the east side of Thirty-eighth Street. Still, in the context of their day-to-day lives, their nights were largely uneventful.

I pulled up to Aaron's apartment around 10:30 in the morning, and the heat was already bordering on stifling. Loud music was blasting from the open windows of Aaron's second-story apartment, which reminded me that he did not have air conditioning. Layboy met me at the door of the apartment with his customary greeting, "TimTim." I responded as usual, "WhatWhat." This response always amused the boys. The apartment was less empty than it had been a few months earlier. Aaron had an older couch and loveseat, TV, Xbox, and a small table purchased at a thrift store. The apartment reeked of marijuana smoke, and two girls in their late teens were lounging on the couch. They did not seem particularly interested in me, and they were still groggy from waking up. The boys were more alert and seemed ready to leave the apartment. Aaron was notorious for his endless pursuit of women. His sexual indiscretions often created more problems than they were worth. On more than one occasion, a betrayed boyfriend had sought retribution by shooting at Aaron, and as a result he usually carried a gun. I did not know these girls, but Aaron clearly had no more use for them. He angrily told them they needed to get out of his apartment and walk home.

This day was like so many others in the course of this research. Most of the day was filled with monotonous activities capped off with a brief but significant set of interactions. Theoretical insights were often hidden in mundane events, and I could never predict when they would be revealed. Shawn and Layboy got into my car, while Aaron left with a friend. The boys' agenda for this day was to submit some job applications, get lunch, and meet up with other DFW Boyz. We canvassed the city in pursuit of potential job opportunities that never produced even one interview. This was normal. Despite our efforts throughout the summer, Shawn, Layboy, and their cousin TJ could not find jobs. They rarely managed to get an interview. After a few hours, which included a customary stop at McDonald's, we gave up searching for jobs and began to focus on meeting up with other members of the gang.

The fragmented structure of the DFW Boyz often created challenges when attempting to hang out with members outside of Layboy and Shawn's immediate social circle. Without access to a centralized hangout, we usually drove to different houses or apartment complexes hoping to meet up with other members of the gang, only to find that they were out in the streets or at another location. Members of the DFW Boyz were difficult to track down, even for Layboy and Shawn. Much of the data used in this research was gathered only after long days spent in persistent pursuit of gang members. On this day our efforts proved to be unproductive, and we found ourselves aimlessly driving through the city. We eventually decided to reunite with Aaron and arranged to meet at a convenience store on the city's northeast side. As we stood in the shaded area on the store's west side, Layboy, Shawn, and I talked about sports, school, and their plans for that night. Such moments were not very exciting, but they accurately reflected the day-to-day events in the lives of these youth. The threat of violence in gang members' lives might have been ubiquitous, but the average gang member in this study was only sporadically involved in violent incidents, and most days in Indianapolis were uneventful.

I did not doubt that Shawn and Layboy were gang members and that the DFW Boyz constituted a gang. The group certainly reflected various descriptions and/or definitions of street gangs offered by other gang researchers (see Klein 2005). More importantly, the boys defined themselves as gang members, and they were quite persistent in their efforts to demonstrate to me that the DFW Boyz were taken seriously in the streets. Remember, for example, the hyperbolic statements made by Layboy, Shawn, and other DFW Boyz about the group's elite status in the streets. The gang was known and could take over a city block, apartment complex, school, or neighborhood if members desired to take over. However, my opinion did not matter. By claiming gang affiliation, the boys identified themselves as belonging to the intergang field. They considered themselves to be real gang members and believed that peers should also recognize this fact. Shawn and Layboy also dismissively labeled other so-called gang members or groups as fraudulent. Such skepticism was a dominant characteristic of intergang interactions, and the boys were not immune to such negative evaluations. Therefore, the assessments made by other environmental participants were of more concern to Layboy, Shawn, and other DFW Boyz than those made by a relatively detached researcher. Although I was confident that the DFW Boyz was in fact a real gang, I had not forgotten the possibility that others in the intergang environment might view Layboy, Shawn, and the DFW Boyz as gang imitators.

Aaron eventually arrived at the store and suggested that we go hang out with some of his older associates. These individuals were not members of the DFW Boyz, nor were they familiar with Layboy or Shawn. With nothing else to do, the boys agreed, and we all got back into my car. Aaron directed me to an eastside neighborhood that I was relatively unfamiliar with. Earlier in the research process, I had spent some time with an individual in the same hood who had just been released from prison after serving time for two involuntary manslaughter convictions. Two men entered his home with the intent to steal his drugs and drug money, so he killed them. Free and on the streets, he had reverted back to dealing drugs and operated out of a house in this neighborhood. With the exception of the few hours I spent in that dealer's home, I had little working knowledge of this area. However, I knew that this area south of Thirty-eighth Street was also in the middle of another hotspot for crime and violence.

We stopped near a large, two-story house that had a crowd of people sitting on the front porch. Some of these people were members of Aaron's crew, and he got out to see if they were interested in talking to me. I got out of the car with Shawn and Layboy, but we stood by the car waiting for Aaron to verify that it was okay to approach the house. After a brief and unsuccessful attempt by Aaron to explain what I was doing, I decided to approach the porch and talk to the crowd myself. As I left the car, Layboy said, "I'm not going up there," and he stayed in the car with his brother and sipped some fruit punch that I had purchased for him earlier.

The individuals on the porch ranged in age from mid-teens to late forties. They were all relatives, and as I approached the porch, they were deeply engaged in a discussion about professional basketball. Being an avid sports fan, I contemplated adding my own thoughts, but past attempts in similar situations had proved to be awkward. The individuals in this study did not seem to be interested in my insights about the NBA. I explained to them that I was a graduate student from a local university and I was researching local gangs. Interested, they looked over and signed my consent forms but agreed to talk to me at another time, since the ninety-degree temperature was too hot for an interview. However, during the course of a conversation about gangs, one of the older men said that he was from Chicago and that he had been connected to Larry Hoover, the well-known leader of the Gangster Disciples. He said that he would be able to tell me all about how they operated in Chicago, and he alluded to shootings and drug trafficking. He then gestured toward Shawn and Layboy, who were still at my car, and shouted, "Why you with them? They're not gang members, they just wannabes. They don't know Hoover or how it's really done. They just wannabes." As we left, a visibly angry Layboy sat in my front seat mumbling quietly about how everyone knew Hoover, and the man on the porch did not know what he was talking about. This brief but significant interaction between Layboy, Shawn, and the OG on the porch illuminated a fundamental dilemma on the streets. Layboy and Shawn embraced a gang identity, but they were immersed in an environment that was inherently skeptical about their claims.

In an environment where all gangs displayed high levels of internal confidence about the status of their gang and also claimed that most gang members falsely claimed affiliation, contradicting appraisals were bound to happen. This was most evident when someone had the audacity to openly challenge another person by labeling him or her as being a fake gang member, a false flagger, or a wannabe. Such dismissals represented an attempt by someone or some group to invoke the boundaries of an intergang field. Some self-defined gang members belonged within the boundaries of the intergang field, and some did not. Those who did not belong were to be mocked, challenged, and made aware of their inferior status.

The accusation of being a wannabe was indeed damning. The wannabe label did not refer to one's desire to become a gang member, nor did it denote a fringe member. It involved a clear declaration about the invalidity of one's claim to gang membership (Garot 2010).

Ironically, in an earlier conversation, Shawn and Layboy explained the significance of his term:

SHAWN: Somebody that's a wannabe just wants to fit in with the crowd.
LAYBOY: Yeah.
SHAWN: Just want to fit with the crowd.
LAYBOY: They don't want to feel left out. They think everybody else in the gang, and they got to get in the gang. . . . They ain't real.

Much like the individuals who were labeled as false flaggers or Internet gangsters, youths identified as wannabes claimed membership and played the part of a gang member, but they were not considered real. Their motivation for claiming membership was inappropriately based on fitting in and being like others. So-called wannabes claimed membership and mimicked gang affiliation by altering their appearance to look like gang members, using gang terminology, and learning superficial expressions of membership. These alterations were deemed false representations by outsiders who claimed to have inside knowledge about what was in fact real. However, the term "wannabe" was not just directed toward the social misfit who sought belonging through mimicry. The label could also be applied to groups and used to distinguish real gangs from wannabe gangs. Entire groups that defined themselves as gangs could be quickly dismissed as being a bunch of wannabes or a fake gang. According to the OG on the porch, the members of the DFW Boyz were not real gang members. Layboy and Shawn's internal certainty about their status as viable gang members was matched by external skepticism. In this context, they had been cast outside the boundary of the intergang field.

When confronted with an overt dismissal, the boys were limited in their ability to prove that they were indeed legitimate gang members. They could not access objective cues or boundary objects that would have communicated to the OG on the porch that they truly belonged in the intergang field. Any effort probably would have been discounted or used as evidence that gangs had become diluted in Indianapolis. This is the paradox of legitimacy, and such an experience was not uncommon in Indianapolis. Youths embraced a gang identity but encountered both overt and covert dismissive sentiments about their claims to gang membership. They had limited means to demonstrate their status as real gang members. The resulting question, then, becomes, how do gang members demonstrate their authenticity to skeptical peers?

CONCLUSION

In Indianapolis, evaluations of legitimacy permeated intergang interactions. As members of different gangs, cliques, or hoods gathered in various social settings like school, parties, or clubs, they observed each other and made assessments about each other's right to belong. Such assessments were not, however, grounded in objective standards that were universally recognized by all gangs. Self-defined gang members displayed gang symbols, colors, or secret codes, but these superficial signifiers could not legitimize a person's rightful place within the intergang environment. The dilution narrative was too strong, and environmental participants remained dubious about such displays of affiliation. Therefore, the focal gang or gang member was potentially the source and target of environmental skepticism. Each gang member continuously struggled to demonstrate to peers that he or she was a legitimate gang member.

Indeed, the label of "gang member" was meaningful in the streets of Indianapolis, as it was constructed and used by gang members themselves. It was not just created by criminal justice personnel, school administrators and teachers, or parents and then thrust upon undeserved youth. It was not, as some have noted in other cities, a reified concept primarily used by researchers, criminal justice practitioners, policy makers, and the media to create public hysteria and reinforce the status quo (Brotherton and Barrios 2004; Cyr 2003; Fleisher 1995; McCorkle and Miethe 1998).[3] In Indianapolis, invested adults and criminal justice personnel were actually somewhat reluctant to use the term "gang." Shawn and Layboy, for example, often mentioned that their mother consistently denied their gang involvement. On numerous occasions, I observed a director of a nonprofit organization, who frequently interacted with gang members, publicly claim that the so-called gang members were just wannabes. Police, at least in public forums, also seemed more likely to deemphasize rather than exaggerate the gang problem in the city.[4] But to self-defined gang members, the notion of being a gang member was both important and problematic. They were invested in the concept, and the notion of being a real gang member served as a building block, category, or social construct that helped define their social reality.[5]

The construction of that reality often occurred during routine interactions with peers. Constructing reality is a dynamic and reflexive social enterprise that is responsive to the input of individuals but, in turn, also influences their perceptions and behavior. This inherently social endeavor is best observed during routine conversations (Hollander and Gordon 2006). The self-defined gang members in this study routinely examined the way things were in their social environment. They observed the behaviors of peers and then, through conversations with close peers, framed that behavior according to an understanding of "real."[6] As noted in chapter 3, they collectively talked about how the notion of "gang" had become diluted, how many so-called gang members were not real. As I will show in later chapters, gang members were actively involved in constructing characterizations of both themselves and others through gossip and conversation. These conversations relied on and reinforced the subjective boundaries of the intergang field. They also established an understanding of how real gang members should behave, and self-defined gang members were often motivated to "do gang" in social settings.

The impetus behind doing gang is, therefore, largely found in the intergang environment. One's understanding of being a gang member is constructed through interactions with close peers and significant others, but it then must be performed in public settings. These performances are tailored explicitly to one's peers; gang members are not particularly concerned with the opinions of detached outsiders. A teacher's actions and opinions, for example, are only problematic if they cause peers to question one's status as a real gang member.[7] In effect, being called a wannabe or being labeled as a deviant gang member by a teacher is inconsequential to a gang member's sense of self, but it may induce a reaction if peers are nearby. An attack on one's gang identity is only perceived to be serious if it is accompanied by social consequences. If it comes from someone who is largely considered irrelevant, it is easily ignored. Yet gang members are often immersed in social settings where the assessments of peers do matter, and the social consequences of one's actions are a paramount concern. It is in these situations where one's certainty in his or her gang status may be juxtaposed against environmental uncertainty. In these situations legitimacy in the intergang environment becomes problematic, and gang members struggle to demonstrate their place within the intergang field. This process is guided by the enduring question, what does it mean to be a real gang member?

CHAPTER 5

Known in Naptown

WHILE I WAITED FOR Shawn and Layboy in Aaron's apartment, I sat on an older black loveseat and listened to music blaring from a nearby stereo. Considering the close proximity of neighboring apartments, I was always surprised at how loudly the boys played music during the day. Given that windows were ajar and a sliding back door was fully open, the music drowned out any attempted conversations and left the confines of the apartment for all to hear. I recognized the song; it occasionally played in my car when we drove around the city. It was written and performed by a local rapper, E-Weez, or the Prince of Nap, who had not managed to get a record deal or get his music on local radio but was gaining popularity in streets of Indianapolis, or Naptown.[1] Shawn and Layboy had somehow gotten a copy of his mixed tape (CD) as it was being passed around at a party, club, or another other forum used by rappers seeking to become popular in the streets. The song insightfully captured the struggle for legitimacy in both the streets of Indianapolis and in the lives of Shawn, Layboy, Aaron, and other DFW Boyz. As usual, those around me rapped along with the song.

> I'm a real nigga, ain't nothing fake about me
> A lot of niggas doubt me
> But shit I yell it proudly
> "I'm a real nigga"
> "What?"
> "I'm a real nigga"
> "Who?"
> "I'm a real nigga"
> "How 'bout you?"
> [Chorus 2X]

You niggas rap about the whips[2] and the guns and the clips[3]
Rap about moving work, getting chips[4]
Keep it real nigga, you ain't really 'bout that
26s sitting high[5]
You ain't never had that
You ain't never sold crack
You ain't had a pistol cocked ready to react on anybody
    talking about getting at cha'
I guarantee that's a fact, bra'
I ain't never killed but I swear push me to that stage I'll
    detach ya'
Leave ya' skull fractured
All that tough talking going get ya' ass clapped, bra'
Handcuffing bitches, don't know how to act bra'[6]
Hair and nails did, trickin' off ya' last, bra'[7]
You ain't never killed shit
See the hood going feel this
Maybe if you hear this you'll go rewrite ya' songs and talk
    about some real shit
'Cuz ya' niggas fiction and I ain't feeling it
Why?
'Cuz I'm a real nigga

The lyrics focused on a street identity that was broader than being a gang member, yet those around me closely related to the basic message. Their lives seemed to be consumed by a constant need to validate their authenticity. Although the issue of being a "real nigga" or a real man is a salient concern for many young minority males living in poor urban communities (see Anderson 1999; Hannerz 1969; Oliver 1994 and 2006; Wilkinson 2001), the dominance of the dilution narrative in Indianapolis ensured that gang members experienced this concern more intensely than their non-gang counterparts. And interactions between members of different gangs often involved, either directly or through the subtle subtext of communication, the statement "I'm real, how about you?"

Much like the rapper, Shawn and Layboy were eager to demonstrate their authenticity and prove to a skeptical environment that they were, indeed, real gang members. They were equally willing to publicly disparage other people's claims to gang membership. For the boys, however, authenticity was difficult to prove or disprove. Amid an uncertain environment characterized by innumerable self-serving definitions of "street gang," they had to convincingly communicate their gang identity to peers. Although self-defined gang members often questioned superficial displays of gang status, and there were no other clear methods for demonstrating affiliation, individuals immersed in the intergang environment did embrace a common expectation: gangs and gang members should be willing and able to use violence.[8]

Public displays of violence could legitimize one's place in the intergang field, but violence was not immune to the dilution narrative. As a result, legitimacy was often gained not through violent events but through the establishment of a widely accepted reputation for violence. The larger the number of environmental participants who accepted a focal gang or gang member as being willing and able to use violence, the less likely he or she was to be viewed as illegitimate.

VIOLENCE AS AN ENVIRONMENTAL EXPECTATION

The expectation of violence in the intergang environment is closely linked to a broader cultural system that emphasizes hypermasculine ideals of toughness, respect, and the use of violence to resolve disputes (see Anderson 1999; Fagan and Wilkinson 1998; Horowitz and Schwartz 1974; Oliver 1994; Papachristos 2009). The intergang environment, after all, is part of the general street environment, and it embraces similar ideas. For gang members, however, violence is not just an accepted consequence of violating aspects of the street code, nor is it just a normative response to being disrespected. It is a defining trait of the real gang, and one's capacity to establish legitimacy in the intergang environment is often grounded in his or her willingness and ability to use violence.

The expectation of violence is developed and reinforced through routine interactions between environmental participants. Self-defined gang members routinely discuss the legitimacy of other environmental participants. A gang member's relative position in the intergang environment often depends on his or her willingness and ability to use violence.[9] Thus, external symbols of gang status become somewhat irrelevant if one's capacity for violence can be verified. Self-defined gang members who are perceived to be violent are accepted as authentic, while those perceived to be soft or weak are summarily dismissed. Moreover, gang members continuously reinforce the centrality of violence by advertising themselves as violent. Although such advertising includes a requisite physical demeanor that is embraced by many street participants (Anderson 1990 and 1999), overt discussions about one's own violent exploits is a more important factor. Gang members talk and act as if they are ready and willing to use violence. These routine performances are designed to communicate legitimacy to peers, but they also reinforce the centrality of violence to one's conception of a gang. Each environmental participant is, therefore, routinely subjected to social interactions that communicate the expected association between gangs and violence. Each gang member also participates in communicating that expectation to peers.

Violence and legitimization are also linked through more practical considerations. In the Indianapolis streets, gang symbols, speech patterns, and licks may be dubious, but an act of violence resonates clearly. Violence is unambiguous (Anderson 1999; Jacobs and Wright 2006). When violence erupts, there is usually a clear winner and a clear loser. Furthermore, violence often occurs in public settings, where peers observe the violent event and ultimately judge the outcome. An individual's capacity to publicly humiliate another person through violence resonates with observers who will probably not question his or her status as a legitimate gang member. When symbols and speech patterns lead to disagreement and confusion, an act of violence does not. In the moment, violence is impervious to the dilution narrative. Peers observing the act become fully aware of the actor's capabilities and unquestioningly accept his or her status as a gang member.

Despite the inherent clarity of violence, a violent event has only a limited impact on one's position in the intergang environment. Violence is momentary and witnessed by a finite number of people. The clarity of violence, therefore, wanes over time and social space. A violent event is not going to become known to all environmental participants. Peers who are unaware of a violent event cannot use it to develop an accurate characterization of involved parties. In this case the aggressor is still subject to assessments of illegitimacy. Some peers who did not witness the act of violence will undoubtedly hear about it, but their understanding of the event may not accurately reflect the actual events. Through gossip and evolving versions of the event, the precipitating events are altered, the victim can become the perpetrator, or the aggressor can become demonized or idolized. Stories of the event become distorted, and the aggressor may not reap the legitimizing benefits of the violent act. Confusion remains, even when the intergang environment establishes an agreed-upon expectation that can be used to validate membership.

BEING KNOWN

Given that an act of violence is limited in its ability to demonstrate legitimacy to the intergang environment, gang members must cultivate a violent reputation that transcends their immediate social setting.[10] This endeavor is largely governed by one's ability to become known to a broad array of environmental participants. The street, after all, is an arena where one's identity is displayed for all to see, hear, and evaluate (Anderson 1990 and 1999; Fagan and Wilkinson 1998; Garot 2007b and 2010; Wilkinson 2001). In public spaces, individuals observe and interpret the actions and mannerisms of people they encounter. However, interactions vary considerably. Some are brief, while others are extended. Some interactions involve people who are familiar with each other, while other interactions involve complete strangers. Familiarity stabilizes the interpretive process, as a history of encounters has already allowed both parties to form opinions of their counterparts. When two acquaintances meet, they usually do so with a preset understanding of each other, and their interaction will not drastically alter the relationship. This history does, however, significantly shape the immediate encounter. Hostility breeds conflict and increases the probability of an explosive outcome. Mutual admiration typically leads to more mundane, congenial interactions. In either situation, identities have been previously established and are unlikely to change in the course of one encounter. Both parties have already assessed their counterpart's capacity for violence in addition to his or her position within the intergang field. Yet not all interactions are grounded in familiarity. When strangers meet, subtle behaviors cause both parties to form opinions. During this formative stage of the relationship, interactions alter relational dynamics, but the effect lessens over time. Hostilities gradually become engrained, admiration is reinforced, likes and dislikes become routine, and jealousy and anger or intimacy and respect are forged. Relationships are malleable, but less likely to drastically change if familiarity is high.

In an uncertain environment marked by skepticism and dismissive assessments, gang members strive to become known to other environmental participants. Being known reduces uncertainty by establishing a preset understanding that is relatively stable. Thus, gang members struggling to gain and maintain legitimacy in the intergang environment rely heavily on this basic dictum to overcome the dilution narrative: the larger the number of environmental participants that are familiar with and accept a focal gang as being legitimate, the less likely the group is to experience dismissive appraisals. Being known in the streets is vital to the gang or gang member, but it does not guarantee legitimacy. Gang members also need to adequately control how peers view them (see Horowitz 1983). The lives of gang members often focus on building and establishing reputations that are congruent with the environmental expectation of violence. If members of a group are known for being weak or soft, large numbers of environmental participants will dismiss them as being frauds. Thus, self-defined gang members experience constant pressure to broaden the number of peers who accept them as being real gang members.

Small Social Circles and Reputational Agreement

Most people routinely interact with an established and relatively small group of people, so relational familiarity is common. This is generally true among the youths in northeast Indianapolis. Most hang out with peers from their neighborhood and apartment complex. In these places, groups of youths and young adults congregate in public spaces like corners, sidewalks, front porches, or gas stations. Within a limited geographical area or one's primary social network, issues of identity are well established. Here, acquaintances come and go as they please without worrying much about questions of legitimacy. Youths remain concerned with their relative position among close peers (see Anderson 1999; Whyte 1981). Some youths are seen as weak, while others are seen as strong. But reputations are additive, shifting only slightly in most interactions.

In these limited social networks, everyone is known, and each person has gained a reputation through the collective appraisals of his or her peers. One's reputation within one's neighborhood, apartment complex, or primary social network is important for negotiating that immediate social environment. Reputations provide some youths with a competitive advantage while placing others at a significant disadvantage. In the streets, these advantages lead to concrete rewards like sex, money, and invitations to parties, or intangible benefits like esteem and respect. Although numerous personal attributes are admired and demand respect (see Oliver 1994 and 2006), gang members' behaviors must be congruent with the environmental expectation of violence. If not, they will be seen as illegitimate and become routine targets for mockery and violence.

In smaller social circles, reputations for violence are clear and well established. Some street participants are known for being willing and able to use violence, while others are known for being weak or soft. Individuals known to use violence gain some esteem from peers they are good to have around when conflicts arise. They are also granted some respect from peers who fear being the targets of that violence. For example, during one conversation, Shawn, who was standing in his front yard, motioned to a house two doors down and spoke fondly about how his neighbors did not mess around during conflicts and how they were quick to use guns. Within thirty minutes of his comment, one of his neighbors walked past us in shorts and a winter coat and stood at the end of the road just beyond Shawn's yard. Confused as to why someone would have a winter coat on in the middle of summer, I must have looked puzzled. Shawn seemed to recognize my naïveté and explained that his neighbor had a gun in his jacket. Apparently, someone involved in a street beef with Shawn's neighbors had been seen in the neighborhood, and his neighbor was planning to address the problem if necessary. Shawn did not look concerned, and he seemed to think this behavior was normal for his neighbors. It was consistent with their reputation. Moreover, everyone on the block could reasonably expect that challenging, disrespecting, or threatening Shawn's neighbor would lead to a violent response.

Not all youths benefited from the familiarity created by their immediate social setting. Just as some youths developed reputations for violence, others were known for being soft (see also Wilkinson 2001). This reputation was most problematic for youths who tried to embrace street life but could not demonstrate to others that they belonged. James, for example, was an awkward eighteen-year-old who did not seem particularly intelligent or tough. He appeared insecure when interacting with peers, and they, in turn, seemed annoyed by him. James was not a teenager who would have been popular in any social setting, but he desperately wanted to fit in. Having dropped out of school, and being unable or unwilling to find a job, he did not have access to conventional outlets for establishing friends. In fact, he often spent his days in his mother's house smoking marijuana. His desire to fit in led him to the streets, and he made efforts to hang with the youths in his neighborhood. James's social deficiencies only made his softness more transparent, and, as the following story suggested, his peers targeted him accordingly:

> Ok, I was over there chillin', and then I am getting ready to leave and this dude, he loses his dope. I am leaving, so everybody thinks I got it, since I am leaving now. So I gets halfway home, and then they comes talking about, "Let me check your pockets" and whatever, with a gun pulled out on me. So I let them check my pockets and they didn't find it. So we goes back into the house and look for it. They ain't find it. So I am on my way out, leaving the house, and this dude hit me in my eye. So I kind of like stumbled a little bit. And then I stumbled into some bushes to hold myself up. Then that's when three more people came and started swinging on me. But I was like ducking and blocking my face so I wouldn't get damaged up a lot. And then when they got off of me, my momma had came outside and she broke it up. Then found out the next day the boy ended up finding his dope on him. 'Cause my momma talked to his momma about it, and she was like, "He claimed he had found it on him."

Through routine interactions, James had developed a reputation among the youths in his neighborhood. In addition to being socially awkward, he was not threatening, and he was not closely affiliated with anyone willing and able to use violence. As a result, neighborhood youths could unjustly target and assault him without fear of retaliation.

The only consequence in this situation was that they upset his mother. This assault would not have happened to Shawn's neighbor, as everyone involved would have known his reputation for responding with aggression.

Unfamiliar Social Settings and Reputational Ambiguity

Although youths spend most of their time in these smaller social networks where familiarity is high, there are ample opportunities to encounter a relatively unknown person on the streets. This is especially true in communities that are not socially isolated and where youths move about the city interacting with different people. At parties, clubs, or when walking down the street, gang members routinely encounter people they do not know. These interactions are dominated by uncertainty, and both parties warily observe each other. In most situations, everyone involved has little desire for conflict, but problems occur frequently enough that people stay sensitive to events around them (see Anderson 1990). Even without the advantage of familiarity, most of these interactions are not problematic, as people merely intersect and continue past each other. Typically, those involved in these brief interactions observe, interpret, and assess the behavior of their counterparts, but the process leads to little usable information. Most teenagers and young adults in poor urban areas adopt general patterns of public presentation that are common in the streets (Anderson 1990 and 1999). Baggy jeans, colorful shirts, large cubic zirconium earrings, and tattoos are all customary signals that communicate to people passing by that one belongs on the streets. Teenagers adopt offensive speech by swearing profusely and saying "nigga" or "nigger." They talk loudly enough in public settings to make outsiders feel uncomfortable and walk with a confident air to communicate their toughness to peers. This style of presentation is so universal that without additional information even local residents often cannot discern individuals who are heavily involved in street activities from individuals who are not. When encountering an unknown person, these cultural cues are an accepted form of presentation, and they are not immediately perceived as threatening.

The meaning of an interaction significantly changes when someone implies gang membership. This claim is accompanied by an expectation that gang members are willing and able to use violence. This expectation transcends the intergang environment and is embraced in the streets and beyond. Therefore, in most social contexts, claiming gang membership is perceived as a statement that one is prone to use violence or associates with people who use violence. Yet this claim remains difficult to verify. When people don't know the claimant, his or her willingness to use violence is truly not known until he or she either engages in a violent act or submissively avoids a conflict.

Some youths enter social situations where they are unknown, and they claim gang affiliation. A claim to gang affiliation can lead to the desired effect if peers are unwilling to risk being victimized by questioning that claim. Yet uncertainty still remains, as peers are unsure of the individual's capacity for violence. Is this a person like Shawn's neighbor who will aggressively respond to a challenge? Or is this person like James, the socially awkward teenager who is claiming gang affiliation because it evokes images of violence and demands respect? Such questions do not exist in one's immediate neighborhood or more intimate peer networks where familiarity is high and the claim of gang affiliation is accompanied by a history of encounters.

When entering new social situations, a person may benefit from his or her alleged ties to a street gang, but for many self-defined gang members, being unknown is a problem. Without an established reputation, they are especially vulnerable to the dilution narrative. Peers who are looking to be held in higher esteem and are emboldened by a supportive group of peers may openly mock an unknown person claiming to be a gang member. This may involve a direct affront, or the circulation of gossip through information back channels. Or, confident in their ability to handle the situation and fueled by the belief that most youths falsely claim gang affiliation and are unable to defend themselves, they may initiate physical aggression. As gangs signs are displayed and hood or clique names are shouted, actions are being observed, assessments are being made, and the seeds of future conflicts may be planted. Being known alleviates this problem. The potential for conflict may still exist, but at least everyone involved proceeds with an established understanding of their counterparts. Familiarity breeds certainty and affords the gang member a set of expectations that allows him or her to negotiate potentially hostile or violent interactions.

REPUTATION: THE INTERPLAY OF VIOLENCE AND PEER ASSOCIATIONS

Being known greatly enhances a gang or gang member's ability to negotiate the paradox of legitimacy. Theoretically, if all environmental participants are familiar with a group or person, interactions are guided more by history or reputation than by misguided assumptions. Furthermore, if a group is universally known as being willing and able to use violence, there will be little doubt that it is a gang. All environmental actors will place that group within the boundaries of the intergang field. Individuals genuinely invested in gang life, therefore, become preoccupied with ensuring that their reputation for violence is known as broadly as possible.[11] These efforts are not guided by a formal agenda or goals, but rather by a constant awareness that they are being observed and assessed. Reputations are gained and lost both in social settings and through social contacts. Being known in the Indianapolis streets requires the use of violence, often in public spaces, and a broad network of associations that can transmit a reputation beyond one's immediate social network (Horowitz 1983).

Scholars consistently note that developing and managing reputations is integral to gang life. For example, Ruth Horowitz (1983) argues that status concerns among gang members are intimately linked to their capacity for developing well-known reputations for toughness within their peer environment. Moreover, although these reputations are developed and maintained through public behavior and conflicts with other gangs, they are rather fragile and subject to change. Gang members are, therefore, motivated to promote and/or defend their reputations in social settings. Similarly, Andrew Papachristos (2009) argues that a gang's social status is largely contingent on its ability to establish a proper, or honorable, reputation in the streets. Honor is accrued when a gang demonstrates, through intergang interactions, that it can protect its members, act as a cohesive group, and respond aggressively to external threats or public slander. Any intergang interaction is an opportunity to build, maintain, or lose social standing in the intergang environment. These ideas certainly translate to Indianapolis, where concerns about legitimacy are seemingly ubiquitous, and the need to develop a well-known reputation for violence is essential for gang members.

Throughout my time with the DFW Boyz, members consistently told me or talked about how well they were known in the streets of Indianapolis. These descriptions seemed exaggerated, as the boys claimed to be one of the most known cliques or gangs in the city. During one recorded conversation with Layboy and Shawn, I tried to get a better understanding of how the group had become known. My initial question improperly assumed that being known was a rational goal pursued by the group.

"You said the point of your clique is to represent and be the hardest, the most known. How do you become the most known?"

"Most known," Shawn paused as if I had overemphasized that being known was an openly stated goal of the gang. "See, we been out here, everybody know us because somebody say something smart and we jump, we all take care of that problem."

Layboy reminded me that, "Police have a file stacked against us like this [showing me with his hands]."

"Get money," continued Shawn, "walk around with our names out. Another clique say something smart, cliques come out and talk, everybody going to hear about it."

Their pursuit of being known in Indianapolis paralleled that of an average teenager with aspirations of popularity more than an organization in pursuit of a formal goal. To Shawn, being known was an inevitable consequence of his role in the streets. Everyone knew who he was, and everyone knew the DFW Boyz. Police attention apparently validated the boys' claims that they were heavily invested in the streets, and this was a piece of evidence used to convince a potentially skeptical researcher. They used different techniques to convince other possible skeptics. Although remaining visible in the streets and at parties was important for building and maintaining a reputation in Indianapolis, as was using social settings to shout out gang or hood affiliations, the DFW Boyz proclivity for violence ensured that they were known in the streets. They took care of problems and effectively dealt with other cliques that talked too much or talked negatively about the DFW Boyz.

To develop a reputation for violence, a gang or gang member had to successfully control the perception of a wide range of peers. Shawn's statement "Everybody going to hear about it" provided a clear reminder that discussions or events within a group or between groups became part

of the environment's general conversation. Many youths tried to reinforce their reputation by rapping, or talking negatively, about other
gangs. At times, this negative talk occurred in a public place and was
directed at someone close by, but this type of talk more typically
occurred during public conversation when the rejected person was not
present. The information then entered the teenage gossip channel and
eventually got back to the targeted individual. In each situation, both
parties gained, maintained, or lost their reputation. If insults were not
addressed properly, they could become a fixture in the general street
knowledge base. Members of the DFW Boyz were highly motivated to
manage that information system and control their reputations.

If group members were willing and able to use violence, public
dismissals could be opportunities to reinforce and broaden their
reputation. If their response was brutal and observed by peers, that
information quickly spread through the streets. A set of individuals
became fully aware of the gang's violent capabilities, and peers who were
only mildly familiar with the group increasingly accepted its identity as a
serious gang.

Seeking more information, I asked, "So how do you take care of a
situation or problem?"

"How do we take care of it?" Shawn habitually repeated my
questions as he thought through his response. He always seemed to
analyze questions and situations. He responded casually, "You could go
either way. You could go gunplay or you could fight it out. It really
don't matter."

I hesitantly prodded the boys for more information. "Do you want
to share any situations from the last year?"

"Oh yeah, we got a lot of situations. A lot of them," replied Layboy.

Man, Shawn was at a party. It was me, him, and some other friends
from another clique that we was claiming. We was out on the east
side. One of the dudes in our clique from Post Road, and there a lot
of people from Post Road at the party. So we in there claiming
DFW Boyz, and they claiming Post Road. We claiming Haughville
or whatever, but they don't know that some of the people from our
group is from Post Road too. So Shawn gets to the party and
screams out "Haughville." They claim Post Road. He turns around,

and the dude hits him in the back of the head. So this is where I come up. I hit the dude, and everybody starting to fight at the party. The main thing is we get outside. He, Shawn, busts out the dude's window. So we deep, but they deep too. They call a lot of Post Road people to come over there, so it's basically Post Road against me and him. The other dude in my group is from Post Road, so he's trying to break it up. So we stay apart, and we go back over there and do what we have to do. Since then they ain't said nothing. That's one way how we got our name out there.

We got into it with a lot of cliques. We fight a ton. Most cliques respect us because we don't start nothing, we cool. A person walking around and they claiming stuff, we don't say nothing. We not like "f that, f that." We don't do that. Other cliques do, but we don't. We just cool. 'Til somebody disrespect us. Then we got a problem.

The vagueness of this response ("we do what we have to do") was indicative of the boys' hesitancy during the earlier stages of research. They trusted me, but not enough to tell me all the details of how they handled such situations. In the ensuing months, they loosened up and described rare occurrences of gunplay, but not at this juncture. Fearing that I might alienate the boys, I was not ready to ask them to explain. Still, violence was intimately related to the process of becoming known in the streets of Indianapolis. The individuals initiating the violent episode were unaware that Shawn, Layboy, and the DFW Boyz would respond aggressively. The initial violence was either caused by resentment that an unknown person was claiming gang affiliation or by ingrained hostilities between two hoods. Either way, the boys used the situation to clarify their capacity for violence to a new group of peers and reinforce or broaden their reputation for violence. During the incident that Layboy described, people at the party became more familiar with Shawn and Layboy.

Layboy's assertion that the DFW Boyz did not instigate conflicts was somewhat inaccurate. In other conversations, Layboy and some other DFW Boyz admitted that they liked to "talk shit" about other groups. They certainly were not bashful about mocking or dismissing the members of other cliques. These criticisms were usually based on a history of interactions, and the boys did seem to refrain from such activities when they or someone else was not known. In this sense, they did seem less aggressive than other groups. Some self-defined gang members, according to the boys, incessantly "talked shit" about anyone they encountered. When they did this to the DFW Boyz, problems emerged and reputations were developed further.

Although violence was an essential component to establishing a reputation in the streets of Indianapolis, violent behavior did not ensure that one would become known. Some individuals routinely resorted to violence, but if they had no means to transmit that tendency beyond their closest associates or immediate neighborhood, the breadth of their reputation would be limited. Reputations for violence could only be transmitted through street gossip, as expansive networks of teenagers and young adults continuously discussed events in the streets. Two mediums allowed individuals to efficiently communicate their violent tendencies to a broad social environment. The first involved the establishment of widespread social relationships. Expansive personal networks provided the means to communicate beyond the neighborhood to other parts of the city. Each acquaintance represented a transmitter of street gossip capable of spreading vital information to new people. The second involved orchestrated behavior in public spaces. When large numbers of peers observed a person's behavior and formed an opinion of that person, each peer was capable of transmitting that opinion to a broader audience.

A few weeks later, I was standing around with Layboy and Shawn in front of their mother's house, but this time we were accompanied by their younger brothers and fellow DFW Boyz Dre and C-Note. With the tape recorder on, we discussed the boys' numerous moves over the previous few years. Gangs are stereotypically territorial, and the boy's movement from the west side to the far east side and again to the northeast part of Indianapolis could have been cause for concern. But mixed interactions in the streets of Indianapolis produced expansive social networks that seemed to make stereotypical gang territories somewhat irrelevant.

"How did that move go for you?" I asked, referring to their latest move.

To my surprise, C-Note replied, "It went cool. It's cool."

"Nobody cares?" I asked, trying to figure out why a group of teenagers claiming both a west-side hood and an active clique did not have problems in their most current location along the east side of the Thirty-eighth Street corridor.

"Nah, everybody knows who we is," clarified C-Note. Apparently their reputations were not limited to a small geographic area in Indianapolis.

I replied by asking, "How do you get known?"

C-Note responded, "I got known because my brothers." An individual's reputation in Indianapolis was often connected to the reputation of their older relatives. If Layboy and Shawn were known in Indianapolis, C-Note would have experienced the benefits of this.

"I just do me," added Shawn as if to dismiss the notion that he needed any help in building and maintaining his reputation.

"Plus, like, we move constantly," said Layboy. "We live in a lot of places so everywhere you move people is going to know you. Plus we put in work, so everybody know us."

This last point was especially relevant to the establishment of their reputation in Indianapolis. As they moved from place to place during their formative years, Shawn, Layboy, and other DFW Boyz established a far-reaching network of associates. In each place of residence, they established a reputation with peers in their neighborhood, apartment complex, or immediate social network that was predicated on "work," or violence. When Shawn and Layboy moved away from a neighborhood, their contacts remained. Although Layboy and Shawn lived and operated on the northeast side of Indianapolis, my time with them was not limited to that area. We spent time in select west-side, near north side, far east side, and near south side neighborhoods. Their associations were wide-ranging, and a large number of peers would have known that Shawn and Layboy were prone to violence.

Although Layboy and Shawn had an expansive social network at their disposal, the connectedness of the DFW Boyz was even broader. Founded in one neighborhood, the group had dispersed over time. The group's interaction patterns were less dense than in previous years, but the scope of their influence was much broader. As members moved into different areas, they maintained the gang's name but started their own independently operating subgroups. Shawn and Layboy closely interacted with a small group of DFW Boyz who lived with or around them, and they continued to attract new members. This fracturing and expanding of the gang also happened with other members of the DFW Boyz in other neighborhoods. The entire gang got together periodically, but most members spent their days hanging around with a few select members.

This expansive but loosely affiliated network was ideal for building and maintaining reputations. As a general rule, information is diffused more efficiently through loose but expansive social networks (Granovetter 1973 and 1983). In contrasting networks that are characterized by dense routine interactions, members spend most of their social energy on each other, and they do not routinely interact with people outside the group. Therefore, information tends to circulate quickly throughout the group, but it does not flow beyond the group. When social ties are loose, however, each group member interacts with people outside that group. Information circulating within the group is more likely to be disseminated to a broader social environment through the loose but expansive social ties. Layboy and Shawn's response to the aforementioned fight probably circulated throughout the extended DFW Boyz' network. Moreover, the story was told repeatedly at social gatherings with old acquaintances who were eager to hear about the latest street gossip. As more people heard about their exploits, the reputations of Layboy, Shawn, and the DFW Boyz became solidified to a growing number of people. They became known in Naptown.

"We put in work," agreed Dre. "When you say, 'DFW Boyz,' people just know."

I knew what "work" meant, but I wanted them to clarify the meaning of the term, so I asked, "What's work?"

Dre responded, "What's work? A lot of work. Fighting people, hanging around letting people know who we is."

"Walking around all day," added C-Note. "You know, if someone asks who we is, we tell them who we is. We let them know. They ain't going to try nothing."

For clarification I asked, "Is fighting how you got your reputation?"

"Something like that, something like that," responded Dre.

Shawn, always in tune with the nuances of social life, also acknowledged the role of relationships in developing his reputation. Likability

mattered in the streets, even if one was disposed to violence. His reputation, though grounded in a propensity for violence, was greatly
enhanced by a broad network of people who liked him and remained in
contact with him. "I wouldn't say that's how I got my reputation. Me
being me, doing what I do, I play lots of sports, so people know me from
that too. Me just standing my ground wherever I go. I been to almost
every IPS [Indianapolis Public Schools] school, put out for fighting
basically. And that's it. I done lived in a lot of places anyways. What
we did, moved from house to house, grandma, aunt, uncles and all that.
I was just about everywhere, I know just about everybody. From south
to north—it really don't matter."

"I earned my reputation in school," said Dre. "Being bad, clowning
in school."

"So how did you get your reputation in school?"

"Clowning in school," replied Dre.

"Doing what?"

Dre attempted to clarify, "Talking back to the teachers. Clowning,
clowning on people who think they hard."

Shawn, aware that we sometimes spoke a different language, directed
Dre, "Explain clowning, he don't understand clowning."

"Ho'ing [embarrassing] people basically," he clarified. "Ho'ing
people who think they hard [tough]. Walk around the hallways, skip
class all day. Get with friends all day."

School is a staging area (see Anderson 1990). It is a public place
where a large number of peers come together and struggle to establish
reputations. Interactions, especially those that are violent or intended to
intimidate, occur in front of a sea of peers who are eager to tell others
about the unfolding drama. Identities are presented, assessed, challenged,
and maintained or destroyed (Garot 2010). For the boys in this conversation, the school setting was a great place to both embarrass peers and
become known.

"How many fights have you been in at school?"

Layboy ended his silence by answering, "I haven't been in that
much at school, like three. Three, four, like three."

Shawn explained how his willingness to fight in middle school
established his reputation, and he did not have to fight anymore. "Well,
back in the day I used to fight all the time in school but lately I ain't. Last

time I been in a fight was eighth grade, 'cause I used to fight all the time
in middle school. I used to fight all the time in the streets. When a new
kid came to school he don't really know a lot about what's going on.
Biggest dude in the school, everybody like, 'Shawn slap him real quick,
see what he going to do.' He like 'Don't touch my face,' but you know,
me being me, I slapped him anyways. He pushed me against some tables.
I sat there and thought about it real quick. Should I bang him up and get
suspended for five days or should I let him slide? For one, me being me,
everybody like, 'He pushed Shawn and he didn't do nothing. He got
ho'ed in front of everybody.' So I had to turn him around and bang
him up. After that everybody already knew so during freshman year
everybody like 'there he go' whoopty woo woo. Spread the word.
Everybody already know me from middle school anyway."

"Do you have any problems going into other parts of the city where
people don't know you?"

"Sometimes," replied Shawn. "It depends on how we going over
there. If we going over there disrespectful type stuff, then you going to
have problems. If you just going over there to walk around, then somebody, whoever thinks they the hardest will come up to you, 'who is you,
who is this?' Know what I'm saying? Other than that, some people is
neutral, they cool. Somebody might give you a little look, might not say
nothing, though. If we go over there all wild, if we go over there with
some problems and be hyper or whatever, then we go over and start
something."

Layboy again reiterated, "We don't talk though."

Shawn agreed, "We ain't about to go over there and rap to people."

Layboy responded, "We don't rap to people, actions speak for
themselves."

"We about to go outside and split him right here [beat up]," agreed
Shawn. "It's going to be that, plain and simple."

"There's all those niggas that just be rapping," said Layboy with a
noticeable amount of disdain.

"So you just react?"

"Yeah. Be down for whatever."

This was the message that members of the DFW Boyz wanted to
communicate to the rest of the intergang environment. They were
down for whatever. Too many self-defined gang members embraced the

superficial symbols of gang members. The so-called gang members were willing to talk like gang members, question other members' affiliation, and even threaten or demean other groups, but they were not real gang members. They were wannabes who were unable to support their ganglike performances with actual acts of violence. The DFW Boyz, by contrast, demonstrated a willingness and ability to engage in violent activities. They were known for violence and were, therefore, considered legitimate gang members. Anyone not recognizing this fact was either trying to look tough by talking shit or was ignorant of the Indianapolis streets. The behavior of the boys was congruent with environmental expectations, and, according to their accounts, many in Indianapolis accepted this to be true.

Still, developing a wide reputation did not happen quickly. Shawn and Layboy confidently maintained that the DFW Boyz quickly became known in the streets of Indianapolis, but their reputations had not become fully established. I once asked Michael, who was a few years older and loosely associated with Shawn and Layboy, about the boys' reputations.

"Are Shawn and Layboy individually known?"

He affirmatively responded, "Yeah, they individually known. I talk to people who know them. They like the leaders of the thing [DFW Boyz]."

"What's their reputation?"

"It's decent," Michael replied, but then added, "They ain't too big because they young. But I give them a few years doing the same stuff. Because DFW Boyz just started not too long ago. So I give them a few years and they be known all over the place."

For teenage gang members in this study, the struggle to become known was a continuous endeavor. As their reputations for violence expanded, their legitimacy in the intergang environment also increased. When Shawn and Layboy entered unfamiliar social settings where peers questioned their legitimacy, their need to expand their reputations continued. Even if they were to establish themselves as legitimate gang members within the intergang environment, maintaining that status would become a paramount concern. Legitimacy in the intergang environment could be lost, so reputations had to be cultivated and safely guarded. As long as the boys remained invested in their position within the intergang environment, the need to build and maintain their reputations would never cease.

CONCLUSION

In a skeptical environment where participants employ innumerable subjective and self-serving definitions of gang, one's capacity for violence can potentially clarify any ambiguity. An act of violence effectively communicates to both the victim and outside observers that a gang member's behaviors are congruent with environmental expectations. If a gang or gang member is subject to dismissive appraisals, an act of violence is a proper and effective retort. However, violent behavior is not impervious to the dilution narrative, as time and social distance can mute the effect of a single violent act. Gang members must work to establish well-known reputations for violence. They must become familiar figures in the intergang environment and continuously convince peers that they are willing and able to engage in violent behavior. They must use peer networks to disseminate information that supports their claims of gang affiliation.

A reputation can become widely embraced in the intergang environment, but it may not always reflect one's actual willingness and ability to use violence. In the streets of Indianapolis, as in other social environments, some gang members are adept at self-promotion, while others are not. Some gang members are able to convince peers that they are willing to use violence, while others are not convincing. To some extent, this ability is grounded in one's actual proclivity for violence. The few gang members who demonstrate an extreme capacity for violence presumably do not have to work hard to cultivate a reputation. Conversely, extremely passive gangs or gang members are probably limited in their ability to generate a believable reputation for violence. Most gang members, however, are neither extremely passive nor extremely violent. Most gang members sporadically engage in violent behavior, in part to build or maintain a reputation, but they also use those episodes to create an exaggerated reputation for aggressiveness. The perceived ubiquity of violence in the intergang environment is, therefore, both a reality and a myth. Relative to their non-gang counterparts, gang members do engage in exceedingly high levels of violence, they talk about violence, and they are always aware of the threat of violence.

But, for most gang members, actual acts of violence rarely occur in the context of day-to-day life. Indeed, the need to cultivate a reputation for violence is more salient than the need to actually engage in violence.

Most reputations in the intergang environment are loosely based on gang members' actual behavior. This is good in the sense that gang members' violent public personas tend to be more extreme than their routine behaviors, but it can also be problematic. If building a well-known reputation in the intergang environment offsets environmental uncertainty, questions about the accuracy of one's reputation undermines a gang member's pursuit of legitimacy. Like the status of being a real gang member, one's reputation can also be questioned. Gang members continuously work to become known in the streets, and they try to control how they are known. Short of engaging in excessive levels of violence, there is no guarantee that gang members will be able to fully control how others perceive them. Lacking this control, many gang members may not be able to fully resolve the paradox of legitimacy. Skepticism and derision continue even as they become known to a greater number of environmental participants. They are left pursuing an illusion of legitimacy, which, they believe, will come as they convince skeptics that they are indeed willing and able to use violence.

CHAPTER 6

Teenage Gossip and
the Presentation of Self

THE NEED TO ESTABLISH a violent reputation can, quite naturally, cause one to engage in violent acts. Often, gang members slowly develop reputations by interacting with a variety of people. Within the context of these social relationships, a single violent act or a series of violent acts can provide the basis for building a reputation. Yet gang members must broadcast their capacity for violence beyond their immediate social circle, which remains a significant challenge. Loosely connected but extensive social ties maximize the diffusion of information, and, as noted in the last chapter, gangs' and gang members' capacity to become known is largely based on the expansiveness of their social network. This chapter examines the type of information that is often spread through gang networks. Gang members frequently use their varied social contacts to receive and transmit street gossip. These interpersonal networks produce a continuously flowing channel of information that functions as an important tool for developing and managing reputations.

Controlling a reputation through street gossip is a constant endeavor, since the flow of information in the streets frequently changes. Few, if any, reputations are universally accepted in the intergang environment, and all can be altered. The pursuit of legitimacy through building a reputation for violence involves an ongoing process whereby the illegitimate can become accepted, and the legitimate can be rejected. Within the vast network of intergang interactions that constitute the intergang environment, gangs and gang members are the focus of both positive and negative information. They can be labeled as weak just as quickly as they can be labeled as violent. Gang members with broad social networks and well-established reputations have a greater capacity to influence perceptions of both themselves and others. When compared to their less-connected or less-violent peers, these well-connected gang members are considered legitimate by a greater percentage of environmental participants. However, assessments of legitimacy can change, so gang members remain heavily invested in manipulating the information that circulates through street gossip. Being known in the streets can be beneficial, but only if one is viewed as being a legitimate gang member. Gang members who are labeled as illegitimate are often the targets of widespread derision. They are victims of the dilution narrative, and gang members are heavily motivated to avoid this unfortunate position.

TEENAGE GOSSIP AND DISCUSSIONS OF VIOLENCE

On another warm summer day, I accompanied Shawn and Layboy to an apartment complex where fellow DFW Boy Lil' Crazy resided. Aaron, the boys' older brother, and Lonnie, another DFW Boy who frequently participated in my research endeavors, accompanied us. Lil' Crazy was on house arrest for bringing a gun to school, and the boys tried to stop by his place whenever possible. I also liked these occasional visits, as Lil' Crazy was a sixteen-year-old who loved to talk, and those around him often followed suit. He, like many gang members, embraced a self-characterization that paralleled the values of street and his clique yet set him apart from his peers. He claimed to be the crazy one in the clique:

> It's like, you know how you got your friends, you got your cool friends, your laid-back friends, and the friends who just don't give a fuck. That's what I am, the one that just don't give a damn about nothing. You feel me? See a nigga, "Hey man I don't like him." "You want me to split [beat up] him, you want me to knock him out?" Then I just run over there and "Bop," lay him out. He's out. That's why they call me Lil' Crazy, the crazy one out of the clique, DFW Boy for life. I'm just the crazy one. . . . Like how they is [Shawn, Layboy, Lonnie, and Aaron], they don't give a shit to a certain extent. Me, shit, I slap motherfuckers around if I don't know you. We be walking down the street, whooping niggas' asses

or whatever, shit like that. But I do shit out of the blue. We just be walking around we ain't even splitting [beating] anybody today, and I just be walking and "Pow." They just look at me, "What you just do that for man? That was unnecessary." [Everyone laughs]. I don't know. There's just something wrong with my anger problems and shit. Like when I get in that mood and just want to hit something, see a nigga walking down the street, "You, come here." But like me, I slap on grown people. If you run your mouth you get busted. There ain't no talking it out or shit like that.

Other DFW Boyz also liked to provide characterizations of themselves, but they did so in less colorful terms. These self-descriptions always seemed tied to one's role in or approach to potentially violent situations. Shawn, who once described himself as being copacetic, embraced an identity of being the intelligent one, most likely to observe and analyze a situation before acting. Layboy was the muscle and the one who quickly resorted to physical violence. When asked why, he seemed to have little insight into his personality, replying, "I don't know, that's just me." Their younger brother Dre often instigated confrontations by "running his mouth." When asked why, he simply replied, "'Cause that's me. I rap [talk shit]. Just having fun . . . but I ain't the type of person that will get things started and not fight you." A large part of the boys' lives, from their individual and group identity to their routine daily conversations, focused on violence.

The centrality of violence in gang members' lives reflected a need to build and maintain an acceptable reputation within the intergang environment. However, these reputations were not simply the natural derivatives of violent events. They evolved as a continuous flow of information was transmitted from person to person through street gossip. If violent episodes birthed reputations, street gossip then worked to spread and solidify reputations. Each gang member was heavily invested not only in violence but also in controlling the characterizations that stemmed from a violent or potentially violent episode. As gang members interacted with peers, they worked to access and manipulate the information being spread throughout the intergang environment. They heard new information about events in the streets or about other gang members. They participated in the dissemination of information by telling stories about or providing characterizations of other gangs or gang members. Perhaps most importantly, they used the flow of information to transmit a self-image that was intimately attached to violent behavior.

Clarifying the Environment and Gaining New Information

As we stood outside Lil' Crazy's apartment, our discussion quickly transformed from an interview to a natural conversation between associates. The boys seemed to forget that my tape recorder was on and began to discuss their social environment. It was a conversation similar to many others that I had heard. Members of the DFW Boyz continuously focused on the people and events in their social world. During such conversations, the boys reinforced the rules of the street, disseminated information, and presented and evaluated self-characterizations.

"Nowadays, people be talking about Post [Road], but they ain't been there, they just moved there," said Aaron.

"False claiming hoods and shit like that," agreed Lil' Crazy.

Aaron agreed, and explained how some false claimers were able to get away with their fraudulent claims. "They get cool with everybody over there, so everybody want to have his back. Talking about being from Post Road and you really ain't."

"You say you from where?" countered Lil' Crazy, as if he was talking to someone claiming Post Road. "Nah, you ain't from the hood. This nigga ain't from my ghetto. That's how we call niggas out down here, I'm telling you. Niggas rap and shit, and you tell them smash [quit] all that."

Aaron looked at me and said, "The dudes you going to interview, that's my little squad. There's four of us, and every one of us got their own squad. I run with the niggas you seen, all those niggas from Chicago. That's my little squad. I got a couple that be on their own shit, but if something go down I can call them up. One of my niggas got a lot of niggas from his hood. I just mess with a lot of people that know a lot of people. Like, if I get into it with somebody, I call up this dude and then Post Road is over there. He known in Post Road, so all he do is got to make a call and that's when all the cars surround. That's why I'm cool with a person in down near every hood, so I don't get into it with hood niggas. I get into it with lame-ass niggas that want to roll around in their cars and stunting and shit." ("Stunting" refers to an outward display of toughness that has no merit.)

"Stunting and all that shit," agreed Lil' Crazy. "Those are the types of niggas I get at with the heater [gun]."

During only a few minutes of conversation, Aaron and Lil' Crazy established two important elements of street life in Indianapolis. First, labeling someone as illegitimate provided gang members an internal justification for acting violently. Although it was difficult to determine if Lil' Crazy actually shot at "stunters," or if Aaron limited his aggression to "lame-ass niggas," they were both adding to the dilution narrative and providing a moral to the story. In short, violence was an appropriate form of retribution for fraudulent gang members. Second, gang members negotiated a skeptical intergang environment by establishing informal social relationships with relevant street participants throughout the city. Aaron benefited from his relatively loose associations with the members of his squad. Those loose ties produced a more expansive social network, as each squad member routinely associated with people outside the clique (see Granovetter 1973 and 1983). Aaron was, therefore, known to people in different hoods, and he had access to a wide range of people who would assist him when needed. The only problem that could arise from these relationships was when someone substituted informal associ- ation for genuine belonging. Aaron might have been associated with selected individuals from Post Road, but he could not claim Post Road. If he had claimed Post Road, his associates might have mediated the subsequent consequences, but other peers would have still viewed him as falsely representing the hood. Some youths in Indianapolis made this mistake, as they tried to build their reputations by name-dropping and then used those contacts to establish legitimacy. They did this most often when they were unable to establish a proper reputation independently and tried to gain a reputation through false association.

"You don't catch me getting into it with anybody that like, '4-duece on, 4-duece on [Forty-second street],'" continued Aaron. "I'm cool with everybody, but them dime-life niggas. I don't like none of them. I don't fuck with Tenth Street at all. Them like the East Side Boyz, that's what they call themselves."

"They run their mouth too much." agreed Lil' Crazy, providing a clearly negative description of Tenth Street. "Like, down here, it's cliques and hoods. You got some niggas from Chicago that is reppin' [representing] gangs and shit like that. But down here in Nap [Indianapolis] it's like hoods and cliques. You can be a GD in the same clique with a Vice Lord down here."

Reinforcing the role of informal social relationships in Indianapolis, Aaron added, "They [Indianapolis gang members] don't care about that really, they just care if you his nigga or not."

Lil' Crazy agreed, "If you loyal to your set that you reppin'. Like Shawn and Layboy, he [Layboy] Vice Lord and his big brother [Shawn] is GD. But you see, they're still together, they still family."

Noting the difference between Chicago and Indianapolis, Aaron added, "'Cause in Chicago they really do all that. If you a GD and you a Vice Lord we going to go at it. But down here you could be a Vice Lord or GD, whatever, and be still hanging together and shit like that. People down here, they don't really care about all that. They just care about what hood you from."

"What clique you claim," agreed Lil' Crazy. This was the most salient issue in Indianapolis.

Aaron shifted the conversation back to local gangs by telling us some newer street gossip. "You could walk the Baltimore apartments, and I heard those niggas starting to get crazy. Where they be like 'Where you from?'"

Shawn entered into the conversation by further validating his brother's information. "Ah yeah. All those niggas 'on the five' anyways [Vice Lords]. They [say] if you a regular, and it gets up [to have problems], they'll get the choppers [Tech 9, a small semiautomatic firearm] and all. I know a lot of niggas over there."

Apparently, even a widely respected hood had problems with false flaggers. "They got some people that come over there that ain't even from the Balt," responded Aaron, implying again that people falsely represent affiliations.

"Don't even know who you are," agreed Shawn. Everyone in the streets, after all, knew him. He was known. To Shawn, other people's ignorance was a sign of their illegitimacy.

The flow of information in this conversation was bi-directional; each member of the DFW Boyz contributed and received new information about other groups or hoods. Some basic characterizations had been presented and accepted within the group. Tenth Street talked too much, the Baltimore apartments was a serious hood, and false flaggers were ubiquitous and deserved retribution. This information would likely have been passed on to a broader network of DFW Boyz or other associates, and it would have helped shape reality in the street of Indianapolis.

Gossiping About Others

As the boys continued to talk, their conversation transitioned from a discussion about general hoods to one that focused on specific people in the intergang environment. Such conversations typically involved a process in which the group discussed selected individuals and then summarily disparaged them. Although this process resembled more generic versions of teenage gossip, the content and consequences of these conversations were quite abnormal. They often relied on the dilution narrative to openly criticize peers, while they also built or reinforced their own reputations for violence.

Gossip is not unique to gang life; it is common in all areas of society and is especially common in adolescent social circles. Indeed, gossip is, a universal social process that facilitates emotions and behavior in many different contexts. The function of gossip in social life can also be wide-ranging. For example, scholars studying aggression note that gossip can be used as a form of social or relational aggression that is intended to damage a peer's social relationships, self-esteem, or social status (Crick and Grotpeter 1995; Galen and Underwood 1997; Underwood 2003). Gossip can be used as a nonphysical instrument that is designed to humiliate peers and undermine relationships between close peers (Crick 1996 and 1997). Although such aggression is not overt or physical, the consequences for the victim can be severe. Sustained exposure to relational aggression can cause the victim to withdraw from social interactions, to negatively alter his or her self-image, or to struggle with various psychological illnesses like depression (Crick and Bigbee 1998; Hawker and Boulton 2000; Prinstein, Boergers, and Vernberg 2001). Gossip can also lead to anger and an underlying desire to retaliate against peers (Crick and Bigbee 1998). Given that many gang members are teenagers, some of their behaviors are age appropriate and common in other teenage social settings. Still, these generic social processes can help facilitate atypical behavior.

Within the DFW Boyz, gossip was, in part, used as a form of social aggression. Rather than seeking to damage a peer's personal relationships, members of the DFW Boyz used gossip to publicly question a peer's status as a real gang member. They sought to humiliate their peers by disseminating negative information through channels of street gossip. To do this, they relied heavily on the beliefs emanating from the dilution narrative to openly question a peer's rightful place in the intergang environment. More importantly, the group established characterizations of specific gang members that became part of the street knowledge base. This is not to suggest that everyone in the intergang environment embraced the statements made by a few DFW Boyz. Rather, the characterizations created during informal conversations between friends dispersed into the gossip channel and led to questions about the legitimacy of a given person. In the struggle to maintain one's reputation, this information could be damaging, and it could both insight anger and force one to seek a method of reversing the negative stigma.

Although gossip can be used to inflict social harm on victims, it also serves other functions within the group. Gary Allen Fine (1986) argues that gossip in adolescent social settings helps establish moral codes and standards for acceptable behavior. Within a small group, youths can reach a consensus about appropriate behavior by talking about, and ultimately evaluating, the actions and/or characteristics of peers. Most notably, they castigate peers by labeling them as being morally defective or constitutionally unable to abide by acceptable behavioral standards. The targets of gossip are then used as a standard for what not to do in a given social environment. Like most teenagers, the gang members in this study used gossip to establish boundaries of acceptable behavior, though their understanding of acceptability was somewhat different than that of their non-gang peers. Through gossip, they creatively established what was and what was not appropriate behavior in the streets of Indianapolis. The labels of wannabe, false flagger, or fake gang member provided ideal models of unacceptable behavior that helped clarify what was acceptable.

Some gang scholars have already noted that gossip is instrumental to establishing a gang's collective sense of identity. Ann Campbell (1987), for example, observed that female gang members used gossip as a means to reject peers and solidify a gang's identity. They gained a sense of self by contrasting their behavior with the inappropriate behavior of other females in their social setting. Although talking about peers establishes the boundaries of acceptable behavior within the group, it also provides an image of the group to outsiders. In fact, for the DFW Boyz, gossiping about peers effectively communicated the group's defining characteristics to loosely affiliated peers. If the group mocked a peer for falsely claiming a hood, clique, or gang affiliation, an outsider could infer that the group's claims were authentic. If the members of the DFW Boyz criticized a group for being soft, outsiders could assume that the DFW Boyz were tough. In a skeptical social environment, where one's social standing was based on his or her ability to establish a violent reputation, denigrating others through gossip was an important tool for clarifying and reinforcing that reputation.

As my conversation with Shawn, Layboy, Aaron, Lonnie, and Lil' Crazy continued, the boys began to disparage some of their peers.

Aaron said, "I got into it with a dude named Shorty."

With that, both Shawn and Lil' Crazy flippantly shouted, "That nigga's from north-north, slap him!"

Layboy added, "They be protecting them, too, false claiming hood niggas, protecting them."

"That nigga is from Post Road. I seen him," said Aaron as he mimicked someone vouching for Shorty, protecting him from harm.

"Like half of them niggas that live on Post is just living over there," agreed Lil' Crazy. "And they got cool with the motherfuckers."

Aaron mocked, "I call them dick riders. Dick rider, you move into the hood and start claiming, because you don't want to get your ass beat over there. It's a dick rider."

This trend was a source of great frustration for the boys. Temporary residence in a hood was not a sufficient standard for claiming hood affiliation. Instead, it was viewed as a pathetic attempt to build a reputation through false pretenses. The DFW Boyz did not consider Shorty a real gang member. The phrase "north-north" implied that Shorty was originally from an area too far north to be considered a real hood. As such, he had no rightful claim to any serious hood affiliation. According to the gang, Shorty was illegitimate and undoubtedly weak. Shorty himself probably did not take this subjective rule about his hood affiliation seriously and most likely viewed himself to be a real gang member, believing that if hood members accepted him as being a part of the hood, then outsiders should also accept him. Yet the conversation was both the product of and a contributor to the channel of gossip that flowed through the streets. The DFW Boyz characterized Shorty as a dick rider and questioned his legitimacy as a gang member. If such labels gained momentum in the intergang environment, Shorty would have to adapt by disproving the labels or by admitting his weakness and looking foolish.

Lil' Crazy cited another specific example, "I know a nigga over there named Tyrone. This nigga all the way from the west side, and he moved in Sutton Place, and now he's claiming Post. You can't do that."

Lonnie, who had been quiet in this conversation, jumped in, "Like that dude from Naptown Boyz, what's his name, C-Money?"

As soon as Lonnie mentioned C-Money, the entire group feverishly gossiped about how C-Money was falsely representing his hood affiliation. Lil' Crazy dismissed the opposing clique member, "He's from Twenty-ninth, man, and I don't even know if he's really from Twenty-ninth. He's my blood, but shit, you feel me? And that's another clique we into it with, Naptown Boyz."

Shawn further disparaged the Naptown Boyz, "Them guys need to watch their shit, bro', they scared, bro'."

"I know when I was locked up," replied Lil' Crazy. "I was locked up with a few of them little niggas. My cousin in the clique or whatever. I told him, shit, when it all boils down to it, he's choosing them niggas over family. So I tell him, 'When we get at your clique you're going to be the first one I knock out.' You my blood and everything, but you choose those niggas over family, so shit, fuck it. You can get your ass ran up along with them niggas . . . they ain't even that deep [they don't have access to large numbers of supporters]. That's why I didn't go when you all went with Lonnie. It ain't even really that deep. 'Cause I like to get buck wild when I fight, and I get out of control. Like, real out of control. Like stomp your head on the ground."

The Naptown Boyz were a source of anger for the DFW Boyz, and for Lonnie in particular. The day before this conversation, members of the Naptown Boyz had outnumbered Lonnie in his apartment complex and tried to beat him up. This incident was part of the only ongoing street conflict that surfaced during my time with the DFW Boyz. The moralistic overtones that surrounded this conflict were intimately tied to issues of legitimacy. The boys viewed the Naptown Boyz as a group of wannabes who spent their days acting tough, "talking shit" online, and backing up their talk only when the numbers were in their favor. They were the quintessential group that violated almost every supposed rule embraced by members of the DFW Boyz. The Naptown Boyz were frauds, and they deserved retribution.

The confidence exuded by Shawn and Lil' Crazy reflected both their belief in the DFW Boyz and an underlying skepticism that the Naptown Boyz were legitimate gang members. Such an assessment could only reflect an assumption loosely based on reputation. The street beef had not evolved beyond some minor confrontations, and the DFW Boyz could only make an assumption about the capabilities of the other clique. The only way they could verify their assumption was to confront the Naptown Boyz and force them to either act violently or back down. In any case, the DFW Boyz had developed a characterization of the Naptown Boyz that was likely to be transmitted throughout the inter-gang environment. The DFW Boyz did not take the Naptown Boyz seriously, and everyone would know this soon enough. The precursors of intergang conflict had been established earlier, and momentum for the conflict was building as members of the DFW Boyz collectively labeled their counterparts and spread negative information about them throughout the intergang environment. I suspected, although I could not verify it, that the Naptown Boyz were having similar conversations about the DFW Boyz.

Presentation of Self

Up to this point in the conversation, Shawn, Layboy, Aaron, Lonnie, and Lil' Crazy had developed characterizations of multiple groups and individuals, but they mostly left themselves out of the conversation. As they discussed the Naptown Boyz, they began to develop violent self-characterizations. If they were claiming that the Naptown Boyz were weak, they had to demonstrate that the DFW Boyz were strong. During conversations gang members often develop violent self-images and communicate these self-characterizations to peers around them. Often, the development of a violent self-image can be accomplished by revisiting past events that properly display one's capacity for violence. During this conversation I was the audience, but in other conversations the boys had the attention of relatively unfamiliar or loosely affiliated peers.[1] These contacts were vital to the spread and solidification of their reputations.

"We don't call the troops unless we need them," said Shawn. "We go over there about ten deep and we cool with that. It starts getting ugly, we get twenty to fifty and starting making the phone calls. Tell peeps to bring the goons. He come about one hundred strong. Big bro'."

Being deep, or having access to large numbers of gang members who were willing and able to help in a conflict, was vital to Indianapolis gang members. The more people they could pull into a situation, the stronger they were as a group. It is difficult to determine how many people Shawn, Layboy, and the DFW Boyz could have accessed in a given situation. Their recollections of numbers seemed exaggerated to me.

The number of people involved in an incident dramatically shaped the interpretation of the situation. Being outnumbered during a conflict usually reduced an individual's desire to pursue a violent outcome, and it might have caused him or her to defer to the adversary. When the numbers favored someone, he or she was more willing to follow through on threats of violence. Interestingly, retrospective accounts of these incidents were skewed to make the storytellers appear strong and their counterparts weak. If, for example, the DFW Boyz outnumbered another group, they retold the story in a way that affirmed the group's strength. In such a situation, their depth was evidence of group superiority. When numbers were not in their favor, however, the DFW Boyz retold the story to make the other group appear weak. After all, only cowards needed eight people to beat up two DFW Boyz. This was an indication of a weak group merely trying to act like a gang. Such contradictions in the DFW Boyz stories were common and largely reflected the agendas of gang members.

Layboy revisited a previous observation that many so-called gang members could not back up their tough image. "There be niggas that stunt, and niggas that want to run off at the mouth."

"Like dude I got into a fight with," remembered Aaron. "He says he's from Haughville, don't nobody know that nigga though. I don't care, you can be from Haughville, I'll fight any of you all. I don't care."

Lil' Crazy agreed, and added to his self-characterization, "That's the thing about me. I done beat up niggas from my hood. Niggas get greasy [not abiding by the "rules"] over there. They robbing niggas that's from the same hood and shit like that. I done beat the hell out of niggas that's from my hood. You see, I'll fight niggas from every single hood. I don't give a fuck."

"That's what I do," replied Layboy, as if he was trying to keep up with the statements made by Lil' Crazy.

"But I'm cool with a whole bunch of hoods," acknowledged Lil' Crazy. "I'm telling you, that's why they say I'm the crazy one." He then continued to talk about C-Money, from the Naptown Boyz. "He need a slap for real. And the thing that crack me up 'cause he little. Telling you, that's the thing. I'm the littlest nigga, but I love to fight big boy. I don't like to fight little bitty dudes like my size. I like fighting nothing but big dudes. Telling you, I like breaking noses and shit."

"Like when your brother got into it with that big dude," replied Layboy.

"Yeah," Lil' Crazy affirmed. "Like when my brother beat up someone that was from 'The Bricks' [an apartment complex]."

"Smashed him," verified Shawn.

"Got to running his mouth and shit like that," explained Lil' Crazy. "I'm like, shit, I don't give a fuck how old you are, you a grown man, I don't give a damn. We'll still knock your big ass out."

"He was scared," mocked Shawn.

Lil' Crazy continued, "To make a long story short, my brother ended up grabbing him out, whooped his ass real bad."

"In front of all of his people, they all watched him get beat up," added Shawn.

Lil' Crazy agreed. "Embarrassed him in front of his whole little hood. Watched him get his shit busted. And they just standing there like, 'damn.' 'Cause they already knew what would happen if they would have hit my brother, you feel me?"

Aaron reentered the conversation by proudly stating that Indianapolis was a serious gang city, even if smaller cliques were more common than larger and more organized gangs. "That's how we do it down here. No GDs or Vice Lords, you out here in the hood, you banging out here, there ain't going to be none of that 'on the five,' 'on the six.' Don't nobody do that shit down here. That's why in Chicago you hear them saying, 'Man there ain't no real gangsters,' but you can't really say that just because people don't do that gang shit down here. Talking like, 'You ain't real.'"

Lil' Crazy added, "Yeah, and that's the thing, like how people is from Chicago. Yeah, they really strict about their gang shit, and they know all their lists and shit up there. Half of the people down here, we know our lists and shit like that, too, because we done got blessed in or we done got jumped in VL or GD, or whatever gang that you in. Like, some niggas from Chicago come down here, and you claiming Vice Lord. They think you false flagging. Just because you ain't from Chicago and shit like that. Like, motherfuckers think it don't be crashing [getting violent] down here in Naptown."

The subjectively formed notion of an intergang field extended beyond the boundaries of Indianapolis. Only a three-hour drive from Indianapolis, Chicago was home to the original and more organized versions of the Gangster Disciples and Vice Lords. Indianapolis gang members frequently compared themselves to the gangs in Chicago and resented the notion that they were somehow inferior to their bigger-city counterparts to the north. Indianapolis gangs might have been less organized than Chicago gangs, but they were still legitimate gangs. The parameters of the intergang environment were virtually endless. Even if a group were universally known in Indianapolis, its status as a gang would be doubtful when exposed to nonlocals. In Indianapolis, this trend was most noticeable between Indianapolis and Chicago gang members, but it extended to other cities as well. Familiarity bred certainty, but interactions with relatively unknown persons generated skepticism.

Aaron added, "That's why I say you see niggas come down here and get their ass whooped."

"Every time," agreed Shawn.

Lil' Crazy again boasted, "We done beat up guys from Chicago. We cool with niggas from Chicago, but me and my brothers beat up some motherfuckers that came down here from Gary, Chicago, all that. That's when motherfuckers mistaken. They don't think Naptown [Indianapolis] crash because we ain't all on TV and shit like that. Once they come down here, they see how we get down."

"It's over," agreed the confident Layboy.

Lil' Crazy began to laugh and recounted a game they used to play. "We catch your ass walking down the street and it's this thing, well I call it 'see a nigga split a nigga.' That's what you call it. 'See a nigga split a nigga day.' That's when you walk down the street with your niggas out, doing shit and all that, and, you see a nigga that you want to split. You like, 'Shit, fuck it.' See a nigga split a nigga day. You see a nigga. You split him. It don't matter who he is. He could be a motherfucking grown ass dude. Shit, get his ass whooped."

"I told you," interrupted Aaron, "like dude from St. Louis. He was down here but a couple years ago. He was on a bus, and I guess he said, 'Fuck Haughville.' 'Cause he was from St. Louis. Everybody on the whole bus looked at him stupid. But me, I wasn't about to hit him cause of that. I was about to hit him because he kept rapping [talking shit]. I don't give a fuck. He can say fuck Haughville. I ain't trippin'.

"My nigga from Kenwood [apartments] was like, 'You going to let that nigga say that bro'?'

"So I was like, 'On my daddy I'm going to split you.' He thought I was going to hit him the same day, so he watching his back. I'm like, I'm going to get that nigga when he ain't paying attention. The next morning, you know, when it be morning but it be dark outside, I'm on the bus easing my shit off. Then I just got up. Pop. I'm like, 'Nigga, where you from?'

"'I'm from the Lou' [everyone is laughing].' I'm banging him.

"Then my nigga from Kenwood jump up, 'Nigga this is for my hood.' Bap, bap, bap, we banging this nigga on the bus. Bus driver didn't do nothing.

"This nigga get off the bus, and everybody at breakfast talking about him. He just sitting there, looking stupid.

"'I'm trying to graduate.' Trying to graduate?"

Apparently, the excuse of trying to graduate hit a nerve with the five DFW Boyz involved in this conversation, as they all simultaneously said, in some form or another, "That's everybody's excuse."

"People be lying and shit, 'Ah, I'm under contract [a formal agreement about behavior in school], if I get in any fights I get expelled and I'm trying to graduate,'" explained Lil' Crazy. "See me, I don't give a damn. They put me under every single kind of contact, and I still be whooping niggas' asses. 'Cause I don't give a damn. That's the thing about me though. Like how motherfuckers see me out and shit, at parties, we banging with motherfuckers and all of that. I'm bad [act poorly] in school, but when it comes down to schoolwork I'm acing it every time. Telling you it's not a problem for me. Motherfuckers see me and be like, 'Damn, why the hell you act like this when you got damn near all As and Bs?' Because I just don't give a fuck, just don't give a fuck. Motherfuckers in school, boy, that's the best place to embarrass them."

"That cafeteria," agreed Shawn, as he provided another reminder that public spaces filled with teenagers were ideal for establishing a reputation. Each observer was capable of transmitting information to peers.

Lil' Crazy offered another example. "Like I done broke this nigga's nose, and he had on snatch-out golds [fake teeth or 'grill']. I done broke his nose and his golds with two hits one time when I was in school. Fucked him up bad."

"Why?" This was the first question I had asked in a long time.

"'Cause he was yip-yapping at the mouth," replied Lil' Crazy.

Aaron added, "That's what they do, they think you in school so you ain't going to hit them."

"And that's the thing," Lil' Crazy explained further. "He be by the police officer rappin'."

Lonnie ended his silence. "I hate it when they do that shit. That's pussy shit."

Lil' Crazy continued, "I'm like, 'All right, when we get outside of school I'm knocking you out.'"

"Is that the dude by the busses I was talking about?" asked Aaron as he laughed.

"Yeah, I cocked back real far and boom, hit him in the nose. Hit him in his mouth, gold fall out break in half. Like how I am, motherfuckers been rappin' and I know he's been rappin' there's no coming up and asking. I'm hitting you off the tops."

This was the image that gang members wanted to express to peers. "I am willing and able to use violence, and if you question me or test me I will not hesitate to respond with violence." If peers heard this conversation and accepted it as accurate, no one would have questioned the legitimacy of Shawn, Layboy, Lonnie, Aaron, or Lil' Crazy. The DFW Boyz would be viewed as a legitimate gang worthy of respect. Moreover, they would presumably broaden the reputation of the DFW

Boyz by diffusing this information into their personal networks. If this happened, a growing number of street participants would hear that the DFW Boyz were down for whatever.

A DEGREE OF REALISM

Gang members are violent. When compared to their peers, they are more likely both to engage in violent behavior and to be the victims of violence (Battin et al. 1998; Esbensen and Huizinga 1993; Esbensen and Weerman 2005; Gatti et al. 2005; Huff 2004; Melde, Taylor, and Esbenson 2009; Taylor 2007; Taylor, Feng et al. 2008; Taylor, Peterson et al. 2008; Thornberry et al. 1993 and 2003). Hanging out with gang members can certainly give one the impression that violence is a routine part of their lives. The dialogue between Layboy, Shawn, Aaron, Lonnie, and Lil' Crazy is merely one of many day-to-day conversations between members of the DFW Boyz. They also told numerous stories about violent incidents that I believed to be relatively accurate, though skewed in their favor. Some stories focused on severe beatings, while others recounted collective efforts to intimidate other gangs through mass displays of weapons. However, these conversations and stories do not provide an accurate depiction of the daily lives of gang members. They merely represent reinterpreted highlights of past incidents that develop an identity in response to a skeptical environment. The pursuit of being known is grounded in these violent episodes, but gang members use them to create an exaggerated violent self-image. The reality of gang members' lives is relatively monotonous. Violence occurs only sporadically. Gang members present themselves to be more violent than they actually are.

This contrast between a gang member's behavior and his or her public persona does not mean that occasional acts of violence are trivial. Nor does it mean that discussions of violence and street gossip are inconsequential to the behavior of gang members. There are a number of relatively severe problems caused by the dissemination of such information into the broader social environment. First, the conversations reinforce a general expectation within the intergang environment that gangs are inherently violent. As self-defined gang members interact and regale each other with these self-characterizations and stories of violence, they define how things should be in the streets. Individuals unable to live up to expectations, however vague, are delegitimized. Self-defined gang members who are demonstrably willing and able to use violence are lauded, while those who are only mimicking a proclivity for violence are openly rebuked. Thus, the expectations of violence embraced by gang members are commonly discussed, exaggerated, and then transmitted back to the intergang environment. Violence in the intergang environment is indeed a self-sustaining subcultural expectation.[2]

Second, the management of their gang identity places strong pressures on gang members to live up to their reputations. Although the process used to broaden and strengthen one's reputation can insulate someone from the dilution narrative, in some circumstances it can also force an individual to respond with violence. If a self-proclaimed violent gang member responds passively to a challenge, physical confrontation, or incident of public ridicule, his or her reputation is at risk. A self-defined gang member who readily submits to an adversary will probably create an explanation for this passive behavior that will neutralize his or her vulnerability among his or her closest associates. However, other peers will begin to talk, and that information will disperse throughout the intergang environment. Rumors about the incident will grow and the individual may increasingly be labeled as a wannabe, false flagger, or stunter. This problem is increasingly accentuated the more he or she talks about his or her violent exploits. Self-defined gang members who frequently talk about their violent endeavors without actually demonstrating a willingness and ability to engage in violence are despised in the streets. When challenged, physically confronted, or publicly ridiculed, the gang member with a violent reputation must respond with violence. Failure to do so will lead to a growing belief that the person's seemingly violent reputation is just a façade, and that he or she is just a wannabe. Gang members face constant pressure to prevent this from happening.

Third, gang members do not just develop self-characterizations. They also openly gossip about peers in their social environment, which often fuels intergang conflict. The intergang environment is characterized by an endless flow of gossip and information transmitted between teenagers. Those involved in this gossip channel are the creators and recipients of petty, mean-spirited, and childish information that is intended to disparage other gang members. All participants in the intergang environment become transmitters of this information, and all can be victims of this information. Negative or dismissive information spreads through the streets and is often carried back to those individuals or groups that are the targets of criticism. Such information often precedes intergang conflict. Individuals from different gangs observe each other in social settings. They watch and listen to each other. Characterizations are presented, accepted or rejected, and then transmitted through social relationships. Gang members note the negative comments made by others in their environment. They are aware that another group is calling them weak, soft, or fake. They know when they have been labeled as a false flagger, a dick rider, or a wannabe. This awareness breeds animosity and demands action. It represents the infancy of intergang conflict.

CONCLUSION

Legitimacy in the intergang environment is not static; gang members continuously develop reputations for violence by telling stories or gossiping about peers. The intergang environment is host to an endless stream of information designed to both build and undermine reputations. Violent or potentially violent events become distorted as they are reconstructed to fit the agendas of the storyteller. Some self-defined gang members are labeled as weak, while others are labeled as strong. This constant flow of information pressures gang members to perform in front of their peers. Circulating gossip that strips away the believability of their violent reputation can victimize even those known for violence. As a result, the struggle for legitimacy and the enduring need to control one's reputation is a constant endeavor in the streets of Indianapolis.

Of course the use of gossip to build or dismantle reputations is not unique to gang life. Researchers have long noted that gossip is common to many different social settings (see Eder and Enke 1991; Fine 1986; Gluckman 1963; Goodwin 1980; Paine 1967), and one can reasonably suggest that non-gang members also voraciously gossip about peers. The use of gossip by Layboy, Shawn, and their associates should remind the reader that the boys are, quite simply, adolescents struggling to find their place in a meaningful social environment. In this respect, they are very similar to the hordes of teenagers who navigate the petty and, at times, mean-spirited social world of middle school and high school.[3] They are invested in what peers think of them, but they also contribute to their environment by gossiping and spreading rumors about peers. Amid discussions of violence and crime, outsiders may be tempted to mislabel gang members as being wholly different from their non-gang members or nonoffending peers, but this is not entirely accurate.

What is different about gang members' struggle is not their fixation on a peer environment, their concern for reputations, or their use of gossip, but rather the socially constructed meanings that guide this behavior. They are uniquely positioned in an uncertain environment that questions their status as real gang members without providing the means to establish legitimacy. They are uniquely invested in an identity that is ambiguous and open to attack from other environmental participants. The gang member, therefore, continuously faces real or imagined pressures to prove that his or her gang identity is authentic. Conversations tend to focus on building or reinforcing that identity, while gossip attacks or tears down a peer's claim to real gang membership. The meaning of "real gang member" guides how self-defined gang members talk about peers, how they talk about themselves, and, ultimately, how they respond to peers.

The notion of "real gang member" provides an idealized construct for self-defined gang members to pursue, and too often the meaning of "real" is intimately connected to violence. Despite high levels of uncertainty in the intergang environment, most self-defined gang members in Indianapolis considered violence a defining element of gang life. The DFW Boyz exemplify this: violence was a core element of their collective identity. In addition, they frequently tried to cultivate strong reputations by both talking about their violent capabilities and openly questioning peers' capacity for violence. Indeed, to the degree that gang members' understanding of "real" was associated with violence, they focused on violence during their conversations with peers. Although they used these conversations to build reputations for violence, the authenticity of these reputations remained tenuous. Just because a gang member could skillfully communicate his or her willingness and ability to use violence did not actually mean that he or she was violent. Many gang members acted tough, but they might not have been tough, and discerning those who were willing to use violence from those who were not was difficult for individuals invested in the intergang environment.

CHAPTER 7

The Violent Encounter

INTERGANG INTERACTIONS are imbued with meaning. In various social settings, gang members observe, interpret, and assess the behavior of their peers. They freely use dismissive labels such as "wannabe," "weak," "false flagger," or "dick rider" to signify that a peer is not a part of the intergang field. The need to prove otherwise, to legitimize one's self or gang to other participants in the intergang environment, is a focal concern for gang members. An act of violence legitimizes, but its effects are limited. A person or group must, therefore, build a reputation for violence that is broadly accepted in the intergang environment. Thus gang members routinely discuss their violent exploits, and each storyteller favorably recounts his or her role in various violent events. During the process, they mock other environmental participants and characterize peers as being weak or soft. Legitimacy is directly linked to violence, in that violence provides the means for gang members to establish their place within the intergang field. But legitimacy is also indirectly linked to violence, as negative labels and disparaging comments circulate through channels of gossip. The diffusion of inflammatory information across gang networks slowly builds animosities between various street gangs and increases the need for gang members to aggressively respond to the negative information circulating through gossip channels. By ignoring such talk, gang members risk irreparable harm to their reputations, so they often respond aggressively with violence or escalating threats of violence. This chapter examines the history and evolution of intergang conflict. Although intergang violence is often motivated by concerns about legitimacy, a violent act is merely the by-product of evolving hostilities that are fueled by gossip and reinforced by repeated antagonistic interactions.

GANGS, STREET BEEFS, AND
A HISTORY OF EVENTS

Gang violence is a complex problem that cannot be fully explained by a single theoretical concept, and scholars note that gang violence often stems from either instrumental or expressive motivations (Papachristos 2009). Instrumental violence occurs when gang members are involved in disputes over tangible material goods. For example, they may commit a violent act in response to a drug turf dispute or use violence to punish an individual who stole from the gang or from a single gang member (Levitt and Venkatesh 2000; Mieczkowski 1986). Expressive violence, by contrast, occurs when gang members respond violently to threats that offend or challenge their status. A common theme in gang lore is that colors automatically trigger a violent response from rivals, as a particular color represents a symbolic threat that merits reprisal. Expressive violence is, however, more commonly the end result of a pattern of interactions between one or more gang members, and it begins with an insult or an act of disrespect and escalates when neither of the involved parties submits to his or her counterpart. Concerns about legitimacy in the intergang environment simply add to a general cultural milieu where personal status is already closely guarded and expressive violence is all too common. The status of gang members is easily questioned, and so-called members face added pressure to protect their reputations by engaging in expressive violence.

Getting killed over turf or colors may be a reality in some communities, but these stereotypical motivations for violence are generally not a dominant element of the intergang environment in Indianapolis.[1] Instead, violence is often the byproduct of escalating confrontations that are largely motivated by considerations of legitimacy and reputation and are fueled by the diffusion of gossip through gang networks.[2] Although the intergang environment produces the motivation for conflict, violence is directly caused by contextual factors that influence two or more interacting and potentially hostile gang members.[3] Scholars call this the foreground of criminal offending, or the immediate context in which the decision to commit a crime is activated (Jacobs and Wright 1999; Katz 1988). During these moments, considerations of legitimacy and building a reputation intersect with an adversary who is unwilling to be intimidated or submit to threats of violence. When this happens, the probability of violence substantially increases.

All intergang conflicts have a beginning. They start with mundane interactions as peers observe, interpret, and assess each other. Gang members form opinions of peers, which are then disseminated throughout the intergang environment. Negative assessments ("fake," "soft," "wannabe") breed gossip and increase the possibility of a confrontation. A gang member may hear that a peer is "talking shit" about him or her, or may be openly mocked and challenged in public. A public challenge forces the individual to make a decision about a suitable response. Passivity brings forth serious negative social consequences, since other environmental participants are likely to assume that the individual is indeed weak, fake, or a wannabe. The establishment of such negative labels can lead to escalating insults while also generally undermining a key element of a person's identity. Moreover, the negative labels reflect poorly on the individual's gang, and the entire group can be labeled as a collection of wannabes. An aggressive response, however, is a display of strength and an administration of punishment (Jacobs and Wright 2006). It reinforces an individual's position within the boundaries of the intergang field and establishes legitimacy in the streets. When an individual is a victim of humiliating criticism and chooses to respond with aggression, the intergang conflict or street beef becomes solidified.

There are no clear guidelines for the amount of aggression that should be used in response to public humiliation or a personal affront. Bruce Jacobs and Richard Wright (2006) suggest that at minimum an act of retaliation should be equal to the affront. This restores relational equilibrium and balances the negative image circulating throughout the intergang environment. Many participants in street beefs seem content with this balance; they often reciprocally posture or gossip without significantly escalating the conflict. Over time, however, responses can become more aggressive so that the probability of a physical confrontation increases. Another strategy for dealing with public humiliation involves an extreme response designed to clearly communicate one's violent capabilities to the perpetrator and other environmental participants. In such situations, even a minor offense is perceived to be a serious threat to one's reputation, and the victim responds with a force far greater than the initial offense. A person reacts to a perceived insult with an offer to fight, a threat of gunplay, or an actual act of violence. Each reaction substantially escalates the conflict and forces the new victim to either respond with aggression or back down from the conflict. This response is also accompanied by an awareness of the potentially serious social consequences of appearing weak, which provides ample motivation for a gang member to further escalate the conflict.

Although an intergang conflict can emerge from a reaction to a single insult, it often evolves slowly. As members of different gangs routinely interact and share social spaces, they develop negative characterizations of their counterparts and increasingly resent each other. This period of an intergang conflict resembles an incubation phase in which hostilities fester and gossip circulates. A conflict may take weeks or months to produce an act of violence. During this time, members gossip about each other to their peers through conversation or on social networking websites like MySpace. They might even engage in a series of potentially violent scenarios, in which threats are presented or guns are shown. Each of these encounters also involves a more nuanced series of interactions that can produce violence (see Athens 2005; Fagan and Wilkinson 1998; Felson 1982; Felson and Steadman 1983; Hepburn 1973; Hughes and Short 2005; Luckenbill 1977; Oliver 1994; Wilkinson and Fagan 2003). If neither participant backs down during a potentially violent encounter, violence is likely to erupt. More commonly, however, people on one side back down. They usually have a justification for their actions that allows them to save face, such as being outnumbered or outgunned.[4] A nonviolent outcome to a single contentious interaction is not a final resolution to the street beef, however. The winner of the conflict will publicly recount the story, emphasizing how his or her gang is deep, while also telling peers that the other gang is weak. The loser reinterprets the story to diminish the exploits of the other group. Both messages are presented to the intergang environment.

In Indianapolis neighborhoods where the code of the streets tends to govern the actions and perceptions of some local youth, interpersonal conflict is not uncommon, and youths must periodically negotiate the microcontext of potentially violent situations (see Anderson 1999; Brezina et al. 2004; Kubrin 2005). Yet for gang members, these hostile interactions and enduring street beefs are more significant, as they provide an honest glimpse into one's capacity to "do gang." Conflict-ridden interactions are ideal forums for self-defined gang members to prove to peers that they are, indeed, legitimate members of the intergang field.

The social consequences of winning or losing such an encounter are greater for self-defined gang members than for most of their non-gang peers. The label of "gang member" generates expectations among peers. When a self-defined gang member also publicly constructs a self-characterization based on a willingness and ability to engage in violence, the pressures to perform increase further. Appearing soft in a potentially violent situation can undermine one's reputation, and gang members, compared to their non-gang peers, are more motivated to prevent that from happening.

Although considerations of legitimacy provide additional motivation for gang members to engage in conflict, their skeptical assessments of peers can create a false sense of confidence during potentially violent encounters. Those involved in a conflict are often blinded by a naive confidence in their ability to dominate members of the other gang. They genuinely believe that they are strong and that the other group is soft. They also operate under the illusion that they can control the outcome of the conflict. With enough force, they can compel the other group to submit permanently, so they do not have to fear violent retaliation. This confidence is largely based on an assumption that most self-defined gang members are unwilling or unable to commit serious acts of violence. Previous experiences with gangs or gang members who were easily intimidated or were unwilling to retaliate reinforce this assumption. However, every street beef involves a risk that the other group will not be intimidated and is willing to escalate the conflict from mere threats to actual violence.

If both groups are heavily invested in gaining and maintaining legitimacy in the intergang environment, everyone involved in the street beef may be unwilling to back down from the conflict as hostility between the gangs escalates. Consequently, a simple street beef can escalate into a process of contagious violence, whereby assaults or shootings ricochet back and forth between the gangs (Decker 1996). The consequences of contagious violence can be devastating for both gang members and the broader community. For example, Andrew Papachristos persuasively argues that murders in Chicago are often embedded in "institutionalized networks of group conflicts" (2009, 76). Ongoing gang conflicts create relatively stable patterns of violence, and members on both sides are at risk of being either the victims or the perpetrators of murder.

The Birth of a Street Beef

During the course of my research, Layboy, Shawn, and their closest associates were involved in only one ongoing street beef. They periodically talked about other incidents that involved violence, but the victims in those circumstances quickly learned not to talk negatively about the group, so the conflict ended quickly. Members of the DFW Boyz generally acknowledged that their interactions with other gangs were uneventful because everyone knew who they were and accepted their status as serious gang members. However, the origins of a prolonged street beef between the DFW Boyz and the Naptown Boyz began in the spring of 2008 with some minor confrontations at school. It developed more fully a few months later during a routine interaction between Lonnie, a sixteen-year-old member of the DFW Boyz, and a few members of the Naptown Boyz. The conflict maintained momentum for the next few months and still was not resolved when I left the research field.

The day after the incident, Lonnie recounted his antagonistic encounter with some Naptown Boyz. "These motherfuckers talking shit. I wasn't going to worry about it, tell you the truth. I was trying to call these niggas [Shawn and Layboy] before the shit went down, but bro' wasn't answering the phone. So we walking in the parking lot, and he [one of the Naptown Boyz] started talking shit about me. I was cool with one of them, and they just started talking shit to me out of nowhere. He got into an argument with one of my niggas, and he was going to bring me in it by talking shit about me. So shit, I took off my shirt and was like, 'What's up?' Motherfuckers holding me back. He got on the phone and started calling his little niggas up. Niggas came out of the car, came out about twelve or thirteen deep. That little nigga a ho'. He didn't do shit. He had to get his cousin over. His cousin a ho', too, because he didn't do shit. He ran up and didn't do shit."

Lil' Crazy added, "And the niggas he got into it with was some of my hood niggas, like some of them niggas is from my hood. So I'm like, damn, both sides is my bro's, and they getting into it. I don't know. Want to squash that [mediate a peaceful resolution] between them, but, shit, he [the aggressor] done lame shit, so they going to have to bang it out."

Publicly challenged, and somewhat confused as to why he was targeted, Lonnie was confronted with a choice. He could have ignored the aggressor, or he could have responded with equal or greater force.

If he chose to ignore the aggressor, his response would have been noted by observers and disseminated into the broader social environment. Many peers would have heard that Lonnie had backed down, which would have caused some peers to label him as soft. To prevent this, he needed to react aggressively to the affront. Despite being outnumbered, he tried to initiate a physical confrontation. Being held back only fueled his resentment and gave him a justifiable reason to label the other group as being ho's or as being soft.

Hostility between two parties does not automatically produce an ongoing conflict, and many street beefs are actually resolved through informal mediations by third parties. Social networks among street-oriented urban youths are so broad and loosely connected that one can be in an active conflict with someone without realizing that both individuals are tight with (close to) a third person. When this occurs, the third person has the power to either choose a side or mediate a peaceful end to the conflict.[5] The third party often mediates a peaceful resolution to the conflict, and he or she will remain close to both conflicting parties. At times, however, the third party cannot intervene and he or she must chose sides. Lil' Crazy would have had the power to mediate a peaceful end to the conflict between Lonnie and members of the Naptown Boyz, but he was not present during the incident. Moreover, he viewed the member of the Naptown Boyz to be lame and deserving of punishment.

Shawn agreed, "If you ain't there, then there's nothing you can do."

"That's what I'm saying. If I ain't there, well, shit."

"So they came out there twelve or thirteen deep?" I asked.

Lonnie responded, "Yeah, get out of the car like, 'What's up' woo woo. Dude pointed me out. His cousin like, 'Who was rappin' [talking shit]?' He ran up, and I was squatting up. Then they start surrounding me like in their little car and shit. So I'm backing up, and, shit, my niggas didn't know what to do, so they walking away. Other niggas park somewhere else, and they still try to jump me and shit."

Aaron asked, "They didn't actually hit you or nothing like that?"

"No, my nigga called his little stepdaddy up and told him to come up there. He came up there and had his little 9 [9 mm pistol] and shit. He took us to my nigga's crib. They try to come and apologize to my bro'. Wasn't going down though, we still going to get at them, though."

I tried to further clarify the events that had unfolded, "Is that why they didn't jump you, because he had a gun?"

"Yeah, when my nigga's stepdaddy came, he had his little 9, and they chilled out for a minute. We all rolled out with him."

During a single interaction, an insult turned into a physical challenge, and a physical challenge turned in a collective display of strength. The Naptown Boyz were trying to intimidate Lonnie by surrounding him with twelve or thirteen guys. If no one had intervened in the situation, the Naptown Boyz might have beaten up Lonnie. Such violence would have communicated to Lonnie and the DFW Boyz that the Naptown Boyz were willing and able to use violence and, therefore, should not be messed with. Possibly however, this display of strength was a collective demonstration designed to intimidate Lonnie, and none of Naptown Boyz actually had any intention of engaging in violence.

It is somewhat ironic that gang members were concerned with establishing a violent reputation but purposefully called in extra help when a fight seemed imminent. The irony in this situation was accentuated because Lonnie was not very big. He was a wiry sixteen-year-old who stood under six feet tall and probably weighted less than 150 pounds. He did not have a weapon, and he was not accompanied by intimidating peers. In his in-depth study of Kansas City gang members, Mark Fleisher (1998) noted that most of the gang members in his study were cowards who masqueraded as hardened criminals. Perhaps this was also an accurate description of many Indianapolis gang members; they might simply have been scared teenagers who tried to look tough in the midst of an intergang environment that emphasized violent behavior. They constantly sought to cultivate violent reputations by talking tough, telling stories, and intimidating peers in public settings. They produced a self-image that was more myth than reality. When actual confrontations did emerge, they called for backup and hoped for the best. The DFW Boyz certainly recognized the absurdity of the situation and characterized all of the Naptown Boyz as wannabe gang members. Still, the interaction between Lonnie and the Naptown Boyz had escalated quickly. A simple argument quickly became a gun-related incident. Fortunately, the gun was not used, but the street beef had become well established, and hostility between the two gangs was readily apparent.

"Is it going to continue?"

Lil' Crazy responded affirmatively to my question, "Yeah, it going to continue until we finally get at them. That's the thing. These niggas [Shawn, Layboy, and Lonnie] ain't from my hood, but I be knowing them for the longest. We lost touch when growing up and shit like that, yeah. They [the Naptown Boyz] from the hood and shit, but when it comes to bro' and me, I'm DFW Boyz for life. Shit it's on and poppin'. Knocking heads, breaking skulls."

After the incident, the DFW Boyz were angry and motivated to retaliate. However, efforts to retaliate were not always immediate; street beefs could linger for months without action. Following the event, the DFW Boyz readily talked about the incident and gossiped about members of the Naptown Boyz. Over the next few weeks, discussions about the Naptown Boyz subsided, and Layboy, Shawn, and the gang focused on other events and other people in their environment. I also stopped asking about the beef, in part because I did not want to unnecessarily stir any latent hostility. As weeks passed without another incident or further discussion about the Naptown Boyz, I gained the impression that, somehow, past transgressions had been forgotten. I was wrong.

THE POTENTIALLY VIOLENT ENCOUNTER

As I noted earlier, I spent a lot of time in my car with several members of the DFW Boyz. This time was invaluable, since it enabled me to closely observe the boys interacting naturally. However, the choice to spend so much time driving gang members around the city of Indianapolis was initially difficult and, in retrospect, probably unwise. As the owner of the car I was, after all, responsible for the people in the car, and there were no guarantees that I could avoid being involved in criminal activity. Perhaps the biggest risk involved in chauffeuring gang members around the city was the possibility that they were carrying drugs. I frequently worried about being pulled over by the police and having someone drop illegal drugs onto the floor of my car. Earlier in the research process, I had allowed drug addicts to ride in my car as I drove about the city. This decision made me very uncomfortable, but such risk was inherent to field research. When I began to hang out with the DFW Boyz, I asked them if they had any drugs on them before they got in my car. From the back seat, Shawn once responded by intentionally regurgitating the rhetoric of antidrug campaigns, "We just say no to drugs."

Although the boys partied and smoked marijuana occasionally, drugs did not seem to be a central element of their lives. I saw little evidence of drug sales, so I stopped worrying about the potential problem.

There was also a risk that their newfound mobility could induce random violence. Over time, however, my concern diminished as I became more comfortable with the day-to-day events surrounding the DFW Boyz. The repetitious pattern of the boys' lives dulled my fears and produced a (retrospectively) foolishly relaxed approach to driving them around the city. They talked about violence, but I had not seen much evidence of such activity, so I simply drove them to their desired locations without asking many questions. As I became more familiar with the neighborhoods I was able to navigate between the gang's favorite locations without directions. If gang members told me to go to one of those locations, I agreed to drive them with little thought for any potential negative consequences.

One afternoon, about a month after the incident with Lonnie and the Naptown Boyz, I was in the car with Lonnie, Layboy, and Shawn. Lonnie received a phone call, talked to Shawn, and told me drive to a strip mall near one of the gang's major hangouts. The conversation between Shawn and Lonnie was inaudible over the blare of loud hip-hop music in the car, and I assumed we were going to meet some other DFW Boyz. They directed me into a familiar parking lot and told me to wait while they checked something out. The strip mall was nondescript. A row of small shops anchored the large parking area, and a gas station was situated across the lot near a busy intersection. We were within short walking distance of Lonnie's apartment, which was another favorite hangout for Layboy and Shawn. The boys were gone for an usually long time, so I walked over to the gas station for a snack and then returned to my car to listen to the radio. The boys emerged from the strip mall after fifteen or twenty minutes and walked toward the gas station instead of my car. Shawn and Layboy's older brother, whom I had not yet noticed, was filling his black sedan at the gas station. After a few minutes of discussion, they got into their brother's car and drove back to the other side of the strip mall. The presence of Shawn and Layboy's older brother was not a good sign. They did not speak much about him, and although he was friendly to me, he had no interest in being involved in my research. Shawn and Layboy occasionally mentioned that their brother had "handled a situation for them." I never asked what that meant. The boys reemerged from the mall after a few minutes and came back to my car. At the same time, two police cars entered the parking lot, drove past Layboy, Shawn, and Lonnie, and went to the back of the strip mall.

As they got back into my car and we left the parking lot, Shawn, Layboy, and Lonnie began excitedly to discuss what had transpired in the strip mall. Their narration of the incident was hurried and not focused on recounting the events logically. Rather, they raucously tried to retell the story, with each person focusing on his part in the incident. Unable to keep up with their conversation, I drove to a nearby house where we could rehash whatever had happened. The conflict between the DFW Boyz and the Naptown Boyz was ongoing, and it seemed to me that Layboy, Shawn, and Lonnie had just used me to drive them to a potentially serious gang confrontation.

"I'll tell you what happened," said Lonnie. "I got a phone call from my bro'. There are those Naptown Boyz niggas that I'm into it with and DFW Boyz into it with."

Lonnie impersonated his brother's phone message, "Shit, these Naptown Boyz niggas up here." He had encountered the Naptown Boyz as they were sitting in a barbershop.

Quickly shifting back to his response, Lonnie continued, "'We going to be up here in a minute, nigga.' Got in the car and went up there. There's two of them niggas. Shit, went in there with my niggas, because they going to be banging [fighting] with us too."

Upon entering the barbershop, Layboy, Shawn, and Lonnie initiated an interaction that largely determined if violence would be used to end this street beef. These moments were the foreground of criminal offending, the micro-context of potentially violent interactions when threats of violence could turn into acts of violence (Jacobs and Wright 1999). In this situation, the gang's goal was not to use violence. Rather, the boys desired to publicly humiliate the Naptown Boyz and force them into submission by using threats of violence. For Shawn, Layboy, and Lonnie, winning the interaction without violence was preferable, but they were probably willing to use violence. What ensued from this agenda was a series of threatening behaviors that were designed to intimidate. These threats were observed, interpreted, and then countered by the Naptown Boyz. If both groups were motivated, these interactions could have quickly escalated to a point where serious violence was inevitable. Both parties had to weigh the costs and benefits of violence with the costs and benefits of submission.[6] Thus each group was making nearly instantaneous calculations about its ability to physically handle the conflict, in addition to the reputational consequences of backing down. Each group knew that its counterparts would have labeled them as soft if they had backed down. Each group was heavily motivated to avoid being viewed as inferior. Verbal threats could have escalated as each group tried to convince their counterpart that the consequences of a conflict were too great. Posturing could have turned into physical challenge, which could have turned into a discussion of guns, which could have turned into a display of firepower. If no one had been willing to back down, both groups would have been left with guns drawn, thinking that the last one to shoot would be the victim.

Lonnie continued, "They said, 'Alright nigga, shit, meet us outside.' So shit, I went outside, I don't know what they [Shawn and Layboy] was doing. They probably was talking shit to them."

"I was in there muggin' them niggas," replied Shawn, letting us know he was holding his own. "Muggin'" simply referred to carrying oneself in a manner that communicates to others that they are in a dangerous position. He was posturing in a threatening manner and letting the Naptown Boyz know that he was down for whatever.

"I was talking shit," chimed Layboy, who had admitted to me earlier that he was much louder than his brother during such confrontations. Shawn liked to stand back and observe, while Layboy jumped into such situations emotionally and verbally harassed potential combatants.

Lonnie continued to tell the story, "We was up there at least seven or eight deep. Shit, it was us three, and then some of my niggas was there. They was going to bang with us, too."

"Some more niggas pulled up," affirmed Shawn.

If necessary, the DFW Boyz could quickly draw a crowd. In the twenty minutes between getting the phone call and the beginning stages of the conflict, they had doubled the number of members involved in the fight. In such conflicts, being deep, or being able to amass a large number of allies, strengthened the group's position. It was momentarily advantageous to appear deep during a conflict, as it could have motivated the other group to back down. If violence did erupt, being deep also increased the group's ability to handle it. In these moments, notions of honor and fair fighting that were well developed in street lore were irrelevant. Pragmatism defeated idealism during intergang conflicts, so the DFW Boyz called for backup.

Backed by these numbers, and a violent reputation, Layboy continued to challenge the Naptown Boyz. "I was like, 'Which one you got a problem with, my brother Lonnie? What's up nigga?' There's one of them talking about how he from Haughville, I mean, shit."

At this point, Shawn took over the role of primary narrator. "They got beef [a problem] with us. They scared. They kept walking away. So his uncle came out there and some more dudes came out there at the barbershop.

"He's like, 'I'll bang with him one on one.'

"We like, 'There ain't one on one when it comes to fam.'"

Ironically, members of the DFW Boyz had previously described scenarios in which they had been outnumbered in a situation and had disdainfully characterized peers who would only try to fight or intimidate them with skewed numbers as cowards. The Naptown Boyz had tried to intimidate Lonnie with skewed numbers during their previous encounter. Of course, the actions of the Naptown Boyz were viewed as cowardly, while the actions of the DFW Boyz during this conflict were somehow justified. Indeed, discussions of norm-violating behavior, bravery, and honor often became irrelevant when the numbers were in favor of the DFW Boyz. If they had not had the upper hand in this situation, they would have perceived a one-on-one fight to be the only fair option. Using the excuse of being family seemed to be an ad hoc rule created to fit the immediate context.[7]

"Some dude says something. He got some things," Shawn continued, implying that gunplay had emerged as possible resolution to this conflict.

"'So you got some things? Ok, we'll be right back.' Called my big bro'."

The DFW Boyz had access to guns, but they typically did not carry them. During the day, especially while riding with me, they never carried guns. If they needed guns, the boys would call their older brother.

Shawn continued, "He got scared. 'No, I'm talking about my hands, talking about my hands.'

"Some dude called the police while we was right there.

"Dude's uncle said, 'Bang one-on-one, bang one on one.'

"So we said, 'Ain't no one-on-one nigga.'

"So he point out little bro' like, 'Shit, bang with him, then.'

"I was like, 'Nigga nah, ain't no-one-on one.' Layboy walked up on one dude and jumped at him. He damn near fell because he was scared."

"Pussy," agreed Layboy, quite proud of his ability to intimidate.

Shawn continued, "His uncle was like, 'We family, so I'm family too.' Showed his tattoo got family name on there. 'We bang one on one, though. I was in the penitentiary, whoopty woo woo.'

He left, backed up. Someone told us he got choppers [tech-9's] or whatever. My big bro', we met him at the gas station. We rode over there with the pump [shotgun]. Everybody sitting over there quiet against the wall, didn't want to bang."

Layboy bragged, "They walking around paranoid like this." He showed me a defeated walk that signified submission.

"Paranoid, they all walking around the barbershop," agreed Shawn.

"Ain't doing shit," added the temporarily vindicated Lonnie.

"They calling the police," said Shawn. "So we came up around here with you. That was the end of that, but we probably get them later on tonight."

Fortunately, the Naptown Boyz had submitted, thereby mitigating the need for violence. Yet the conflict had not been resolved. Perhaps the Naptown Boyz understood that the DFW Boyz were willing to use extreme measures to win this street beef and would accept their fate as the weaker gang. From the perspective of the DFW Boyz, submission was not an option, and they seemed ready to continue the conflict if needed. The incident at the barbershop was another intense moment in an evolving intergang conflict. Each group was heavily motivated to build or maintain its reputation within the intergang environment. Backing down and being perceived as weak was not an option. Although I could not verify their reaction, the Naptown Boyz were probably incensed over this humiliating experience, and it presumably increased their hostility toward the DFW Boyz. For the DFW Boyz, the incident merely reaffirmed their characterizations of the Naptown Boyz. They were weak. They were wannabe gang members who played the role of gang members but were not willing or able to use extreme forms of violence.

To both the gang and specific gang members, overt affronts deserved punishment, and although Shawn, Layboy, and Lonnie were satisfied with the outcome of this incident, they were not ready to feel vindicated.

"Later on tonight it's going down. You might see some fellas' on the news," said Layboy. I could not tell if he was serious, but I hoped he was exaggerating. I knew what he meant, as I had developed a daily routine of checking the news to see if any of the boys had been murdered.[8]

Shawn continued, "Go to those pumps [shotguns] so we letting all them ride."

"Something going to go down," agreed Lonnie.

"So is this exciting for you, or do you get tired of this?"

At once, they all said, "Exciting."

I was not surprised. Their energy in the last thirty minutes had increased to a level I had not previously seen, and they retold the story at a feverish pace. There was something undeniably alluring about the drama in this situation that would attract a teenager, I thought. The excitement of the moment was also fueled by a general understanding that the Naptown Boyz were going to get what they deserved. Justice, it seemed, was based on a distorted understanding of retribution, with violence the appropriate response not only to the latest threat but also to a series of events that had led to this moment.

Although this incident was produced by interactions between members of both gangs and by the decision of the Naptown Boyz to submit, the conflict itself was grounded in a history of events and motivated by concerns of legitimacy. Hostilities had emerged months prior to this event and were reinforced when the Naptown Boyz targeted Lonnie. Since that incident, each group had developed a characterization of its counterpart and disseminated it to others in the intergang environment. This last incident would circulate through peer networks, as the DFW Boyz were more than willing to tell peers about their exploits. A pattern of escalating, conflict-laden interactions led to this incident, and intergang hostilities probably would have been difficult to stop.

"I been on one of them. He be rapping [talking shit] on MySpace," Shawn added in an attempt to explain what had been fueling the conflict. "He be rapping on MySpace. I tell him I will get him when I see him. He was scared. He didn't even want to fight. He backed up. He was by the door."

"He didn't even say nothing," scoffed Lonnie. "The big dude, he was the one rapping, talking shit. He soft."

"He got put in a body cast," added Shawn.

"Yeah. That nigga got put in the hospital. One of my niggas whooped his ass and put him in the hospital," affirmed Lonnie, referencing an incident that had happened months earlier.

Negotiating reputation invariably causes one to diminish peers in a public forum (Horowitz 1983). Social networking Web sites created a false sense of security for gang members who sought to build or maintain violent reputations, and the DFW Boyz often dealt with other youths talking negatively about them online. These Web sites were, however, public staging areas, and the gang did not tolerate inflammatory online banter. There had to be consequences for the child who sat at a computer and publicly challenged the DFW Boyz. The boy's operating premise was, after all, that most self-defined gang members were frauds. They delighted in incidents that suggested this belief to be true, and they took great satisfaction in the perceived weakness of the Naptown Boyz.

Trying to clarify the emergence of guns in this episode, and the decision to call their big brother, I asked, "Why did you call your brother for this one?"

"'Cause they said they got some things. And then . . ." replied Lonnie before Shawn interrupted him.

"One dude showed his pistol, 'See I got mine here.'"

"No thing, we can call them if you want them."

These last statements were indicative of the mindset held by members of the DFW Boyz. Many teenagers carried guns in the streets of Indianapolis, and when they felt threatened or afraid, they revealed their weapon to others by simply lifting their shirts or by pulling the gun out, pointing it at the sky, and shooting it. Often, this caused everyone else to disperse. However, Shawn and Layboy had been taught that, if they were going to show a gun, they had better be ready to use it. If someone else showed them a gun, they were free to respond accordingly. If they had a gun in the moment, they should use it. If not, they should go get one and return. By bringing up the idea of gunplay, the Naptown Boyz had pushed the ongoing conflict to a new level. No longer was this conflict a simple street beef that built up or tore down reputations. The idea of guns invoked issues of life or death, and the

DFW Boyz were seemingly prepared to come out on the right side of that option.

Conflicts are not uncommon in the streets, and most of the time they do not lead to extreme violence. Indeed, the most common responses to disputes or conflicts in poor urban communities are nonviolent, as people demonstrate a remarkable ability to live with and manage prolonged conflicts (Felstiner 1974; Merry 1979). Yet gang members are not just average residents in these communities. When compared to those of other community members, their responses to public disputes are more often guided by the need to defend their identity and combat environmental skepticism. Still, violence is not deterministically bound to petty conflicts, and many gang members walk away from fights (see Garot 2007a, 2009, and 2010). Cooler heads prevail, as someone involved may realize the cost of a street beef is not worth the benefit. Others may step in and mediate a peaceful resolution, especially when two of their acquaintances are engaged in a conflict. The outcome of any conflict or street beef is unpredictable, however, and gang members can only reference their counterpart's reputation to estimate the probability of a violent outcome.

Given that he was related to a member of the Naptown Boyz, perhaps Lil' Crazy would intervene. I asked hopefully, "Is there any way this is going to get squashed [end peacefully]?"

Each replied, "Ah, hell no."

"No."

"Hell no."

Shawn added, "Even if it's squashed, we going to beat their ass every time we see them."

"They're probably going to beef with us," agreed Lonnie. "Every time I see one of these niggas, I'm muggin', talking shit to them or something."

"How's it going to end?" I asked, still searching for the hope that someone would back down.

Shawn answered, "Us beating their ass. One of them getting popped [shot]."

Lonnie countered, "Tell you the truth, I don't think we have to take it that far. That's how soft they is, man. We don't have to take it that far. Them niggas don't really want it."

This was an odd, and rather troubling, gamble that could only be based on reputation, teenage gossip, and brief interactions. All these forms of information, I thought, were tenuous at best, and it was certainly not a game that should be played by teenagers.

FRIGHTENING CONSEQUENCES

The gang members in this study viewed intergang violence with a naive sense of invincibility coupled with an equally naive assumption that they could control the outcome of any conflict.[9] Each gang member assumed that a threat of violence would not be reciprocated with an actual act of violence. In their experience, the threat of violence was often enough to get another group to back down. If not, an act of nonlethal violence was sufficient. Of course the outcome of each potentially violent encounter was unknown to participating gang members in advance. They often downplayed, but remained aware of, the slight possibility that another gang or gang member was willing to respond to their threats or violent actions with lethal force. This was always a possibility, but the boys often gambled that their reputation for violence would deter anyone from using such extreme measures. Such violence could also be delayed, as their counterpart waited for a more advantageous moment to exact revenge (see Jacobs and Wright 2006). This led to a general awareness of lurking violence, but few gang members believed they would be the victims of that violence.

One of my last recorded conversations with members of the DFW Boyz included Layboy, Shawn, EZ Man, and Shon-Shon. The latter members were not heavily involved with this study, but they happened to be around during the conversation and were willing to participate. By this time in the research, I had established enough rapport with Shawn and Layboy that they told me about their criminal activities and street beefs, but we had never openly discussed the use of potentially fatal violence. With only a few more weeks left to collect data, I tried to resolve some lingering questions.

"How do you know that when you get into a fight with someone, they're not going to pull a gun out and shoot?"

EZ Man replied, "If you beat them up, you know they going to come back. They going to come back to fight you again, or they'll come back with a weapon because they know they can't beat you up."

"They going to come back," agreed Shawn.

Shon-Shon added, "You get them before they get you."

EZ Man agreed, "After you beat them up you get to that point, you get it in your mind where, he's going to come back, so I'm going to take care of him before he take care of me."

The certainty of retaliation in these statements starkly contrasted with the tone of prior conversations. Generally, the DFW Boyz assumed that other groups were too intimidated to continue a prolonged, violent street beef. The boys were confident that their capacity for violence caused other groups to avoid additional confrontations. They often told stories about beating someone up, and the individual never messed with them again. Their apparent admission of inevitable retaliation did not fit with what I had witnessed or heard for the last few months.

Before I could ask them to explain this disparity, Shawn clarified, "If we beat them, and we see them come back, we know they strapped. They not going to come back to fight you hands-up again if you beat they ass. You see them coming at you running, 'Ah ok, hey bro' bring up the things.' We sit there and let them keep coming until the pumps start spraying. Then they start going the opposite way."

EZ Man added, "Especially with us, when we beat somebody up, we really beat them up."

Shawn agreed, "Ain't none of this beating them up and, 'Ah nigga you can walk away.' Don't pick up the phone and act like you going to call somebody. I'm going to get you again. That's what I did to that one dude. He got on the phone. I was like, 'Nigga, you calling somebody?'

"'Nah, I'm calling my boss to tell him I'm going to be late for work.'

"Yeah, ok. Don't be on the phone. I'm going to beat your head so you have to go to the hospital. I don't play that shit. I'm not going to let you get me."

Although the boys assumed that their peers were not willing or able to retaliate, they remained aware of the possibility. Members of the DFW Boyz believed that they could mitigate the inherent risks of such violence, regardless of the threat involved. They could offset the consequences of delayed retaliation by recognizing an attempt and responding with extreme aggression. They could also proactively diminish the probability of retaliation by reducing their victim's will or his opportunity to respond violently. When possible, the DFW Boyz beat up someone to a point where he could not immediately retaliate.[10] Given that youths often called their associates to come and handle a street beef, the boys recognized that an opportunity to make a phone call could mean impending retaliation. Extreme violence prevented this simply because the victim would be incapable of organizing a response. Such aggression was also intended to make the victim rethink instigating additional confrontations with the group. It also reinforced the group's reputation, which acted as a deterrent in future conflicts. To the boys, retaliation was controllable, and they were confident in their ability to handle the risks involved with intergang conflicts.

Shawn continued, "Yeah, everybody shoots with choppers."

"What's choppers?"

Shon-Shon answered, "A motherfucking automatic."

While acting like he was shooting an automatic, Shawn said, "That shoot, that spray."

To verify my understanding of another gun-related slang term, I asked, "Pump is a shotgun?"

"Yeah," verified Shawn. "That's a shotty. We got a lot of pumps." With that statement, they all talked excitedly about the sound and feeling of shooting a shotgun. Everyone was laughing, and during the chaotic conversation someone said, "It sounds good."

Shawn added, "Those pumps ain't no joke, especially when you learn to shoot the motherfucker."

Layboy agreed, "And the motherfucker's spreading."

"Have you ever shot at people?" This was a question I had not yet felt comfortable asking.

"Last time . . .," said Shawn, thoughtfully, but he was not able to fully respond.

EZ Man quickly added, "I have with my older cousins and them . . ."

"I don't know if I be hitting people," interrupted Shawn. "Somebody could get hit, but you can't tell until afterward. I spray the motherfucker. I let loose. I don't give a fuck. Especially at night, I wait till night anyways. Hit that boy and duck out. Get the throwaways, and put them in the sewer somewhere."

Even after spending months hanging out with Shawn, Layboy, and their DFW Boyz associates, this was a startling admission. The boys had previously admitted that some gang members were labeled as hot boys because they liked to shoot at people. The capacity to shoot, however, seemed to be an individualized trait not universally embraced by all legitimate gang members. I often wondered what distinguished the so-called killer from the average violent gang member.[11] I hoped that Shawn's admission was merely tough talk, but everyone in this conversation knew him very well, and nobody challenged his statement.

Shon-Shon added, "I'm to the point where I don't give a fuck. If a nigga talking about that gunplay, I ain't going to give him no chance."

EZ Man interjected with a harsh reality of street life, "I been shot at a lot."

"I been shot at too many times," agreed Shawn. At least for the moment, he abandoned the illusion of control and admitted the inherent danger of gang life and street beefs.

Layboy added, "I done seen the bottom of the barrel. That motherfucker's bigger than a bitch. I was scared as a motherfucker. Start praying, nigga."

"What was this?"

Shawn replied to my question, "That was on Fortieth. That dude went past with his car. He came up too fast."

Layboy recounted, "I was knocking on everybody's door. 'Hey, call the police. This nigga's got a gun.'"

"Did he shoot?"

"He didn't shoot," responded Shawn. "He wanted to."

"He didn't shoot," verified Layboy. "I was wearing a big ass red coat. I was like 'I'm hit. Fuck, I'm hit.'"

Shawn added, "Pops and them took care of that one, though. I was like, 'Damn, that a wrap.'"

The extended social networks of gang members make street beefs complicated. Shawn and Layboy had connections throughout the city, and their position within a large extended family full of gang members gave them options when dealing with a problem. Just as their brother had intervened in the situation at the barbershop, their father, and his associates dealt with the prospective shooter. If conflicts with the DFW Boyz escalated to the point where shootings became an option, the boys had access to a pool of older family members who were capable of overwhelming the opposition with force. These connections only emboldened Layboy and Shawn and reinforced their illusion of control.

EZ Man added, "You basically don't have to worry, though, because if someone shoots one of us, there's somebody above us that's going . . ."

With that, everyone else chimed in, "Yeah."

Layboy elaborated, "We know people. I'm telling you we know people. If people come at us, we got big bros. They got big bros."

Shawn agreed, "All of us got big bros. Everybody got big brothers, and big brothers got niggas."

Shawn, Layboy, and other members of the DFW Boyz thought that they were safe. After all, they believed that most other self-defined gang members were not real and did not have the ability or willingness to use violence. The gang's reputation alone would convince most other gang members not to question the gang's status. Yet when someone did "talk shit" about the gang, the DFW Boyz responded aggressively and used the opportunity to reinforce or expand their reputation. Although most offenders learned from their mistake and did not continue to dismiss the DFW Boyz, a person or group occasionally continued to insult members of the gang, thereby creating an ongoing street beef. As these conflicts escalated, members of the DFW Boyz remained confident that they were more willing and able to use violence than their counterparts. They believed that their efforts to intimidate other gangs would demonstrate their strength and reveal their counterparts' weaknesses. Their connections to older relatives who had no qualms about the use of violence seemingly insulated them from extreme forms of violent victimization. I was not as confident about the safety of the DFW Boyz, but their attitude was somewhat contagious. I hoped their perceptions were accurate.

CONCLUSION

On the streets of Indianapolis, much was gained or lost during the micro-context of social interaction. For gang members, reputations were built, maintained, or lost during social interactions and the resulting flow of gossip, which efficiently disseminated information. One's performance during a public confrontation was intimately linked to status concerns, as each gang member was aware that he or she might be labeled as soft or, perhaps, as a wannabe gang member. Gang members experienced strong pressures to avoid these labels, as the assessments made by observers would undoubtedly transcend the moment and become part of the general street knowledge base. Appearing soft or weak during these interactions did not just cause a gang member to lose social standing among observing peers. He or she also risked losing status throughout the intergang environment, as a growing number of peers would begin to think that he or she was not a real gang member. The need to prove that one genuinely belonged within the boundaries of the intergang field produced consistent motivation to engage in interpersonal violence. Legitimacy in the intergang environment was, therefore, a status concern that was intimately related to expressive, rather than instrumental, violence. Indeed, the DFW Boyz and other research participants were not motivated by monetary concerns and settling street debts. They were concerned with perceived slights and building or maintaining their reputation in the intergang environment.

Gang members' concerns about their public image are not entirely different from the concerns of their street-oriented, non-gang peers, but the intensity of their commitment to status is greater than that of their peers. Legitimacy is intimately related to respect, a concept that has long been noted as playing a role in interpersonal street violence (Anderson 1999; Jacobs and Wright 2006; Oliver 1994; Wilkinson 2001). For gang members, respect and legitimacy are interdependent concepts. Gang members have to establish legitimacy in the intergang environment to gain respect, but they gain legitimacy by becoming respected in the streets. And for gang members, interpersonal interactions offer a forum where concerns of legitimacy and respect intersect. Personal slights are not only viewed as incidents of disrespect, they also might be perceived as symbolic challenges to one's status as a real gang member. In addition, any overt challenge to or question about one's status as a real gang member is automatically viewed as being disrespectful. Concerns about legitimacy are not as salient among non-gang members. Thus gang members in this study were likely to be more sensitive to personal affronts, and they were likely more willing to respond with violence.

For gang members, respect is connected to an explicit identity that is embraced by an individual, or a collection of individuals, presented to a peer environment, and then questioned by that environment. When compared to the notion of "gang member," few other identities in the street are so easily embraced and performed yet so frequently questioned. Whereas non-gang street identities are often broad, gendered, and connected to vague notions like toughness, virility, or street smarts (Anderson 1999; Oliver 1994; Wilkinson 2001), gang identities are often linked to the unambiguous notion of violence. Gang members must "do gang," or publicly perform in a manner that is consistent with environmental expectations about the meaning of "gang," which invariably means that gang members must engage in or appear to engage in violence. Given their immersion into an environment that is generally skeptical about gang membership claims, gang members are more likely than their peers to have to defend their street identities. And, as some scholars note (see Anderson 1999), violence is a common response to an identity attack.

Concerns about status and social identity were salient among the gang members in this study, and they influenced both gang members' behavior and their understanding of social life. Members of the DFW Boyz, for example, believed that if they consistently demonstrated a willingness and ability to engage in violence, questions of legitimacy would become irrelevant. They believed that if everyone recognized them as tough or deep, the need to engage in violence would diminish. Borrowing from William Muir's classic dictum on the paradox of face, "the nastier one's reputation, the less nasty one has to be" (1977, 101), the boys seemed to assume that building a reputation for violence was a good solution to an array of short- and long-term social challenges. It solidified their sense of belonging, established their place within the intergang environment, and was supposed to reduce the probability that other gangs would dare to threaten them. But in the unending social struggle found within the intergang environment, the increased visibility that accompanied a growing reputation also increased the frequency and intensity of potential intergang conflict. The boys' pursuit of legitimacy in the intergang environment placed them at greater risk for violent victimization.

CHAPTER 8

Hope, Intervention, and Tragedy

MY TIME WITH SHAWN, Layboy, and other members
of the DFW Boyz often led me to ponder their immediate safety
and future prospects. Although I recognized the seriousness of their
actions and knew that, according to research, they were at high risk for
either violent victimization or felony arrest, my concerns were often
suppressed by their illusion of control and the assumed invincibility
of youth. The boys constantly expressed the belief that they were
untouchable in the streets of Indianapolis, and that confidence proved
to be somewhat contagious. In retrospect, I should have been more concerned. The depth and duration of their commitment to both the gang's
collective identity and the appraisals of the broader intergang environment were a potentially fatal combination, yet I was often more worried
about their ability to assimilate into conventional society as they matured
and, I hoped, grew weary of gang life.

My hope for change in the boys' lives was not unreasonable, despite
the array of challenges they faced. Gang membership typically does not
signify an unbreakable contractual agreement with the gang; most youths
only temporarily participate in gang life. For example, one study in
Rochester, New York, found that most youths join a gang for less than
one year (Thornberry et al. 2003). Unfortunately, core members of the
DFW Boyz who were featured in this book were fully invested in gang
life. They considered themselves gang members long before I entered
the research field, and two years later they were still actively representing the DFW Boyz in the streets of Indianapolis. That degree of
commitment to gang life presents an especially difficult challenge for
policy makers, civil servants, and ordinary citizens seeking to address the
gang problem in their respective communities. A mere eighteen months
of field research cannot satisfactorily account for the inevitable changes

that occur in the lives of gang members. Investment in the gang and, by extension, the intergang environment, is in constant flux. Still, my time with the DFW Boyz revealed some fundamental dilemmas relating to change and the prospects of intervening in gang members' lives. There is hope for intervention, but the challenges remain significant.

In this chapter I explore some of the dilemmas of intervention and change. My intention is not to fully develop a comprehensive gang control program but rather to acknowledge the complexity of change in active gang members' lives. Gang members negotiate the prospects of change while still invested in the appraisals of the intergang environment. Even within the small network of the DFW Boyz, this negotiation varied greatly. Some of the boys expressed very little desire to get a job or to finish school, while others appeared quite motivated to do so. Such motivation was accompanied by a degree of ambivalence, however, as they had to choose between, or try to balance, two attractive yet competing social worlds. For anyone seeking to intervene in gang members' lives, understanding this ambivalence is essential, since gang members must negotiate that ambivalence if they are to desist from gang life. Unfortunately, the prospects of change do not protect gang members from the consequences of their behavior.

A Campus Trip and Dilemmas of Intervention

Researchers generally agree that any serious attempt to address the gang problem should include a concerted effort to make conventional avenues for success more accessible to gang members.[1] Active gang members need a realistic alternative to gang life, but providing them with such an alternative is not always easy. They often lack the education, training, or cultural acumen to transition smoothly into a well-paying job, if one is even available (see Fleisher 1998). Many gang control programs, therefore, use job training, job placement, or educational programs to help members find non-gang alternatives (see Spergel and Grossman 1997; Spergel, Wa, and Sosa 2005).[2] When combined with systematic efforts by police to suppress gang activity, some of these programs have demonstrated a remarkable ability to reduce violence (see Kennedy, Braga, and Piehl 2001), but less is known about their capability to transform gang members' lives. Given my close relationships with

Layboy, Shawn, and other gang members, I considered the challenges of intervention to be vitally important.

Sacrificing the ethic that a researcher should not disrupt the research setting, I made consistent efforts to give Layboy, Shawn, and other gang members access to conventional outlets for success. As noted earlier, I helped them fill out countless job applications. I also occasionally drove them across the city so that they would not miss summer school classes. These efforts produced frustration, but they also led to insights regarding the challenges that confronted the boys. They were unable to find jobs, and when I was not around they often could not or would not find transportation to summer school, so they dropped out. My time with the boys led to more questions about intervention than actual solutions. Most notably, while I recognized that access and opportunity were part of the solution, the boys might not have ignored the power of their peer environment for a good job or even a college education. When given a reasonable opportunity to pursue other, more conventional endeavors, how would they negotiate two divergent worlds?

In early July of 2008, I was again in my car with Shawn, Layboy, and their cousin TJ. Instead of driving around the city in search of food, jobs, or other DFW Boyz, we were making the one-and-a-quarter-hour trip to Bloomington so they could witness the university setting. I had first gotten the idea for the trip more than one year before, when I invited Sidney, the OG who was my first reliable contact, to speak to one of my classes. It was the first time Sidney had stepped into a college classroom. Afterward, as we walked through campus, he looked around at the buildings, the well-manicured lawns, and the abundance of blooming spring flowers, and simply said, "Tim, if I had only known this was here." The statement effectively communicated an awareness of the opportunities he lost while running the streets at an early age. His father died of natural causes when he was young, which forced his mother to raise eight children on her own. Soon after his father's death, Sidney's family moved from a large home on the near-north side of Indianapolis to a low-income apartment complex along Thirty-eighth Street. Sidney quickly embraced street life and spent much of his adult life in prison. If he had fully understood the possibilities of college life, perhaps Sidney would have focused his energies on pursuing an education. Perhaps the allure of the streets was too strong, and he would have rejected such a conventional institution. In his mid-forties, he could only ponder life's elusive possibilities.

Throughout the course of my research, Sidney insisted that seeing a college campus would dramatically alter the perspective of a gang member. He continually argued that gang members were just misguided youths in need of direction. Although I thought he underestimated the violent capabilities of Indianapolis youth, his reaction to seeing a college campus convinced me that it might have a similar effect on Layboy, Shawn, and TJ. When compared to other gang members in this study and other studies (see Fleisher 1998; Decker and Van Winkle 1996), the boys were actually in a relatively good position to succeed. Even though they had been expelled from multiple Indianapolis high schools and were behind on their credits, all three were still in school. Shawn, who was entering his senior year of high school, had mentioned a vague interest in going to community college. Although he probably lacked some essential skills for college, he was taking college prep courses in school and seemed to be competent in upper-level algebra classes. I did not doubt Shawn's intelligence. Over time, I grew to believe that Shawn would become a high-achieving leader in whatever he pursued. His leadership ability was already evident, as younger and older peers gravitated to him and were willing to follow him. I only questioned the direction of his pursuits. Would he succeed in the streets, or through more legitimate avenues?

Layboy and TJ were also capable, though probably less talented, but they did not express much of an interest in their long-term future. Perhaps this lack of interest was caused by their inability to anticipate the important transition from high school to adult life, making it easier to remain content in their youthful obsessions. In addition to violent victimization and being arrested for criminal activities, one of the insidious consequences of gang membership is that it tends to disrupt the developmental trajectory of adolescent members (Thornberry et al. 2003). Troubled youths join gangs in response to chaotic life conditions, only to enter a group and intergroup environment that undermines their development. For example, a gang member's need to establish a tough reputation in school supersedes his or her concerns for school performance. Too many youths abandon conventional avenues for success to pursue the illusion of promise offered by gang life. Most gang members eventually become disillusioned with this promise, but upon leaving gang life, they are confronted with the reality that they have squandered important developmental years on the streets. To obtain good jobs, they need an education, which they ignored when they were in the gang, but to get an education, they need a job that is both flexible enough to negotiate the time commitments of school and lucrative enough to cover both living and schooling expenses. A GED may be sufficient to find menial work, but additional education or training is needed to find stable employment. The longer they stay in the gang the more difficult these educational goals are to attain.

The streets are full of older, inactive gang members living day to day by working in menial jobs. Some former gang members are lucky to find moderately well-paying construction or labor-intensive jobs that are not guaranteed over the long term. Others find work in the margins of the non–illicit underground economy that is pervasive in urban areas (Venkatesh 2006). Sidney, for example, had seemingly worked in every type of labor-intensive job available to him. He dug trenches for plumbers, shingled roofs, refurbished cars, hustled for day-to-day carpentry/ construction work, and worked as an unlicensed electrician/repairman. He claimed to be too old to risk the dangers of digging trenches and shingling steep roofs, and he continuously searched for safer jobs that required some skill. Although he was capable of doing skilled labor, his aspirations placed him in competition with people who were properly licensed and had not gotten their only formal education from Leavenworth Federal Penitentiary. Recognizing that such work was unlikely, he constantly came up with new ideas to tap into the underground economy. He frequently mentioned to me that $25,000 would change his life, as it would let him start a landscaping business or allow him to buy and remodel abandoned homes. Although there was nothing inherently wrong with Sidney's struggle, it did produce overwhelming frustrations in his life, and it created persistent temptations to regress into criminal activity. Sidney was not alone. Throughout Indianapolis, and in other cities, middle-aged adults, young adults, and older teenagers become disillusioned with gang life or the streets in general and desperately try to regain what they lost or acquire what they never had. The developmental years wasted in gang life are essential for establishing a lifetime of stability, and many former gang members struggle after leaving their gangs.

Although their school performance was likely substandard, the fact that Shawn, Layboy, and TJ could reasonably expect to obtain their high school diplomas and at least attend a community college placed them at an advantage over some of their peers.[3] Some of the gang members in this study had dropped out of school, while others were substantially underprepared in their formal education. I once helped a teenage gang member with his math homework and quickly realized that he could not learn the algebraic order of operations because he lacked a basic understanding of multiplication.

Layboy, Shawn, and TJ demonstrated an ability to transition seamlessly from the social context of the streets into one where conventional behaviors were expected. I could take them to restaurants and not have to worry about severely loud speech or vulgar language. When applying for jobs, they generally knew how to act in front of prospective employers. On one occasion, Shawn applied for job at a sports store in a mall on the outer edges of the city. The manager was present and interviewed Shawn for a job. Shawn was dressed normally for a seventeen-year-old from Indianapolis and spoke intelligently about his aspirations and previous work experience. His gang tattoos were clearly visible, however, which probably required the prospective employer to deal with an apparent contrast between two different forms of communication. Ultimately, Shawn did not get the job; the tattoos were presumably enough to deter the employer. Still, it demonstrated that Shawn could behave in a manner that was consistent with the expectations of employers and college admissions staff.

Although the boys were heavily invested in gang life and capable of engaging in severe violent activities, I remained hopeful that their long-term prospects did not have to parallel Sidney's experience. They might see the opportunities provided by a university, largely isolated from the concerns of the street, that could alter their perception of life's possibilities. In effect, I hoped that in twenty-five years they would not be saying, "If only I had known." Their prospects of actually attending a university were unknown. I thought they might attend a local community college and perhaps transfer to a four-year school. My agenda for the Bloomington trip was merely to expose them to a world quite different from their own and convince them that such a place was not unreachable.

The university or college setting is a unique social environment that provides an attractive alternative to the intergang environment. To some extent, the recreational activities of university students are not dramatically different from the activities enjoyed by gang members. Both groups party, play sports, hang out late into the night, play video games, and pursue sexual relationships. In fact, some college students probably pursue these activities more vigorously than Shawn, Layboy, and TJ. Therefore, the boys would naturally be drawn to the endless activities available on campus. More importantly, the pressures of the intergang environment would be largely absent on a college campus. Few, if any, of their peers would be immersed in a social system that reinforced the legitimizing power of violent behavior. Most college students would probably avoid self-defined gang members or view gang members as novelty acts on campus. Indeed, college would be accompanied by sudden immersion into a social system quite different from the intergang environment. How would the boys adapt to a social environment that was generally apathetic or wary of gang affiliation? Would this new environment eliminate or reduce the boys' need to endlessly build and maintain a violent reputation, or would the boys enter a new environment seeking to establish a campuswide reputation for toughness? To me, either option seemed possible.

The first place the boys wanted to see was the basketball arena, and we were lucky that the gym floor was accessible. While we stood on the edge of the court and the boys stared at the more than 17,000 empty seats above them, two basketball players were shooting free throws nearby. Layboy, Shawn, and TJ were less impressed by the players than they were by the size of the arena. They had been to professional games with a community organization, but they had never been on the court. They fantasized about the prospects of playing in the gym and talked excitedly about what that experience would be like. I told them about the relatively affordable student season tickets and the excitement of each game. We lingered for about twenty minutes without any disturbances, before they were ready to move on and see the rest of campus. The rest of the tour resembled those moments on the basketball court, though without some of the excitement. They walked through the campus, impressed with the physical surroundings, but they were more intrigued with college life. Like many teenagers, they talked mostly about college girls, parties, playing sports on the fields or basketball courts, working out in the weight room, and eating at some of the food vendors. They were not particularly interested in the library or other academic facilities, but they found the size of some lecture halls intriguing.

As we ate lunch in the student union, they began to ask me more serious questions about the life of a college student. Although I could not comment on the nonacademic life at the school, I could inform them about the academics. This conversation involved a number of basic points. First, students had more freedom in college than they did in high school. The amount of time they spent in class each week was much less than in high school, and the professors would not force the boys to do their work. In this sense, college students were given more autonomy than their high school counterparts. The boys approved of this freedom. Second, I warned them that, with more freedom, they had to be more disciplined than they were in high school. The biggest problem I saw with college students was not lack of intelligence but lack of discipline. To succeed, they had to read, study, and turn in work without prompting. The boys, especially Shawn, seemed to think this was not a big deal. Finally, I told them that the transition from their current academic situation to college would be difficult, and they might be behind some of the other students. This, I said, was not a byproduct of their intelligence but caused by their current inattentiveness to school.[4] They had the ability to succeed, but they would have to work hard to catch up to their peers. They did not seem as excited by those comments.

I had arranged for the boys to meet with a financial aid representative after lunch, but as we passed some time, I asked them what they thought about the university. Layboy and TJ did not have much to say besides superficial comments about the campus and college girls. Shawn, however, said, "I could get used to this. It's quiet down here." For some reason his comments surprised me and reminded me that while life on the streets of Indianapolis often appeared mundane, the threat and prevalence of violence produced a sense of chaos in boy's lives. No campus is perfect, but in Bloomington Shawn would have been free from both the pressures of the intergang environment and the drama that accompanied gang conflicts. He would not have had to worry about episodic violence and the prospects of retaliation. He would not have had to worry about environmental pressures to maintain his reputation. He would not have had to deal with the daily tedium of street life, as there were more than enough recreational options on campus. He would also have been eligible for a campus job, or he might have been able to find one off-campus. Given our failed attempts to find him a job in Indianapolis, this was an important realization. Undoubtedly, he could have found ways to get in trouble, but life as a college student would have been relatively quiet. Perhaps exposure to another world would have been enough to motivate Shawn to desist from gang life.

Despite this, I realized that the expense of college would likely cause practical problems if the boys had actually wanted to attend. A more realistic path would have first involved two years of community college. When we met with the financial aid officer, this assumption changed dramatically. The boys had signed up for Indiana's Twenty-first Century Scholars program in middle school. Essentially, the program provides all students below a certain income level the opportunity to attend a public college in the state with full financial assistance. The only requirements for this scholarship were that one had to sign up for the program in middle school, maintain a 2.0 GPA, and make a pledge of good citizenship. Thus they could have attended any number of colleges in Indiana for free if they met both these requirements and the school's standards for admission (for more information see Indiana.gov). I was surprised to learn about this opportunity and naturally concerned about some of the requirements. The boys had been arrested multiple times, but they had never been convicted.

Shawn would have likely benefited from the opportunity to attend college and immerse himself in a social environment that was largely detached from the intergang environment. But thousands of teenagers enter college every year, and it would be naïve to suggest that these students and their parents would not have justifiable concerns about the presence of Shawn on a college campus. Moreover, college administrators and professors might reasonably be uncomfortable with Shawn in their dormitories and classrooms. After all, he had repeatedly demonstrated a willingness and ability to engage in excessively violent behavior. How much of that behavior was directly produced by his social environment, and how much of that behavior had become internalized and would translate to other social settings? He was immersed in a social system that emphasized violence, but through conversations and actions he also reinforced the use of violence. To what extent would he change in a new environment? Would he compartmentalize his gang identity to the streets of Indianapolis and conform to the college campus? Was his role as a gang member such a dominant and unwavering part of his personal identity that he would not dramatically change in a new social setting? Perhaps the more difficult question should be directed at decision makers who can help change gang members' lives. How much are you willing to risk by providing an opportunity to someone who desperately needs assistance?

Unfortunately, the answers to these questions cannot be found in this study or others. Gang scholarship as a whole lacks sufficient micro-level theory to explain gang member behavior. Thus, we do not understand important differences between gang members, nor do we understand the psychological effects of gang membership. Many scholars argue that gangs arise out of adverse socioeconomic conditions, but researchers do not understand how gang membership influences an individual's decision when he or she is given the opportunity to attend college. This study suggests that intervention is not just about exposure, opportunity, and assistance; it also involves complex issues of identity. The gang member embraces a violent identity and negotiates an environment that both reinforces and questions his or her commitment to that identity. The challenge is in explaining variation in commitment to the gang identity and understanding members' capacity to develop alternative identities.[5]

As we left campus, I began to think about the ramifications of Shawn's attending college. Layboy interrupted my thoughts by saying, "Where do you live? Can we see your house?" Given their willingness to open their lives to me, I thought it would send a poor message to the boys if I denied their curiosity. Therefore, I drove the short distance to my house and pulled into my driveway. My 1,350-square-foot house was something of a disappointment to the boys, who seemed to expect something more substantial. They looked around the neighborhood at the other modest houses, which differed primarily in upkeep from the houses along East Thirty-eighth Street. Layboy asked me why I did not lock my car here, when I often did in Indianapolis. It was a good observation for which I did not have a good response. I took them through the house and, again, they did not seem impressed. My pregnant wife and nine-month-old daughter were home, and the boys awkwardly talked to my wife while I held the baby. As I write this, I am reminded that most of the DFW Boyz I met in the course of my research currently have young children.

The significance of this scene was not that it foreshadowed events in the boy's lives, but that I was quite comfortable bringing violent gang members into my home to meet the two people I hold most dear. In retrospect, this decision was not misguided or foolish. Layboy, Shawn, and TJ were undoubtedly gang members who were heavily involved in violence and other criminal activities, but they generally seemed like normal teenagers. At a time when some scholars and practitioners like to use the term "super predators" to describe violence-prone youths (Dilulio 1995), the complexity of gang members' characters is largely underappreciated. In one context, they will try to intimidate teachers, rob strangers, harass or assault peers, or even participate in lethal acts of violence. In other situations, they are friendly, honest, courteous, and even hardworking. They are not, as some have suggested, immersed in a negativistic normative system that takes pleasure in the pain of law-abiding citizens (see Cohen 1955). The gang members in this study also did not seem to suffer from a psychological deficiency like low self-control or "psychopathology" (see Fleisher 1995; Yablonsky 1967). Instead, they were immersed in a skeptical social system that routinely demanded proof of legitimacy. As a result, their behavior was largely guided by the need to demonstrate a willingness and ability to engage in violent behavior. Detached from that pressure, gang members were unlikely to offend, and their presence in my home was not particularly concerning.

As I drove back to Indianapolis, Shawn and I discussed the possibility of his going to college. The visit had clearly exposed him to an attractive option, and he was aware of the short- and long-term benefits of college. We also talked about the problems that he might deal with at college. He knew that it would be academically challenging. He understood that he would have to live with peers from dramatically different backgrounds. He seemed to understand that disruptive behavior or criminal activities would not be tolerated in class, on campus, or in the city of Bloomington. Our discussion ended as I made a few brief comments. I told him that at college no one would know who he was, and most students probably would not care who he was. His reputation in

Indianapolis would not matter much at school, and he would be sacrificing status in the streets for the peace and quiet of a college environment. If he went to college talking about Haughville or the DFW Boyz, throwing signs up at parties and trying to intimidate peers, he could be kicked out of school or become a social outcast. From the back seat of my car, he responded with a contemplative tone, "I was thinking about that." He then put his head back and eventually fell asleep for the remainder of the trip.

A Final Conversation and Thoughts of Change

Exposing gang members to an attractive alternative to gang life seems to be an important part of intervening in their lives, but it should also be accompanied by a concerted effort to help them gain access to that alternative. Our trip to Bloomington showed the boys that college was one possible option, but they still needed help getting there. Moreover, the expectation that Shawn, Layboy, and TJ would immediately end their gang activities and focus their lives on pursuing a college education was largely unrealistic. College might have been a turning point, but change would likely have been gradual. If the boys went to college, they would still have had close friends and relatives representing the DFW Boyz. At least for a while they would have continued to define themselves as gang members and remained focused on the evaluations and activities of their peers. They would have continued to participate in street life. Time away from the streets could have decreased their visibility and undermined their ability to establish wide reputations. A new wave of ambitious youths might have taken their place in the streets, while they lived in relative anonymity on a college campus. To most readers the choice between street life and college life seems obvious, but for teenage gang members it is not.

Change was inevitable for Shawn and Layboy, but the direction of that change was difficult to predict. Our trip to Bloomington was only a respite from their daily concerns, and the promise of college was soon displaced by the attractions of street life. Over the next few weeks, Layboy and TJ told me that they had no interest in pursuing their education, but Shawn remained interested. The extent of his interest remained unclear, however, and I regretted my inability to help develop that attraction further. I passed the information about college to Shawn's aunt and hoped that she would help him pursue the opportunity. Despite Shawn's attraction to college, he still remained heavily invested in gang life. More generally, the boys' attentiveness to the intergang environment caused them to reevaluate their standing in the streets of Indianapolis, and they began to discuss new ideas for organizing the gang.

My last conversation with Shawn and Layboy occurred in late July 2008, as they once again escaped boredom by hanging out with a few other DFW Boyz in Aaron's east-side apartment. The conversation began like many others. The boys talked about recent events in the streets, peers, and the gang. As we talked, Shawn appeared uncharacteristically pensive and contributed very little to the conversation. Something, it seemed, was bothering him. The conversation then shifted, as the boys discussed transforming the gang from a well-known clique into one that would be organized and entrepreneurial. Such a change was not what I had in mind, as it seemed to reflect a growing, long-term commitment to gang life. But as the boys talked, their plans for change seemed motivated by a growing disillusionment about petty street beefs and senseless violence.

I said to the boys, "You mentioned earlier that you just started having guys work for the clique, and if they're not bringing in money there are consequences."

Layboy responded, "Yeah. There's consequences, I tell everybody, I was telling people yesterday, 'By Friday if you ain't known and we don't have money we don't need you.' We don't need you sitting here claiming DFW Boyz. What you claiming for if you ain't put in no work?"

Layboy's statement was largely motivated by a crisis of legitimacy. The DFW Boyz, like most gangs, was not formally organized. There was little evidence of a clear leadership structure, formal role differentiation, rules, or a defined system of internal control. The boys seemed content to rely on their loose but widespread connections. Each member seemed to have an understanding of his informal role in the clique, and each enjoyed not having to follow strict rules. Problems accompanied such informality, however. Without clear standards, membership was open to anyone who became a close associate of some, but not all, members of the DFW Boyz. The gang was growing, but only because it lacked standards for membership. Too many new additions were joining the gang because it had become popular. Some newer members were not really down for whatever, and they could not establish well-known reputations in the streets of Indianapolis. In a sense, they were wannabes, diluting the potency of the DFW Boyz. Being able to make money insulated a member from the "wannabe" label, and it was an acceptable alternative to being known. However, if the group became too diluted, its position in the intergang environment would be weakened. The gang, as a collective body, could lose legitimacy in the streets of Indianapolis, so the boys tried to address the problem.

"You just started that policy, right?" Admittedly, the word "policy" immediately seemed too formal given the gang's relative lack of organization.

"Yeah, well it done been like that but we been slippin' [not enforcing it]," replied Layboy. "Now it's to the point where niggas out here need money, and there's a lot of money to get. So we like might as well try to get money, stack up on the low, and by next summer we going to be out there. All of us going to be rolling in cars. We ain't trying to be on that beef stuff right now, trying to get money. About to change our whole swag [approach/appearance] up."

His newfound focus on money surprised me, as did his statement about ending their street beefs. I asked, "What changed? Before, you were talking about beefs and you haven't talked much about money."

Layboy answered my question, "Yeah, we about to change that. We about to change all that beef stuff. We about to change all that up."

"Squash [end] that shit," added Shawn. This was the first time he had talked for a while.

"We about to squash everything with everybody, about to start getting money," clarified Layboy. "We ain't going to be no clique no more. People still going to know who we are, but we ain't going to go around saying 'DFW Boyz.' We going to get money, stacking our chips up, getting bread, getting out here. Everybody going to have jobs, 'cause we ain't going to be dumb. Everybody going to be in school, everybody going to have jobs. Do what you do. We trying to get it the positive way and still be out here. Like people get caught out here selling weed, we trying to do it the positive way, getting money. Have our own house or whatever. You can still sell weed or whatever, but at least have a job so the police stop you [and ask] 'Where you get this money from?'"

This statement surprised me even more. This was the first time I had heard any member of the DFW Boyz express some disillusionment with any aspect of gang life. Their need to change was apparent, but the direction of that change was not. Layboy seemed confused. Money was an important part of his plan, but he was not clearly articulating whether or not the group would pursue money through legal or illegal channels. Gangs can evolve. Although it is rare, some gangs are able to develop into highly sophisticated, well-organized entrepreneurial street organizations (see Venkatesh 1998; Levitt and Venkatesh 2000). At this point, such a transition seemed unlikely for the DFW Boyz. They were, after all, just a loose collection of teenagers who did not understand how to organize or operate an illicit underground enterprise. The idea of owning a house was undoubtedly attractive, but it seemed unrealistic. Layboy's focus on doing things in what he called the positive way was somewhat vague and seemingly inconsistent with prior conversations. Was he implying that the DFW Boyz should quit participating in illicit street activities? I was not sure what Layboy was referring to or why he suddenly wanted to change.

"Yeah, but two weeks ago you weren't talking money, you were talking cliques and fights. What changed in the last two weeks?"

Layboy insightfully and somewhat expectedly, responded, "Ain't nothing change. The other day I was thinking like what we doing this for? It's not necessary. Beefing, it's going to end up getting somebody killed. Then it's going to be somebody else. Then it's going to be a big disaster. 'Cause I know if somebody kill one of my niggas it ain't going to ever stop. It ain't going to ever stop. So I'm saying we going to start doing it, trying to get it the positive way."

"You look like you have something to say," I said to Shawn, who still looked bothered by something.

"It ain't all about the positive," replied Shawn. "Shit, if you get stopped and you got three thousand dollars in your pocket, and they ask you how you get it. What you going to say? They look at your history, and you ain't never had a job. The job ain't nothing but a cover-up."

Shawn had brought this point up before. Anyone trying to make money on the streets also needed to have a legitimate job, which provided a reasonable excuse for having money. I often thought of this while I helped them try to find jobs. Was I helping them access legitimate avenues for success, or just helping them cover up their illicit activities? Shawn had also talked about how pursuing a college education could be used to help the gang. Would he use college to improve his criminal exploits? Perhaps, but he seemed more like a seventeen-year-old who was attracted to college life yet still committed to the gang. Only time would tell how he negotiated that ambivalence.

"So where do you go from here?"

Shawn replied, "Basically we about to get more organized. Have a couple of meetings, and then have these niggas from the far-east control the far-east niggas. The niggas from the west side control the west-side niggas. Then we going to take over the south and the north. 'Cause when we was at the Expo we got into it with some far-east side niggas, some of our niggas from the far east side . . ."

Layboy interrupted, "They ain't doing it."

The Expo refers to the Indiana Black Expo Summer Celebration. Every summer Indiana Black Expo Inc. organizes a ten-day summer celebration in downtown Indianapolis. The Expo's general mission is to advance the economic and social development of African Americans (see Indiana Black Expo, Inc. 2010). The summer celebration offers various business conferences, job fairs, entrepreneurship seminars, and sporting and music events. During the weekend of the celebration, downtown Indianapolis is full of teenagers and young adults. Generally this is a time of uneventful social interaction, but gang members do make up a small percentage of the people in the downtown area. With ample opportunities to interact with other gangs, conflicts invariably occur. In 2010, for example, nine people were shot when a gang member started shooting in a crowded area. Members of the DFW Boyz were not immune to the occasional hostile encounter during the Expo, and a street beef reemerged during that event in 2008. Shawn told the story.

"At the Expo we was walking downtown and Aaron was talking to some little chick. Well, before that Michael, the one you interviewed, beat up this guy, AJ, back when we went to Broad Ripple [high school]. AJ never let it go or whatever. So now every time we see him it break out and shit. So they see him at the Expo. My brother came back and got me and my big bro', and we walked around there. Some little niggas that's from Brightwood was with him. Niggas from Brightwood kept talking right in front of the police center.

"My brother was like, 'Let's go bitch, take it to the street.'

"Niggas scared. They said, 'Get the pistol, go get the pistol.'

"There's sixteen of them and only three of us, and they still going to go get the pistol. So the police came over there, and we kept on walking. Then we went to AJ, 'Why you bump me or whatever, you trying to bang with me?'

"He like, 'Nah, I ain't trying to bang with you man. We cool it's cool.'

"My brother's like, 'Nah bitch, fuck that cool shit.'

"'No it's cool bro', it's cool bro'.'

"We came around the corner and met up with them. First there's just three of us. Then we get with all our niggas, and we see him again.

"I said, 'He cool bro', he cool.'

"From there we went to the crib. The next day we went to church and came back to the crib everybody like, 'Bro' two hundred niggas came over here talking about they going to get you all.'

"I thought about it and saw the spray paint on the door. I'm like, 'Ah, ok, did one of them have dreads?'

"They like, 'Yeah, AJ.'

"Ok, he got ho'd at the Expo by everybody. Everybody seen him get ho'd so, shit, he came back with his little goons. But they already knew there was only two of us there, two boys and the rest of them were females anyways. So they hoes. They hoes for that one. I ain't trippin'. I play it cool though. Then I seen one of the niggas at the Expo. He was like, 'The DFW Boyz, they's some bitches. They scared to do something.'

"I seen that nigga the next day coming out of his cousin's house slipping [being an easy target]. I stopped and hold that nigga. He was all pretending he didn't know shit about shit. So I guess he went and told his little boys, came back, and gathered up the troops to come over there.

"Later, I walked to the front of the apartments by myself where all them niggas be at. There wasn't anybody there, should be taking care of it a little later. We don't retaliate because that's how a lot of shit goes down. Wait till it's died down, everything is good and gravy, go up to their grandma shit and put their shit . . ."

Layboy interrupted with a conclusion. "It's a wrap."

"So it's been a rough week?" I asked.

"It's been a rough week," verified Layboy. "Well, it ain't necessarily been a rough week, it's just tiring, man." This admission was somewhat surprising. Shawn had expressed fatigue with the gang life, but Layboy had not.

"It's been a rough week," agreed Shawn. "My nigga, the one that you interviewed back a few weeks ago, from Post Road. He got robbed. Someone robbed him and took his pistol and shit. He got his shit back."

Killa-Con, a member of the DFW Boyz who was listening to the conversation, added, "I had some motherfucker jump out on me."

One challenge for gang intervention is that the aspects of gang life that can cause disillusionment can also cause members to become more committed to gang life. Conflict, for example, can solidify street gangs by increasing internal cohesion, or it can cause gangs to disintegrate (Thrasher 1967). Until this point in my research, conflict seemed only to fuel the gang's activities and increase the group's solidarity. The boys never seemed tired of their unending street dramas. During this conversation, however, Layboy acknowledged growing weary of fighting with other gangs. For the first time, he seemed to understand the potentially fatal consequences of the gang's activities. Before this, he consistently talked about how he would never stop, and he seemed genuinely energized by the group's conflict with the Naptown Boyz. This internal struggle should be a reason for both hope and concern for anyone trying to intervene in the lives of active and committed gang members. Relative to other gang members, Layboy and Shawn were both heavily committed to gang life and intensely connected to gang peers. Yet Shawn seemed interested in college and, in a candid moment, Layboy admitted to being fatigued with street life. Their ambivalence suggested that the boys were willing to pursue other endeavors, but those pursuits would have been in constant tension with their attraction to gang life. Their conflicts in the street could motivate the boys to seek out other options, or it could increase their commitment to gang life. At the moment of this exchange, the latter seemed more likely.

Shawn clarified the issue by saying, "Now we need to get more organized and shit, I been watching little films and shit."

"Like what?" I asked.

"I watched this Larry Hoover film the other day. See how organized them niggas was. Then I watched this Al Capone film. See how organized they was, how legit they was."

Larry Hoover was the leader of Chicago's Gangster Disciples and was able to organize the gang into a well-structured entrepreneurial street organization. With all of their connections in the streets of Indianapolis, Shawn and Layboy were still forced to watch documentaries to learn how to organize their gang. Their need to watch documentaries reinforced my earlier observations that Indianapolis gangs were largely unorganized. The boys had connections to the Vice Lords and the Gangster Disciples, but the gangs were not well structured. The boys lacked guidance and were trying to grasp the basic elements of an organizational system.

Layboy offered a description of the gang's new leadership structure. "Like us being the generals of DFW Boyz, people like, 'You the leaders.' It ain't necessarily that we the leaders, it's just that when these guys get out there we ain't going to be doing everything. That's what I'm trying to tell these niggas. I'm going to lay low. I'm going to let them niggas control, I'm going to be in the house, I'm going to lay low."

Shawn agreed and added to his brother's description. "Especially like this, we got the generals then we got the commanders. He [Layboy] got his motherfucking troops. He control his troops. He got his main niggers that he fuck with and they go out there."

Oddly enough, I had already met multiple so-called gang generals. The term was used so frequently that I began to question its meaning. Traditionally used to distinguish gang elites, it now seemed to be embraced by any informal leader of an Indianapolis clique, gang, or hood. As the boys talked about their organizational structure, a few other DFW Boyz sat quietly, nodding, clearly accepting their subservient role in the gang.

Layboy continued. "Like me, I'm a general and I got my commander, but he ain't here right now. That's my right-hand man. He [Shawn] got his right-hand man. I got my right-hand man. I tell him what to do. 'Hey tell them niggas.' He go back and tell them. Something ain't poppin' off right, he come tell me. 'Hey something ain't going right.' That's when I go out there. 'What's going on, what's up?' He got his right-hand man that he go to, he's got his little commander tell him what's up. He get back to me, clique up, start talking, something, something. . . . This is what we're going to do. We about to get organized man. These niggas, like lately, we ain't been organized. People been just putting people in—'Ah, you want to be in DFW Boyz? You in.' It ain't going to be like that. I'm about to cut people. If you ain't bringing in money and you ain't putting in work, you about to get out. We don't need you."

"So things just changed recently."

Layboy responded to my question, "Yeah, just changed, it's about to be a whole lot different. DFW Boyz is about to be different, you'll see."[6]

An Unfortunate End

I left Indianapolis in early August of 2008 and did not hear from the boys until the winter months. During that time, I talked to Sidney, my original contact, a few times, and he kept me updated on the events in Indianapolis. I last talked to him in late October. One winter evening, I received a call on the phone that I used primarily for research. Looking at the number, I recognized the Indianapolis area code, assumed that Sidney was on the other line, and answered, "What's going on, Sidney?" There was a hesitation on the other end of the line. I then heard, "This is Layboy. Sidney's dead."

"What? When and how?"

Layboy impatiently answered, "I don't know, a while ago." That's not why he was calling. "Shawn's been shot."

"Is he okay?" I asked, not really knowing what to say.

"Yeah, I think so."

"How are you doing?" Admittedly, this was a dumb question.

"I'm cool," he said. But I doubted that he would say otherwise.

After a short, awkward conversation, I told him to keep me updated and said good-bye. I then called one of the boys' adult mentors to find out what had happened and if Shawn was going recover. He had been shot at a party when a fight broke out during a conflict. Shawn had actually left the house when the fight started and then returned to retrieve his brothers. Doctors initially did not know if he would survive, but he was currently doing much better. His prospects looked good. His mentor lamented that before the shooting, Shawn was heading in the right direction. He was on the honor roll, and he was sending out college applications. His mentor promised to keep in touch as Shawn recovered.

As the phone conversation ended, I experienced an odd combination of fear, concern, and hope. Fear arose as I remembered Layboy's statements that he would retaliate if anyone killed one of his brothers. Would this incident instigate a process of contagious violence that could leave numerous other DFW Boyz injured, dead, or in prison? Or was Layboy merely talking tough in a moment when he did not have to back up his promise? I was naturally concerned for Shawn's health, but the prognosis initially seemed positive. I remained hopeful; Shawn had clearly returned to school with the intention of pursuing a college education. His hospital stay would cause him to miss school, but hopefully it would not distract him from his college aspirations. Perhaps the incident would further motivate him to leave gang life and fully invest in college life. Of course it could also lead him to retaliate.

Although there is no such thing as a representative gang member, Shawn's struggle to negotiate the competing demands of two divergent social worlds provided insight into the dilemmas of intervention. The opportunity to further his education caused him to make changes. Despite his academic activity, his commitment to the DFW Boyz remained strong. He continued to go to parties, challenge peers, and get into fights. The allure of the intergang environment was too strong to be overcome by burgeoning aspirations. As these aspirations grew, and he would be routinely exposed to the college environment, perhaps the influence of the intergang environment would lessen. Or perhaps, he would grow weary of college life and permanently return to the streets of Indianapolis.

I did not hear anything about Shawn's recovery for a few weeks and took comfort in the fact that no news was good news. Then one morning I got to my office, scanned the Indianapolis news online, and learned that Shawn had unexpectedly died from his gunshot wounds. Later that night I again received a phone call from Layboy. What does one say to a sixteen-year-old who just lost his brother and best friend? Years later, I still do not know.

A few days later I drove back to Indianapolis for Shawn's funeral. Arriving an hour early, I had a hard time finding a place to park and had to walk a few blocks to the church. Unmarked police cars were positioned outside of the church, and sheriff's deputies manned the door. Although the church building was not large or extravagant, it was not a ghetto storefront church or a small building in disrepair. The newer and well-maintained building had enough seating for a few hundred people. When I entered the church, only few seats were still available. During the next hour, the sanctuary filled to the point of standing room only. Hundreds of people, both young and old, showed up for the service.

The mood of the sanctuary was generally somber until the gospel choir began to sing. As the deep, soulful timbre of the gospel music circulated through the sanctuary, the mourning began. These were not people numbly responding to another unfortunate death. They were deeply affected by the loss of Shawn, and the service functioned as a collective display of grief. Attendees wept together without any hint of self-consciousness. Layboy was the catalyst for this grief, as he shouted in pain and sobbed uncontrollably on the floor near his deceased brother. Family members and funeral workers surrounded him in an attempt to provide counsel.

Like all other violent deaths, the murder of Shawn should be understood not just as a statistic but also as an event of tremendous personal loss. This was indescribably painful for those who knew him. His death was not less tragic because he was a gang member. It was not more tragic because he was intelligent and seemed to be taking school more seriously. He was a friend, a brother, a son, a grandson, and, on a less personal level, a trusted research participant almost solely responsible for much of this study. True, he was heavily involved in criminal behavior. He beat people up and admitted to shooting guns at people. Such activities deserved formal, rational retribution, but death at the hands of another teenager with a gun was not justice.

Later, the pastor passionately spoke to the younger attendees and urged them not to retaliate. The anger on the faces of Shawn's family, friends, and clique members was discernable. The pastor's message was clear and powerful, but would it convince all of them not to respond with aggression? The allure of retaliation was indeed strong. As I listened to the service and observed the emotion around me, I understood the temptation. I hope they resisted that temptation.

Unfortunately, Shawn's funeral would not be the last for his family or for members of the DFW Boyz. A year later, Layboy and his younger brother Dre were standing on a street corner late at night. An unknown male walked by and briefly spoke to the boys, apparently asking who they were. He later returned and without warning, shot Dre from close range. Layboy saw his younger brother fall to the ground, dead, and then ran, only to be shot in the back multiple times. As he lay on the ground pretending to be dead, the assailant stood over him, without any more ammunition. Layboy survived the shooting, but the violence continued. A few months after Dre's death, TJ was also shot during a gang altercation. This shooting occurred in a public setting in front of a large number of witnesses. Fortunately, TJ survived. Over a year later, Layboy and TJ were victims of another shooting. Layboy was again seriously wounded; he sustained debilitating, life altering injuries.

These tragic events are not unique, or even particularly unusual; thousands of adolescents and young adults are murdered in American streets each year.[7] Each incident has its own explanation, and each victim has his or her own story. Shawn, Dre, Layboy, and TJ constantly pursued a violent reputation in the midst of a skeptical intergang environment, and it probably led to their violent victimization. They paid a severe price to ensure that they were known in Naptown.

Appendix: Researching Gangs

STREET GANGS have long been the focus of scholarly inquiry. Since Frederic Thrasher's (1967) seminal study, researchers have worked to provide both an adequate theoretical background and a solid empirical basis for understanding street gangs. Research consistently reaffirms that street gangs are harmful to communities and gang members alike. Most notably, gang members are heavily invested in criminal activity, and when compared to their peers they are more likely to commit serious acts of violence (Battin et al. 1998; Esbensen and Huizinga 1993; Esbensen and Weerman 2005; Gatti et al. 2005; Huff 2004; Thornberry et al. 1993 and 2003). There is no shortage of people victimized by street gangs. Residents in gang-ridden communities not only have to worry about being victims of crime, they also fear that gangs may attract their children, grandchildren, and other close relatives and friends. If a young person survives gang life, he or she is at much higher risk for being incarcerated, dropping out of school, using illegal drugs, or becoming a parent at a young age (Thornberry et al. 2003). All of these consequences create short- and long-term hardships.

Despite these harsh realities, gang membership is a pathway too commonly adopted by contemporary youth. The most recent National Youth Gang Crime Survey conservatively estimates the presence of about 788,000 gang members nationally (National Youth Gang Center 2011a). There is little reason to be optimistic that contemporary efforts to reduce gang membership have had a lasting impact on the overall problem (Klein and Maxson 2006). After declines in gang membership during the mid- to late 1990s, the number of police agencies citing gang problems has grown steadily since 2001 (National Youth Gang Center 2011b). Although most gang members reside in large cities, nonurban youths are becoming more likely to model their social groups in accordance with the images of gangs that are propagated by mass media

(Decker and Van Winkle 1996). Police in suburbs, smaller cities, and rural areas are reporting increased gang problems in their communities (National Youth Gang Center 2011b).

The persistent gang problem in many communities highlights a continuing need to develop new insights about street gangs. Historically, this need has motivated some researchers to temporarily leave the academic setting to study gang members in their natural environment.[1] This approach is not without its challenges. The criminal behavior that is often the focus of research can impede a researcher's ability to gain full access to gang members. The researcher constantly struggles to obtain a sufficient number of willing participants who can insightfully discuss their gang life. Studying gang members in their natural environment is also accompanied by a degree of risk. Although serious violence is an uncommon event in the daily life of the average gang member, the general population of gang members is at high risk for violent victimization. A year after they had completed their study of St. Louis gang members, for example, Scott Decker and Barrik Van Winkle (1996) reported that ten of the gang members in their study, or 10 percent of their sample, had been murdered. After three years, researchers conservatively estimated that 20 percent of the gang members in that sample had been murdered (Miller and Decker 2001). A study in Chicago reported that if a gang member remained in the gang for four years he or she had a one in four chance of being murdered (Levitt and Venkatesh 2000). Thus, to study active gang members, researchers intentionally place themselves within a network of people that attracts violence. The challenges of research are accompanied by the tension between the need to ensure one's own safety and the wish to collect good data.

The need to continue street-level research on active gang members provided the underlying motivation for this study, and I began to immerse myself in the Indianapolis community about a year before I officially began my research. The relationships I established during that time initially indicated to me that an in-depth examination of Indianapolis gangs would not only be possible but also would be relatively easy to achieve. Numerous supposedly reliable contacts had promised me that entire gangs were willing and ready to contribute to the study. As empty promises began to mount, I quickly traded my naive expectations for a more practical approach to street research. Over time

I forged relationships that eventually allowed me to observe and interview active gang members over a period of about eighteen months. This appendix revisits the research experience, describes the sample population, acknowledges some of the study's limitations, and identifies the epistemological assumptions that guided this research endeavor.

RESEARCH ACTIVITIES

Shawn and Layboy were two of my closest contacts, and they were largely responsible for the success of the study. Their inclusion in this study was, however, part of a larger research process that was divided into three stages. The beginning stages of the sampling process developed slowly. During the first four months of research (early February to late May of 2007), I focused on establishing an effective chain referral system, but a generally unstable and unreliable research population hindered this process. Even individuals who were willing to recruit other research participants often did not follow through on their promises. Therefore, a slow-developing snowball sample began with people who inconsistently followed up on their promises to help. Indeed, most of the referral pathways in this study were unproductive, and those that were fruitful typically produced only a few research participants. During the first four months, I spent approximately twenty-five hours a week in the research field, but I had little success in gaining access to gang members or establishing a productive chain referral system.

During that period, I had assumed that a single contact would introduce me to a group of willing gang members who would grant me access to their daily lives. This did not happen. Repeated assurances from my initial contact caused me to be too passive during these months, and I spent a lot of time waiting for individuals to come by and talk to me. The contact did introduce me to one potentially important research participant, whom I had met during a previous research endeavor. He was a middle-aged, drug-addicted Vice Lord, who, for a week, seemed like an ideal contact. He was knowledgeable, well connected, and willing to show me around the city. During one outing, he took me to a few locations with the intention of introducing me to active gang members. At the first location the gang was disciplining some members, and they had guns in the apartment. He then brought me to a house that was owned by gang members. With his backing, they were willing to talk to me, but they wanted to see my consent forms. Functioning very much like the novice researcher that I was, I had forgotten to bring them with me. We left the house without further conversation, but I hoped the next meeting would be more successful. A few days later my initial contact was arrested and sent to prison, where he remained for the duration of my research. I learned that I needed to be more opportunistic and pragmatic, to be more assertive and develop contacts with a large number of potential research participants.

Just as the sampling process gained momentum, I had unexpected back surgery during the summer of 2007 that required me to exit the research field for two months. Fortunately, when I returned to the research field, my contacts remained willing and able to assist me. During the following four months (mid-July to mid-October of 2007), my slowly developing research pool eventually led to unstructured interviews with fifteen gang members. Many of these gang members agreed to multiple tape-recorded interviews that produced in-depth and wide-ranging data. I also had the opportunity to become more familiar with gang-ridden neighborhoods. For example, Sidney repeatedly took me to the low-income apartment complex where he had grown up, and I was able to witness the living conditions that are commonly associated with impoverished urban neighborhoods. Although these experiences did not lead me to establish connections with gang members, they did substantially increase my familiarity with specific Indianapolis neighborhoods. During this time, I also began to initiate contact with Layboy, Shawn, and some of the other DFW Boyz. The DFW Boyz often came to a youth center to play basketball. Although given my recent back surgery, I could no longer play basketball, I could shoot baskets with them and drive them home after their games. We became comfortable with each other, which proved invaluable when I eventually asked if they would participate in the study. During this phase of the research, I spent about twenty-five hours a week in the research field. I spent this time conversing with Sidney or the other individuals in this study, formally interviewing people in my sample, and getting to know the DFW Boyz. This stage was again interrupted for two months following the birth of my daughter.

I reentered the research field having thoroughly digested my interview and observational data, which led to a number of emergent issues and questions. Most notably, I began to appreciate that gang members were a part of a broad and influential network of intergang relations. To better understand the significance of the intergang environment, I needed to focus more on day-to-day activities of gang members. This stage of the sampling process was, therefore, substantially guided by theoretical considerations (see Coyne 1997). I approached Layboy and Shawn about their participation in the project, and I asked them if they would be willing to give me full access to their lives. They were intrigued with the idea of being the focus of a study or a book. Although I continued to spend time with other individuals in my sample, for the next seven months (early January to late July of 2008) I spent a lot of time with Layboy, Shawn, and the DFW Boyz. Within two months I was spending about thirty hours a week in the research field, much of that time with Layboy, Shawn, and the other DFW Boyz. These frequent interactions lasted for five months (March through July of 2008) and led to a large number of interviews and field observations.

I taped the interviews and structured them minimally. Many interviews occurred in a group setting while I hung out on the street with gang members or in their apartments. This approach proved advantageous for a number of reasons. First, the younger individuals in this study were less likely than their older counterparts to provide good introspective one-to-one interviews. During group conversations, however, they openly and excitedly discussed the aspects of life most relevant to them. Second, they held each other accountable during these conversations. Over time, I became confident in the accuracy of interview content, as some stories were told numerous times by different people with a fairly high degree of consistency. Third, these interviews often evolved into natural conversations between friends, and they tended to gravitate toward issues defined as relevant by the boys. Fortunately, teenager's age-appropriate obsession with their social position among peers often led to discussion that was consistent with emergent issues in the research.

These interviews coincided with consistent observation of a small network of the DFW Boyz and occasional observation of a larger network of gang members. Members of the DFW Boyz allowed me to come and go freely from their places of residence. I spent about twenty to thirty hours a week with the DFW Boyz for approximately five months, a total of four hundred to six hundred hours. This time enhanced my understanding of focal gang members and gang life, led to new research questions, and refined some theoretical insights. I did not accompany the DFW Boyz to late-night parties, when violence was most likely to occur. Instead, I withdrew to my office to transcribe interviews, analyze data, and prepare for future field observations. Although such a decision may have hindered the field experience, it reduced but did not eliminate the inherent risks of studying gangs in their environment.

Even without attending late-night parties, studying gang members in their natural environment involves some risk for the researcher. Each day in the field involves the risk of being caught in the middle of intergang violence or becoming the victim of a crime like robbery. The gang members in this study were not involved in patterns of reciprocal violence in which drive-by shootings or other random acts of violence were a common occurrence. Still, there were times when I was near potentially violent situations. Robbery, by contrast, is unpredictable (Wright and Decker 1997), and I could do little to prevent it. Instead, I took the advice of Sidney, a former serial armed robber, and usually carried at least twenty dollars with me. As Sidney suggested, the last thing I wanted was a disappointed armed robber (see also Jacobs 1999). Even though I occasionally forgot my "robbing money," I rarely felt unsafe in the research field, and I was never the victim of a crime.

The second type of risk involved police attention, and it worried me more than criminal victimization. Other scholars studying criminal populations have recounted numerous antagonistic encounters with the police and suggested that these events helped build rapport with gang members and/or street offenders (Bourgois 1999; Jacobs 1999). The conditions of my research caused me to routinely drive research gang members around the city. I was ultimately responsible for the contents of my car, and every time they got into my car there was no guarantee that they were not carrying contraband items. If illegal drugs, for example, ended up on the floor of my car, I would be held legally responsible. I often drove members of the DFW Boyz to different hangout spots. If different events had transpired when I drove them to the conflict in chapter 7, I could have been unintentionally involved in a felony. I am fortunate that the boys did not commit a serious crime during that incident and then use me to flee the scene. Throughout the entire research process, I never became the focus of police attention.

THE SAMPLE

In total, this study is based on an ethnographic examination of fifty-five individuals. The study relies heavily on ten contacts who closely interacted with me for months at a time. Much like Bruce Jacobs's (1999) "intensive" fourteen or Thomas Mieczkowski's (1986) "high-quality" sample of fifteen, these ten contacts provided my most in-depth data about gang activities. Five of these individuals were older street-oriented individuals who maturely guided me through the ways of street life. The remaining five were a core group of DFW Boyz headed by Shawn and Layboy. Their contribution to this study was immeasurable and evident throughout the book. In addition to providing access to their personal lives, they were responsible for recruiting a large number of the remaining research participants who became the focus of my data collection. The forty-five remaining individuals contributed to the study on a number of occasions. I interviewed some of these individuals multiple times, whereas I encountered other research participants only a few times as I hung out with the DFW Boyz.

Nearly the entire sample was black (98 percent), and it was made up primarily of males (93 percent). Most of the sampled individuals in this study were under the age of twenty-nine (69 percent). Fifty-eight percent of the sample consisted of active gang members, and many were involved with the DFW Boyz. Although this study primarily focuses on gang members, the sample included a number of individuals who had never been involved with street gangs. These individuals had valuable insights into the logic of the street, and they had contacts with gang members. During the initial phases of research, these non-gang members talked at length about street life and guided me through different Indianapolis communities. These experiences allowed me to establish a basic understanding of Indianapolis street life. In addition to Sidney, this group included a person recently released from prison on two counts of manslaughter, an active pimp, and multiple offenders still on probation or parole. The other set of non-gang members happened to be hanging around gang members during taped group discussions, and they had the opportunity to discuss their perceptions of gangs and gang life. They were a part of gang members' lives, even though they did not think of themselves as gang members.

LIMITATIONS

My methods for selecting gang members to study did not ensure that those included in the study were representative of gang members everywhere. Although the sampling strategy did involve a range of participants, it also included a relatively large number of individuals from a single gang. To some extent, I can be confident in my findings if they are consistent with other field studies (see Fleisher 1998). Many of the findings from this study were, indeed, consistent with other research efforts. Gang members generally belonged to amorphous and relatively disorganized gangs that were not oriented around a single activity (Klein 1995). Some gang members claimed affiliation to Chicago-based super gangs, but these affiliations seemed to have very little influence on their daily activities. They engaged in a substantial amount of violent and nonviolent criminal activity but spent most of their time on mundane activities (Decker and Van Winkle 1996). Some of the DFW Boyz sold drugs, but many did not, and drugs were not a salient issue in this research. Most criminal activity was unfocused and opportunistic (Klein 1995). Accordingly, much of what I witnessed and heard was generally consistent with gang research.

Despite such congruence, other studies have identified important variations between gangs that were not accounted for in this research. The preceding chapters develop a theory that does not account for group-level variations between street gangs (see Klein and Maxson 2006). For example, the unstructured DFW Boyz differ greatly from those rare but well-organized street gangs that focus their activities around selling drugs (see Levitt and Venkatesh 2000; Venkatesh 2000). Given that the boys were not heavily involved with drug dealing, they were also fundamentally different from some loosely organized drug gangs examined in other studies (see Fleisher 1998). Expanding the ideas presented here to account for such diversity represents one direction for future theoretical and empirical development. This study also does not sufficiently account for differences between gang members. Although gang scholarship generally lacks sufficient micro-level theory, research has identified important variations in gang involvement (Bjerregaard 2002; Esbensen et al. 2001). Shawn, Layboy, and the core network of DFW Boyz were probably more invested in gang life than the average gang member. For example, whereas most gang members are only involved for less than one year (Thornberry et al. 2003), Shawn and Layboy had been active gang members for at least four years. Therefore, this study may be oriented toward gang members who were more heavily invested in gang life than the average gang member. These limitations should, however, form a basis for future exploration.

Given that this study is based on a single research site, it is also unclear whether the ideas in this study can be generalized to other intergang environments. Some of the ideas presented in this book are grounded in foundational theoretical assertions that should, predictably, transfer to gangs in other areas. For example, gang members are heavily involved in constructing their social reality through daily interactions with peers. I think it is likely that in most locations gang members are actively involved in constructing field boundaries by determining who does and does not belong in the intergang environment. Intergang interactions are also instrumental for social comparisons, and gang members in other locations probably observe, assess, and evaluate the actions of members in other gangs. Gang members in other communities are also likely to gossip openly about their peers and disseminate this information across the intergang environment. Such information probably fuels intergang conflict in other cities as well. Still, these ideas cannot necessarily be generalized from research in one city, and a closer examination of these ideas across multiple sites is needed in order to verify them.

Some of the more specific elements of my argument may or may not be relatable to other research sites. For example, the outcomes of peer interactions are likely to subtly vary, as are the collective outcomes of interactions within the intergang environment. The meaning of "gang," therefore, may significantly differ across locations. The level of disagreement about the parameters of the intergang field and the level of environmental certainty may also differ depending on locations. The dilution narrative might be unique to Indianapolis, or it might be common to many locations. Legitimacy may a salient concern in some communities but irrelevant in others. Therefore, the underlying motivation of gang member's behavior in Indianapolis may or may not be found in other locations. These challenges merely highlight the need to examine the notion of an intergang environment more thoroughly and to develop theory that explains differences across locations.

One of the most notable methodological limitations of this study comes from my conscious decision not to observe gang members at night when they are more likely to encounter other gangs and be involved in criminal activities. This decision did have some positive consequences. First, it dramatically decreased my risk for becoming a crime victim. I was able to interact routinely with gang members and gain unique insights into their lives in a relatively safe manner. Shawn's death following a shooting at a random party highlights the dangers of hanging out with gang members at night. Moreover, my decision also reduced the probability that my research would be ended prematurely if I had witnessed a violent event. I never had to balance my need to gather data with the need to report violent crime. The individuals in this study told me about their exploits, but I often did not witness them. Still, my decision hindered the research process. I generally found that observing gang members provided more insight than interviews alone did, and observing them at night would have enhanced my analysis. I could have provided a more detailed analysis of intergang interactions in numerous social settings. Any researcher developing an ethnographic study of gangs must think seriously about risks and rewards of participant observation. Its use in this study allowed me to become very familiar with the routines and concerns of some gang members, but it was not comprehensive and could have been more thorough.

Given that I had accepted a job in another state, I was working with a relatively inflexible time frame that in itself produced some methodological limitations. More time in the research field would have allowed me to explore additional questions and provide supplementary insights to this analysis. The opportunity to gather data from multiple gangs would have helped develop ideas about intergang interactions and the intergang environment. For example, my analysis of the street beef between the DFW Boyz and the Naptown Boyz would have been more thorough if it also reflected material gleaned from interviews with members of the Naptown Boyz. Examining street gossip from multiple perspectives and sources would also lead to new and unique insights. For this to be done, however, a researcher would need to develop a long-term relationship with a research site.

As I began to write about my time in Indianapolis, I was confronted with the realization that I had no experience developing an argument with ethnographic data. This forced me to negotiate a significant learning curve and to struggle with some basic questions about how to best use my data. Although the structure of my argument was largely dictated by the data, the execution of the argument was, indeed, saturated with my choices. I selected data that best communicated prominent elements of gang members' lives. This selection required sensitivity to both the breadth and depth of data. I sought to include as many gang members in the text as possible, but not all research participants were equal (Jacobs and Wright 2006). Some research participants were naturally more eloquent, insightful, or talkative than others and, therefore, received more attention during the research process. The conversations and experiences of Layboy, Shawn, and some of their associates dominated the preceding pages because I spent a lot of time with them.

While writing the book, I chose at times to develop concepts by sacrificing breadth for depth. To some extent, this approach was beneficial. For example, my use of lengthy conversations as data reflects a concerted effort to provide an intimate look into gang members' lives, allowing the reader to observe gang members in their natural setting as they engaged in fairly routine activities. Moreover, it should allow the reader to observe how peer interactions intersected with the construction of cultural artifacts ("wannabe," "gang member," and "being soft," for example). It also allowed me interpret and explain the self-serving and subjective agendas that exist in conversation but are often hidden during more formal interviews. Such an approach can be limiting, however: some of the concepts in this study are grounded in a single, though typical, conversation. A broader approach would have developed these ideas by using data from multiple gang members over multiple interviews. Although such an approach would have yielded a slightly more representative, and perhaps varied, analysis, it would not have been possible for the reader to be privy to all the conversations. I hope that I have successfully balanced the demands for both depth and breadth of data. The ideas presented in this book are carefully constructed from my experiences in the streets of Indianapolis. Most of the concepts are grounded in carefully recorded data, and they represent major themes in the lives of gang members. My familiarity with Shawn, Layboy, and other members of the DFW Boyz allowed me to select data that accurately reflect salient concerns and common events in their lives.

Indeed, the only exceptional or uncommon data that I used in this book can be found in chapter seven, when the DFW Boyz confronted the Naptown Boyz. This too is an important commentary on gang life. It is not particularly exciting or glamorous, but it is too often interrupted by extreme violence.

DEVELOPING THEORY

Qualitative studies vary in their goals, research activities, and approaches to interpreting data (Adler et al. 1986; Hammersley and Atkinson 1995). Clarifying methodological and epistemological assumptions is, therefore, important, not to diminish other approaches but to justify both the research process and the presentation of data. This study was guided by an analytic ethnographic approach oriented toward creating testable theory in an undeveloped area of study. The research process began with a focus on street gangs and some general questions, but it adapted to emergent issues found in the data. The end product is oriented toward developing theory.

Analytical ethnography seeks to develop a set of logically inter-related propositions that are open to falsification, rely on concepts to make empirical events meaningful, and utilize a discourse to help explain empirical events (Snow et al. 2003). Whereas some ethnographers rely heavily on descriptions of observation or on thick description (see Geertz 1973), analytical ethnographers argue that such practices lead to an analytical black box and a research field that is conceptually impoverished (Loftland 1970; Snow et al. 2003). Both formal theory and substantive theory provide the impetus for empirical discovery, and the analytical ethnographic approach allows for the discovery of grounded theory that is based in observational data (Glaser and Strauss 2006). As Anselm Strauss and Juliet Corbin articulate, "A grounded theory approach is one that is inductively derived from the study of the phenomenon it represents. That is, it is discovered, developed, and provisionally verified through systematic data collection pertaining to that phenomenon. Therefore, data collection, analysis, and theory stand in reciprocal relationship with each other. One does not begin with a theory, then prove it. Rather, one begins with an area of study and what is relevant to that area is allowed to emerge" (1990, 23). The reciprocal relationship between data collection, analysis, and theory creation represents an emergent process whereby the researcher begins with general questions and allows the data and conceptual development to drive the direction of research (ibid.).

Allowing data to drive the research can lead to subtle or even drastic changes in the general focus of a study. For example, William Foote Whyte (1981) explored his research community for eighteen months and dabbled in numerous directions before studying Doc and the corner boys. Elliot Liebow's (1967) classic study on street corner men first began as an examination of child-rearing practices among low-income men. Similarly, the data emerging from this study produced a subtle shift in emphasis. The original intent of this study was to systematically observe the social organization of a street gang and develop micro-level theory explaining variation between gang members. Questions emerged during the first few months of fieldwork that altered the course of the study. True to the idea of theoretical emergence, I began to focus on ideas that had not previously been present in either the formal research plan or the gang literature in general. More specifically, I realized that there was a need to examine gang-on-gang interactions in the context of a broader intergang environment, which quickly took precedence over examining variations within a single gang.

This approach to qualitative research incorporated flexible research techniques adapted to ideas that emerged from the data unexpectedly. In fact, ideas conceptualized prior to field research not only became irrelevant but at times hindered conceptual development. For example, I largely ignored the theoretical foundations for this study for a few months as I filtered my field experiences through the comfort and familiarity of gang scholarship. I initially ignored the significance of the term "wannabe" because I thought that I understood its meaning. After all, the notion of a "wannabe" is not new to gang scholarship. Researchers have often used the term "wannabe" in reference to those who both want to be gang members and try to model their behavior accordingly (for example see Monti 1994). Furthermore, some of my first contacts justified this interpretation of "wannabe" by contrasting local gangs with their more organized counterparts in nearby Chicago (see Knox 2006; Knox and Papachristos 2002; Venkatesh 1998). Since Indianapolis gangs were generally less organized and more informal than Chicago gangs, my contacts argued that many Indianapolis gangs were just wannabe street

gangs. I initially dismissed such thinking as evidence that research participants had only a limited understanding of street gangs. Research on
street gangs accounts for large variations in gang forms, and the organizationally sophisticated gangs of Chicago represent only a small fraction
of all gangs (Klein 1995; Klein and Maxson 2006). Gang members
and other street participants in Indianapolis simply did not have access
to the comprehensive gang research, I thought, and therefore they
provided naive and incomplete descriptions of Indianapolis gangs.
Those so-called wannabe groups were less organized forms of their
Chicago counterparts, but they were still street gangs.

Freedom from my preconceived ideas came only when my back
surgery led to an early absence from the research field and a time of
forced reflection. It was during this time that I began to contemplate the
inherently subjective nature of the terms "wannabe" and "gang member." The notion of "gang" or "gang member" was meaningful to the
individuals participating in this study. Nearly everyone I had talked to in
Indianapolis adamantly claimed that many self-defined gang members
were wannabes, yet no one admitted to being a wannabe. The term was
explicitly used to evaluate and dismiss others. Furthermore, criteria used
for such assessments varied considerably. The consequences of this
variation are potentially profound, even at a basic level. In a dyadic
relationship between two self-defined gangs, it is possible that each group
views itself as a real gang and the other group as a collection of wannabes.
Such a relational dynamic can impact both intergang interactions and the
gang members themselves. This basic idea became the focus of the rest
of my research, and the preceding study is the product of those efforts.

An analytical ethnographic approach also recognizes limitations in
the researcher's ability to fully capture and interpret social contexts.
Alternative perspectives on ethnography focus on descriptive precision
(see Geertz 1973) and herald qualitative methods as sacrificing reliability
for validity through rich description, or an awareness of what is really
going on (Becker 1996). Thus, some researchers argue that ethnography
offers the best method for accurately describing social life. Although
analytical ethnography seeks to embrace rigorous qualitative practices,
it is less confident in the validity of observational data. In short, the
ethnographer cannot be everywhere or see and understand everything.
The researcher's ability to fully capture a situation in which he or she is

present is questionable; even the most detailed field notes capture only a portion of a social situation. Yet upon exiting the field to write, the researcher "[m]aintains the illusion of omniscience by recreating a scene with attendant bits of talk" (Fine 1993, 277). In addition, all situations are capable of multiple interpretations and misunderstandings, or some important events are simply missed, as the researcher does not always fully understand the situation.

Instead of relying on description of data as the primary contribution of ethnography, the analytic ethnographic approach uses data to ground relationships between concepts. Such data provide new ideas and insights into possible associations between concepts, then provisionally verify the logical adequacy of such relationships (Glaser and Strauss 2006). Data in this study are not used to test propositions but to justify the construction of proposed relationships. Although one may be tempted to argue that a standard of provisional verification is not very scientific and may lead to misguided explanations, inductive verification can provide mature propositions to guide future deductive theory testing. It is better to use such data to establish testable relationships than to accept ethnographic description as a form of empirical test or to reject the use of qualitative methods altogether.

With that in mind, I hope the reader will recognize that the concepts used in this book were extrapolated from data, defined, provisionally verified, and then linked to other concepts to explain behavior. Each stage in this explanatory process should be critically examined so that the contents of this book are not blindly accepted as truth or the way things are. The analytic ethnographic approach is intended to create ideas that are later evaluated with other methodologies and subsequently embraced, rejected, or amended. I am confident that my interpretation of these experiences in Indianapolis is accurate, and I hope it will facilitate new ideas and new pathways of research in gang scholarship.

Notes

Introduction

1. The name DFW Boyz is a false name given to ensure anonymity. When I asked the members of the gang about the meaning of their real name, they responded, "because we are down for whatever." I therefore borrowed the first letter of each of the last three words and adopted the moniker DFW Boyz.

2. The phrase "islands in the street" comes from Sanchez-Jankowski's (1991) important study on street gangs. He is referring to how gangs, in general, are socially isolated from conventional society. This represents a common approach of most gang-related theory, which ignores meaningful intragang and intergang interactions. In essence, gang members may generally be isolated from conventional society, but they are not isolated from each other. Members of the same gang meaningfully interact within each other and members of different gangs also routinely interact with each other. Each gang member and each gang is, therefore, not an island.

3. Although unique in its focus, this study is not incompatible with most gang-related theory. Prior theoretical developments have, however, generally overlooked the significance of intergang interactions. They tend to emphasize various theoretical concepts, like social disorganization, social isolation, cultural marginalization, status frustration, and differential opportunity, which relate to the consequences of living in urban slum or poor minority communities (Cloward and Ohlin 1960; Cohen 1955; Sanchez-Jankowski 1991; Thrasher 1967; Vigil 1991; Whyte 1981). These concepts help explain the prevalence of gangs in certain areas and the general cultural or behavioral adaptations embraced by gang members. Although the differences between these theoretical concepts are important, such concerns are beyond the scope of this book. The research methodology employed in this study did not allow me systematically to assess the variations between these concepts. For a review of this literature see Brotherton and Barrios (2004), Bursik and Grasmick (1993), and Decker and Van Winkle (1996). By focusing on the intergang environment I do not mean to imply that such theoretical concepts are unimportant. In fact, one can reasonably assert that any of the aforementioned theoretical concepts help explain the origins of the intergang environment. Yet this focus does allow one to suggest that intergang environments can mediate the effects of more general social structural processes. The continuous pattern of interaction between gangs probably produces enough variation to explain subtle differences in culture and behavior. Accordingly, researchers must cultivate theoretical concepts to explain how gangs and gang members negotiate an array of social interactions with other members of the intergang environment.

Although gang-related theory has often used more general socioeconomic concepts to explain gang formation and gang behavior, some researchers have also identified the gang itself as an influential, albeit less extensive, environment. Beginning with Whyte's (1981) seminal examination of the interactions between gang members (see also Homans 1992), some scholars have argued that intra-group processes influence gang member behavior. Consequently, researchers have examined the cause and influence of leadership, solidarity, cohesion, and role differentiation within the group setting (Dentler and Erikson 1959; Homans 1992; Jansyn 1966; Klein 1971; Klein and Crawford 1968; Short and Strodtbeck 1974; Whyte 1981; Yablonsky 1959 and 1967). More recently, researchers have sought to clarify important variations between street gangs by examining size, structure, role differentiation, rules, specialization, and the existence or absence of rational action within the gang (Decker, Bynum, and Weisel 1998; Decker and Van Winkle 1996; Klein and Maxson 2006). Again, such arguments are not incompatible with the notion of the intergang environment; each group is immersed in a complex web of interactions with other groups. These interactions produce the foundation upon which gang members base their understanding of the meaning of gang life and the expectations for gang behavior.

CHAPTER 1   GANGS AND THEIR ENVIRONMENTS

1. Specific locations of homicides in Indianapolis for 2008 can be found on the Web site for the *Indianapolis Star*, which is the city's dominant newspaper (see *Indianapolis Star* Homicide Map 2008).
2. Researchers have historically noted the intimate relationship between street gangs and poor communities. Intimately linked to their neighborhood environments, street gangs represent adaptive responses to adverse socio-economic conditions of urban slum communities (Coughlin and Venkatesh 2003). Scholars have identified a number of possible rationales for this connection (see Brotherton and Barrios 2004; Bursik and Grasmik 1993; Decker and Van Winkle 1996; Klein and Maxson 2006). Some suggest that these communities are socially disorganized and suffer from inadequate schools and other institutions, as well as the failure of families themselves to properly monitor children. As a result, crowds of unsupervised children spontaneously form play groups ("gangs in embryo") and evolve into street gangs when conflict arises (Spergel 1984; Thrasher 1967). Such communities have also been described as being socially isolated (Whyte 1981; see also Wilson 1987), with gangs emerging as an organizational response that improves the competitive advantages of gang members (Sanchez-Jankowski 1991 and 2001). Others have argued that lower-class youth, unable to compete with their middle-class counterparts, form gangs as create alternative ways to achieve status (Cohen 1955), or that they represent a collective effort by underclass youth to attain money and goods through illegitimate means (Cloward and Ohlin 1960; Sullivan 1989). A few prominent scholars have noted an intimate link between economic and cultural marginalization in Hispanic communities and the emergence of street gangs and gang culture (Horowitz 1983; Moore 1978 and 1991; Padilla 1992; Vigil 1991 and 2003). Given the scope of research in this area, there is little doubt that poor, urban communities foster the growth and maintenance of street gangs (see also Fleisher 1998; Hagedorn 1998a, 1998b, and 2008).

3. See Barrows (1990) for a more thorough review of Indianapolis's social and economic history and for a discussion of why Indianapolis has been resistant to the social and economic consequences of deindustrialization.

4. All census data comes from the American Community Survey, which provides estimates from 2005–2009. City-level data can be found at the United States Census Bureau Web site (see U.S. Census Bureau 2010a). More specific city-level and tract-level data can be found at United States Census Bureau Web site (see U.S. Census Bureau 2010b).

5. Tract-level census data can be found at the United States Census Bureau's FactFinder Web site (see U.S. Census Bureau 2010b). A more efficient way to gain access to tract-level data can be found at the ProximityOne Web site (see ProximityOne: Information, Resources, and Solutions 2010).

6. Poverty areas are defined as having 20 percent of the population living in poverty. Only one census tract in my research site is considered an extreme poverty area with 40 percent living below poverty (see U.S. Census Bureau 1995).

7. Indianapolis homicide data comes from "Indianapolis Metropolitan Police Department 2008 Homicide Information" (Indianapolis Metropolitan Police Department 2009). The homicide rate for this area was calculated in the following manner: reported homicides (114)/Marion County population (668,403) × 100,000. Other homicides rates were calculated by identifying the population of each census tract in addition to the number of homicides in those locations. The geographical distribution of Indianapolis homicides can be found on the Indianapolis Star Web site.

8. For example, Chicago census tract 4002 has an estimated poverty rate of 88 percent. In Detroit, census tract 5205 has an estimated poverty rate slightly under 91 percent.

9. This individual was a potentially valuable resource, and he may have been able to better validate some of these claims. However, he was arrested and sentenced to prison during the early stages of my research.

CHAPTER 2   JOINING A GANG

1. Research on the relationship between poverty and child maltreatment suggests that maltreatment rates are extraordinarily high in poor areas (Coulton et al. 1995).

2. Other researchers have documented how some youth escape their home lives by turning to the streets. At times, these efforts have unearthed shocking stories of violence, abuse, and neglect in the home (see Caputo 2008; Fleisher 1995 and 1998; Hagan and McCarthy 1997; Miller 2001).

CHAPTER 3   THE DILUTION NARRATIVE

1. "Collective identity" refers to a shared sense of "we" within a group. Scholars have long noted the role of collective identity in facilitating and maintaining group or collective actions (see Futrell and Simi 2004; Hermanowicz and Morgan 1999; Horowitz 1983; Melluci 1995; Pelak 2002; Polletta and Jasper 2001).

2. This study does not examine the existence and influence of variations in collective gang identities, but one can reasonably assume that such variations

matter. The emphasis on violence in the DFW Boyz collective identity likely causes this study to emphasize violence more that it would for a gang with a slightly different collective identity. Violence may be more central to the lives of DFW Boyz compared to other gangs. Scholars note behavioral differences between gangs. Fagan (1989), for example, finds important differences in both general criminal activity and drug activity between gangs. Using Fagan's terminology, the DFW Boyz are a group of "serious delinquents." Another example of such variation is found in Brotherton and Barrios's (2004) study on the Latin Kings in New York City. Brotherton and Barrios report that the Latin Kings view themselves as being a politically engaged street organization that actively tries to distance themselves from violence. The DFW Boyz, by contrast, are wholly detached from political events and ideas.

3. Although gang members in Indianapolis were very much aware of and invested in the term "gang," some researchers have studied gangs that were not invested in that term. For example, Fleisher's research in Kansas City and Seattle (1995 and 1998) found that gang members did not use such static terms. Instead, Fleisher argues that these terms are reified concepts largely created by outsiders. In Indianapolis, however, the meanings of "gang," "member," "wannabe," and other similar concepts were vitally important to gang members.

4. "Spit your lick" is a phrase used by gang members that refers to a method of identifying supposedly secret gang codes. If someone spits his or her lick others will know that he or she is a real gang member.

Chapter 4   The Paradox of Legitimacy

1. The lack of objective field boundaries could suggest that the intergang field is nonexistent. From a researcher's perspective this may true, though one could construct a parameter if there were sufficient methodological or theoretical justification. However, the gang members in this study subjectively form field boundaries and use them to disparage peers. Thus, for gang members, the field exists.

2. The definition of legitimacy is consistent across organizational perspectives. However, the processes by which organizations are viewed to gain legitimacy are varied (Suchman 1995).

3. This is not to suggest that the issues of reification and the construction of moral panics are not serious. Some scholars have persuasively argued that they are, indeed, problematic (see Sullivan 2005 and 2006). In their day-to-day life, the gang members of this study were not particularly concerned with the actions and conversations of people outside their peer environment.

4. In Indianapolis the public use of the term "gang" by police and media temporarily increased in the summer of 2010, after I left the research field. This increase was caused by a high-profile mass shooting in downtown Indianapolis, when nine people were shot, but not mortally wounded, during a gang dispute.

5. The notion of a building block or category is an element of language that is used during the process of social construction. Categories sort people, objects, and experiences into contrasting groups. They typically feature both rules of membership that create boundaries and the common traits of members within the boundary (see Fearon and Laitin 2000; Hollander and Gordon 2006).

6. The notion of framing is an element of language that is used during the process of social construction. Framing gives meaning to events and guides the interpretation of an action or event (Hollander and Gordon 2006; Snow et al. 1986).

7. The relevance of a particular label is largely contingent on the source of the label. Some symbolic interactionists and labeling theorists argue that a label must come from a significant other, or a person the labeled individual cares about (Matsueda 1992; Stryker and Craft 1982). For example, a teacher's label may be meaningful if he or she has a close relationship with the pupil. Based on my conversations with active gang members, they did not have close ties with teachers. They were far more concerned about their peers, who can properly be defined as significant others.

CHAPTER 5 KNOWN IN NAPTOWN

1. "Naptown" is a term often heard in the streets. Its actual meaning is unknown. Some have suggested that it is a derogatory term (Barrows 1990), perhaps suggesting that nothing happens in the city (nap-town). Contemporary residents do not interpret it this way, and they use the phrase as a part of everyday street vernacular.

2. Expensive car.

3. A gun clip that holds bullets.

4. Money.

5. Expensive rims on a vehicle, twenty-six inches.

6. Sharing women, being used by women.

7. Being used by women, buying things for them.

8. Decker (1996) argues that violence is a central element of gang life. Moreover, the gang members in his research also used violence as a defining element of gang life (see also Decker and Van Winkle 1996). Yet this intimate connection between gang membership and violence may vary. The DFW Boyz were committed to developing violent reputations in response to a skeptical environment, but other groups may be less committed. Mark Fleisher, for example, studied gang members in Kansas City who did not seem to embrace a violent collective identity. Instead they seemed more focused on using and selling drugs. Violence was only a tangential activity committed by a few gang members. Such variation highlights the need to develop horizontally integrated theory that can explain the causes and consequences of variation between gangs (see Kautt and Spohn 2007). Using Fagan's (1989) typology, the DFW Boyz can be labeled as a group of serious delinquents, while the gang Fleisher studied can best be described as being a party gang. One can reasonably hypothesize that different types of gangs will respond to environmental pressures differently. Unfortunately, explaining this variation is beyond the scope of this study.

9. Korbin, Puntil, and Peluso (1967) found that among street gangs, delinquency, in general, is associated with status. High-status gangs were generally more delinquent than low-status gangs. Korbin and colleagues postulated, in accordance with Cloward and Ohlin's (1960) theory, that gangs who were willing and able to conform to the norms of the delinquent subculture would have the most status. In line with more contemporary scholarship that emphasizes the role of violence in street culture (Anderson 1999), gangs who

were willing and able to engage in violence would most likely be viewed as legitimate and granted esteem in the streets.

10. Scholars have recorded that some gangs and even some gang members have managed to cultivate widely known reputations within major metropolitan areas. In Boston, for example, police and researchers found that two gangs, Intervale Posse and the Vamp Hill Kings, were well known in the city and particularly violent. Specific members of these gangs had also become known in the streets (Freddie Cardoza, for example). Moreover, gangs and gang members with well-known reputations can be used by criminal justice agencies seeking to reduce violence. Through aggressive repression tactics, these high-profile gangs in Boston were targeted by police agencies and used as examples to effectively deter other gangs from engaging in violence. In short, since other gangs in the city knew about the Vamp Hill Kings and Intervale Posse, other gangs noticed criminal justice efforts to arrest and prosecute members of these two gangs (Kennedy, Braga, and Piehl 2001).

11. Within inner-city communities, the pursuit of violent reputations is not specific to gang members. Numerous scholars have observed that non-gang, street-oriented youth and young adults work to cultivate violent reputations (see Anderson 1999; Kubrin 2005; Oliver 1994; Wilkinson 2001). Some have noted that certain street offenders actively work to build and maintain a violent reputation, and this pursuit causes them to respond aggressively to perceived slights (Jacobs and Wright 2006; Topalli, Wright, and Fornango 2002). I hypothesize that environmental skepticism and the pressure to demonstrate legitimacy in the intergang environment increases gang members' need to cultivate violent reputations. Again, gang membership is an added identity that is valued and can be attacked or questioned.

CHAPTER 6   TEENAGE GOSSIP AND THE PRESENTATION OF SELF

1. Erving Goffman argues that the presentation of self to other social actors is a performance, and that it encompasses "all the activity of an individual which occurs during a period marked by his continuous presence before a particular set of observers and which has some influence on the observers" (1959, 22). This performance defines one's place in the social order. Goffman's seminal study has led to a large body of literature on impression management (see Leary and Kowalski 1990). Elijah Anderson (1990 and 1999) has adapted some of these ideas to explain the micro-interactions of residents living in areas of concentrated poverty. His coverage focuses on physical mannerisms and patterns of dress. Robert Garot (2007b and 2010) provides an examination of how gang identity performances shape interactions and behavior. Few, if any, street-oriented studies acknowledge that gossip is often the by-product of such performances.

2. This idea is based on an interactionist view of subculture in that the gang members in this study contributed to the maintenance of culture (Fine and Kleinman 1979). Culture is not just a system of values; it is a set of schematic structures that organize information and develop strategies of action (DiMaggio 1997; Swidler 1986; see also Harding 2007 and 2010; Kirk and Papachristos 2011; Small 2002). Fine and Kleinman (1979) argue that small groups are part of a broader environment marked by innumerable social

connections. They further argue that ties between groups transmit information and create, alter, or reinforce subculture. The notions of "gang," "wannabe," "dick rider," and "being soft" are all cultural artifacts that are constructed through social interactions. They then influence how gang members interpret events during interpersonal conduct. These artifacts are bound together by the dilution narrative, a broad cultural frame that allows gang members to understand ongoing events (Goffman 1974; see also Corsaro 1992). Conversations between gang members reveal that they both contribute to and respond to these cultural ideas.

It should also be noted that the argument presented in this study is not tautological. Violence is caused by environmental expectations that place legitimizing pressures on gang members to perform accordingly, or it is mediated by gossip that leads to intergroup antagonisms, which then lead to violence. It is a cultural adaptation that is grounded in one's interpretation of events. These interpretations are influenced by one's exposure to an array of cultural artifacts.

3. See Donna Eder and colleagues (1997) for a good analysis of peer culture in a middle school located in a medium-sized midwestern city.

CHAPTER 7 THE VIOLENT ENCOUNTER

1. Environmental variations are to be expected, as researchers have noted significant differences in motivations behind violence and the methods used for violence. For example, Edmund McGarrell and Steven Chermak (2001) observed that Indianapolis gangs were poorly structured and not especially territorial. Researchers in Chicago, however, noted that gangs were relatively well organized and heavily involved in drug sales (Coldren and Higgins 2001). Moreover, disputes over drug territory represented almost half of all gang-on-gang homicides (Block and Block 2001). In contrast, George Tita and colleagues (2001) found that in the Hollenbeck community of Los Angeles, gang members dealt drugs, but murders were typically not motivated by territory disputes.

2. Violence between gang members in Indianapolis was, therefore, consistent with Elijah Anderson's (1999) description of violence in the streets of Philadelphia. Not surprisingly, gang members were immersed in the code of the street. As noted at the end of chapter 3, gang members were likely to be more invested in violence because their gang identity was often questioned or attacked. Unlike their non-gang peers, they had to prove that they were real gang members. This pressure increased their need both to appear aggressive in social settings and to respond aggressively to challenges.

3. Historically, the relationship between status and criminal behavior has been a central theme in gang research. Many theorists have conceptualized status in accordance with class disparities (Hughes and Short 2005). Thus gang members were viewed to be reacting or adapting to their inability to access the opportunities or rewards enjoyed by their middle-class counter parts (Cloward and Ohlin 1960; Cohen 1955). Recently, however, researchers have begun to refocus on the notion of status as it relates to other gang members or peers. Classic works from Elijah Anderson (1999) and Ruth Horowitz (1983) have guided these efforts. More recent studies by Lorine Hughes and James Short (2005) and Andrew Papachristos (2009) have added important

insights into the microcontext of gang violence and the network dynamics of contagious violence.

4. See Erving Goffman (1967) for a more thorough discussion of face-saving in the context of social interaction.

5. Network analysts have theorized about the relational balance between, at minimum, three related nodes. Structural balance occurs when two people like each other and they have a consistent evaluation of all other people in the group (Wasserman and Faust 1999). When disagreement exists in a triad, as only one friend likes the third party, the group will move toward a state of balance. Either the two friendly parties will become unfriendly, as one node rejects his or her friend for the sake of another friend in the group. Or, all three become friends. Either solution resolves dissonance or unbalance in the group. Though no researchers have closely examined the concept of structural balance within gangs, Andrew Papachristos (2007) has studied the role of balance between gangs. He finds that intergang conflict, in the form of murder, follows similar patterns that are predicted in balance theory.

6. One of the limitations of this study is that it could not adequately account for the role of emotion during these conflicts or in gang member's lives more generally. The boys periodically noted that they experienced a lot of anger but then seemed willing or unable to insightfully discuss their anger. Emotions probably play a role in these potentially violent encounters, although researchers often write about gang members as if they are making hyper-rational decisions (for good discussion see Garot 2009).

7. Volkan Topalli (2005) argues that street offenders often protect their self-images, which are consistent with the code of the street, by neutralizing or justifying good behavior. Similarly, to save face or maintain their reputations, gang members seem to justify their decisions to not engage in violence when confronted by another gang.

8. This incident actually brings up a difficult ethical issue that did not occur to me when this incident occurred. Researchers are expected to report violence when they know about it beforehand. I made the gang members in this study aware that they should not tell me about any plans that involved violence, and they acted accordingly. This incident involved a vague threat and a reasonable expectation that violence could have ensued later that night. In the moment, I interpreted their comments as just tough talk, and they made no plans to follow through on their threats while in my presence. Only after I began to analyze my data did I question the ethics of my conduct. Although I still struggle with the issue, the information in this conversation only reveals that the Naptown Boyz and the DFW Boyz were involved in an ongoing conflict. To my knowledge, nothing happened between the groups that night.

9. Some researchers argue that youths deal with the inherent dangers of their lifestyle by adopting a fatalistic worldview (Fleisher 1995; Jacobs and Wright 2006; Brezina, Tekin, and Topalli 2009). In short, street youth have little influence over the outcome of their lives, so they discount their fears. The gang members in this study, by contrast, seemed to believe that they were in control and somewhat impervious to consequences. They had multiple rationalizations that reinforced their immunity. For example, Layboy and Shawn discussed the need to be both school smart and street smart. People who could not accomplish both were at risk for death or being arrested.

School-smart drug dealers, for example, would get jobs so that they could provide a legal justification for having money. This would help them evade police. By contrast, people who were not street smart would get themselves into trouble with peers and possibly get themselves killed.

10. The use of gender-specific language here, and in a few other places, is intentional. I never saw or heard evidence that the type of violence discussed in this chapter crossed gender lines. Shawn and Layboy did not get into street beefs with girls. However, the girls in and around the gang did get into fights with other girls. These fights often occurred in public spaces, such as parks, where crowds gathered to watch and cheer on the combatants. At times, these fights would be posted on personal MySpace pages. This is not to suggest that boys never victimized their female counterparts. Shawn acknowledged that, at times, he would hit some of the girls in the gang to toughen them up. Neither the girls nor Shawn seemed to think this was abusive behavior. I never saw such behavior and therefore could not evaluate the frequency or intensity of cross-gender physical confrontations. Jody Miller (2008) provides excellent insights into these issues.

11. To answer these questions, I would have needed to systematically examine the variations between members of the same gang, that is, observe multiple gang members in multiple threatening situations to discern their differences.

CHAPTER 8   HOPE, INTERVENTION, AND TRAGEDY

1. Researchers often argue that gang members and, more generally, individuals immersed in street life, must be given the opportunity to access conventional avenues for success. Perhaps the best-known example of this approach comes from William Julius Wilson (1987 and 1996), who has consistently argued for an array of policies that provide disadvantaged populations with better access to jobs, job training, and quality education. Essentially, he argues that by providing increased access to well-paying jobs, these policies will reduce concentrated poverty in urban areas, reverse the process of social isolation, weaken the influence of street culture, and lessen the prevalence of ghetto-related behavior. It is also important to note that economic fluctuations increase or decrease the difficulties that gang members or former gang members might face when searching for a job. During economic downturns they face an intensely competitive job market where more-educated people with no criminal records are underemployed in the service industry.

2. Responding to the gang problem can involve different goals and strategies. Scholars and practitioners often identify the differences between prevention, suppression, and intervention (Greene 2003; Klein and Maxson 2006; Spergel and Curry 1993). Suppression strategies have been widely employed with varying degrees of success (see Decker 2003). With some notable exceptions (see Esbensen et al. 2001; Schram and Gaines 2005), independent prevention and intervention programs have not been well constructed, properly implemented, or rigorously evaluated.

3. Although I could never verify the boys' academic abilities, they claimed to be doing well in school. Sometimes Shawn would talk to me about his college-prep level algebra classes. He said they were easy for him. However, the boys had been expelled from multiple schools. They had to take summer school courses to catch up on credits and dropped out of summer school after the

first two weeks. Thus, their school performance was likely substandard even if they were able to do well in college-prep classes.

4. It is important to note that I am significantly understating the complexity of the problem. Certainly, the boy's level of preparedness for college is closely connected to economic disparity, the broader educational system, and the multiplicity of decisions made about issues like resource allocation, educational policy, staffing, and curriculum development. Such concerns are outside the scope of this study, and they were not included in my conversation with the boys. See Jonathan Kozol's (1992 and 2006) works for a good discussion of these issues.

5. Scholars have long noted that one's identity is often made up of a multiplicity of self-concepts or roles (Stryker 1968 and 1980). When I was with members of the DFW Boyz, they were fully invested in performing their gang role. This does not mean that they always enacted that role. They might have utilized different, non-gang identities in settings that I did not observe (see Garot 2010). When I asked Shawn and Layboy if they ever experienced conflicts between their roles as gang members and their roles in other social settings (school, church, family, or work), they said that their gang status was generally not problematic.

6. I did not witness any transformation in the DFW Boyz or the members themselves. I left the research field for a new job in Pennsylvania and could only ponder the possible changes in the boy's lives. Although unsatisfying both personally and for the purposes of research, this ambiguity reflects the uncertainty likely to be experienced by social workers, teachers, and others trying to intervene in the lives of active gang members. If a gang member is to change, he or she must consistently choose an alternative path over gang life. This choice requires adequate exposure and access to conventional avenues for success, and perhaps assistance learning some requisite skills that were ignored while they ran the streets. I believe the best that one can hope for is that, initially, gang members are both disillusioned with aspects of gang life and attracted to non-gang alternatives. This ambivalence provides hope for successful intervention.

7. According to the Federal Bureau of Investigations Uniform Crime Reports, 3,304 people under the age of twenty-two were murdered in 2009. In 2008, that number was slightly higher at 3,466 victims (see U.S Department of Justice 2009 and 2010).

Appendix

1. See Fleisher (1995 and 1998); Garot (2010); Hagedorn (1998 and 2008); Horowitz (1986); Klein (1971); Moore (1978 and 1991); Padilla (1996); Sanchez-Jankowski (1991 and 2008); Short and Strodbeck (1974); Sullivan (1989); Thrasher (1967); Venkatesh (2000); Vigil (1991); Whyte (1981); Yablonsky (1959 and 1967).

References

Adler, P. A., P. Adler, and E. B. Rochford Jr. 1986. "The Politics of Participation in Field Research." *Urban Life* 14 (4): 363–376.

Anderson, E. 1990. *Street Wise: Race, Class, and Change in an Urban Community.* Chicago: University of Chicago Press.

———. 1999. *Code of the Street: Decency, Violence, and the Moral Life of the Inner City.* New York: W. W. Norton.

Athens, L. 2005. "Violent Encounters: Violent Engagements, Skirmishes, and Tiffs." *Journal of Contemporary Ethnography* 34 (6): 631–678.

Ball, R. A., and D. G. Curry. 1995. "The Logic and Definition in Criminology: Purposes and Methods for Defining 'Gangs.'" *Criminology* 33 (2): 225–245.

Barrows, R. G. 1990. "Indianapolis: Silver Buckle on the Rust Belt." In *Snowbelt Cities,* edited by R. M. Bernard, 1–24. Bloomington: Indiana University Press.

Battin, S. R., K. G. Hill, R. D. Abbott, R. F. Catalano, and J. D. Hawkins. 1998. "The Contribution of Gang Membership to Delinquency Beyond Delinquent Friends." *Criminology* 36 (1): 93–115.

Becker, H. S. 1996. "The Epistemology of Qualitative Research." In *Ethnography and Human Development: Context and Meaning in Social Inquiry,* edited by R. Jessor and A. Colby, 53–72. Chicago: University of Chicago Press.

Benson, J. K. 1975. "The Interorganizational Network as a Political Economy." *Administrative Science Quarterly* 20 (2): 229–249.

Bernard, R. M. 1990. "Introduction: Snowbelt Politics." In *Snowbelt Cities,* edited by R. M. Bernard, 1–24. Bloomington: Indiana University Press.

Bjerregaard, B. 2002. "Self-Definitions of Gang Membership and Involvement in Delinquent Activities." *Youth and Society* 34(1):31–54.

Block, C. R., and R. Block. 2001. "Street Gang Crime in Chicago." In *The Modern Gang Reader,* 2nd ed., edited by J. Miller, C. L. Maxson, and M. W. Klein, 186–199. Los Angeles: Roxbury

Bourgois, P. 1999. *In Search of Respect: Selling Crack in El Barrio.* New York: Cambridge University Press.

Braga, A. A. 2005. "Hot Spots Policing and Crime Prevention: A Systematic Review of Randomized Control Trials." *Journal of Experimental Criminology* 1 (2): 317–342.

Braga, A. A., D. L. Weisburd, E. J. Waring, L. G. Mazerolle, W. Spellman, and F. Gajewski. 1999. "Problem-Oriented Policing in Violent Crime Places: A Randomized Controlled Experiment." *Criminology* 37 (3): 541–580.

Brezina, T., R. Agnew, F. T. Cullen, and J. P. Wright. 2004. "The Code of the Street: A Quantitative Assessment of Elijah Anderson's Subculture of Violence

Thesis and its Contribution to Youth Violence Research." *Youth Violence and Juvenile Justice* 2 (4): 303–328.

Brezina, T., E. Tekin, and V. Topalli. 2009. "'Might Not Be a Tomorrow': A Multimethods Approach to Anticipated Early Death and Youth Crime." *Criminology* 47 (4): 1091–1129.

Brint, S., and J. Karabel. 1991. "Institutional Origins and Transformations: The Case of American Community Colleges." In *The New Institutionalism in Organizational Analysis*, edited by W. Powell and P. J. DiMaggio, 337–360. Chicago: University of Chicago Press.

Brotherton, D. C., and L. Barrios. 2004. *The Almighty Latin King and Queen Nation: Street Politics and the Transformation of a New York City Gang*. New York: Columbia University Press.

Bursik, R. J., and H. G. Grasmik. 1993. *Neighborhoods and Crime: The Dimensions of Effective Community Control*. San Francisco: Lexington.

Campbell, A. 1984. *The Girls in the Gang*. New York: Basil Blackwell.

———. 1987. "Self-Definition by Rejection: The Case of Gang Girls." *Social Problems* 34 (5): 451–466.

Caputo, G. A. 2008. *Out in the Storm: Drug-Addicted Women Living as Shoplifters and Sex Workers*. Boston: Northeastern University Press.

Cloward, R. A., and L. E. Ohlin. 1960. *Delinquency and Opportunity*. New York: Free Press.

Cohen, A. K. 1955. *Delinquent Boys*. New York: Free Press.

Coldren, J. R. Jr., and D. F. Higgins. 2001. "Evaluating Nuisance Abatement at Gang and Drug Houses in Chicago." In *Policing Street Gangs and Youth Violence*, edited by S. H. Decker, 131–166. Belmont, CA: Thompson/Wadsworth.

Copes, H., and A. Hochstetler. 2003. "Situational Construction of Masculinity among Male Street Thieves." *Journal of Contemporary Ethnography* 32 (3): 279–302.

Corbin, J. M., and A. Strauss. 1990. "Grounded Theory Research: Procedures, Canons, and Evaluative Criteria." *Qualitative Sociology* 13 (1): 3–21.

Corsaro, W. A. 1992. "Interpretive Reproduction in Children's Peer Cultures." *Social Psychological Quarterly* 55 (2): 160–177.

Coughlin, B. C., and S. A. Venkatesh. 2003. "The Urban Street Gang after 1970." *Annual Review of Sociology* 29:41–64.

Coulton, C. J., J. E. Korbin, M. Su, and J. Chow. 1995. "Community Level Factor and Child Maltreatment Rates." *Child Development* 66 (5): 1262–1276.

Coyne, I. T. 1997. "Sampling in Qualitative Research. Purposeful and Theoretical Sampling; Merging or Clear Boundaries?" *Journal of Advanced Nursing* 26 (3): 623–630.

Craig, W. M., F. K Vitaro, L. Gagnon, and R. E. Tremblay. 2002. "The Road to Gang Membership: Characteristics of Male Gang and Nongang Members from Ages 10 to 14." *Social Development* 11 (1): 53–68.

Crick, N. R. 1996. "The Role of Overt Aggression, Relational Aggression, and Prosocial Behavior in the Prediction of Children's Future Social Adjustment." *Child Development* 67 (5): 2317–2327.

———. 1997. "Engagement in Gender Normative Versus Gender Non-normative Forms of Aggression: Links to Socio-Psychological Adjustment." *Developmental Psychology* 33 (4): 589–600.

Crick, N. R., and M. A. Bigbee. 1998. "Relational and Overt Forms of Peer Victimization: A Multiinformant Approach." *Journal of Consulting and Clinical Psychology* 66 (2): 337–347.

Crick, N. R., and J. K. Grotpeter. 1995. "Relational Aggression, Gender, and Social Psychological Adjustment." *Child Development* 66 (3): 710–722.

Cyr, J. L. 2003. "The Folk Devil Reacts: Gangs and Moral Panics." *Criminal Justice Review* 28 (1): 26–46.

Decker, S. H. 1996. "Collective and Normative Features of Gang Violence." *Justice Quarterly* 13 (2): 243–264.

Decker, S. H., ed. 2003. *Policing Gangs and Youth Violence.* Belmont, CA: Thompson/Wadsworth.

Decker, S. H., T. Bynum, and D. Weisel. 1998. "A Tale of Two Cities: Gangs as Organized Crime Groups." *Justice Quarterly* 15 (3): 395–425.

Decker, S. H., and B. Van Winkle. 1996. *Life in the Gang.* Cambridge: Cambridge University Press.

Deephouse, D. L. 1996. "Does Isomorphism Legitimate?" *Academy of Management Journal* 39 (4): 1024–1039.

Dentler, R. A., and K. T. Erikson. 1959. "The Functions of Deviance in Groups." *Social Problems* 7 (2): 98–107.

Dilulio, J. J. Jr. 1995. "The Coming of the Super-Predators." *Weekly Standard*, November, 23–28.

DiMaggio, P. J. 1991. "Constructing an Organizational Field as a Profession." In *The New Institutionalism in Organizational Analysis*, edited by W. Powell and P. J. DiMaggio, 267–292. Chicago: University of Chicago Press.

———. 1997. "Culture and Cognition." *Annual Review of Sociology* 23: 263–287.

DiMaggio, P. J., and W. Powell. 1991. "The Iron Cage Revisited: Institutional Isomorphism and Collective Rationality in Organizational Fields." In *The New Institutionalism in Organizational Analysis*, edited by W. Powell and P. J. DiMaggio, 63–82. Chicago: University of Chicago Press.

Dowling, J., and J. Pfeffer. 1975. "Organizational Legitimacy and Organizational Behavior." *Pacific Sociological Review* 18 (1): 122–136.

Eder, D., and J. L. Enke. 1991. "The Structure of Gossip: Opportunities and Constraints on Collective Expression among Adolescents." *American Sociological Review* 56 (4): 494–508.

Eder, D., with C. C. Evans and S. Parker. 1997. *School Talk: Gender and Adolescent Culture.* New Brunswick, NJ: Rutgers University Press.

Eitle, D., S. Gunkel, and K. Van Gundy. 2004. "Cumulative Exposure to Stressful Life Events and Male Gang Membership." *Journal of Criminal Justice* 32 (2): 95–111.

Esbensen, F., and E. P. Deschenes. 1998. "A Multisite Examination of Youth Gang Membership: Does Gender Matter?" *Criminology* 36 (4): 799–828.

Esbensen, F., and D. Huizinga. 1993. "Gangs, Drugs, and Delinquency in a Survey of Urban Youth." *Criminology* 31 (4): 565–589.

Esbensen, F., D. W. Osgood, T. J. Taylor, D. Peterson, and A. Freng. 2001. "How Great Is G.R.E.A.T.? Results from a Longitudinal Quasi-Experimental Design." *Criminology and Public Policy* 1 (1): 87–118.

Esbensen, F., and F. M. Weerman 2005. "Youth Gangs and Troublesome Youth Groups in the United States and the Netherlands: A Cross National Comparison." *European Journal of Criminology* 2 (1): 1477–3708.

Esbensen, F., L. T. Winfree Jr., N. He, and T. J. Taylor. 2001 "Youth Gangs and Definitional Issues: When Is a Gang a Gang, and Why Does It Matter?" *Crime and Delinquency* 47 (1): 105–130.

Fagan, J. 1989. "The Social Organization of Drug Use and Drug Dealing among Urban Gangs." *Criminology* 27 (4): 633–669.

Fagan, J., and D. L. Wilkinson. 1998. "Guns, Youth Violence, and Social Identity in Inner Cities." *Crime and Justice* 24:105–188.

Fearon, J. D., and D. D. Laitin. 2000. "Violence and the Social Construction of Ethnic Identity." *International Organization* 54:845–877.

Felson, R. B. 1982. "Impression Management and the Escalation of Aggression and Violence." *Social Psychological Quarterly* 45 (4): 245–254.

Felson, R. B., and H. J. Steadman. 1983. "Situational Factors in Disputes Leading to Criminal Violence." *Criminology* 21 (1): 59–74.

Felstiner, W. L. F. 1974. "Influences of Social Organization on Dispute Processing." *Law & Society Review* 9 (1): 63–94.

Federal Bureau of Investigation. 2010. Uniform Crime Reporting Statistics: Crime Reported by Indianapolis Police Dept., Indiana. http://www .ucrdatatool.gov/Search/Crime/Local/RunCrimeJurisbyJurisLarge.cfm. Accessed January 10, 2012.

Fine, G. A. 1986. "The Social Organization of Adolescent Gossip." In *Children's Worlds and Children's Language*, edited by J. Cook-Gumperz, W. Corsaro, and J. Streek, 405–423. Berlin: Mouton.

———. 1993. "Ten Lies of Ethnography: Moral Dilemmas of Field Research." *Journal of Contemporary Ethnography* 22 (3): 267–294.

Fine, G. A., and S. Kleinman. 1979. "Rethinking Subculture: An Interactionist Analysis." *American Journal of Sociology* 85 (1): 1–20.

Fleisher, M. 1995. *Beggars and Thieves*. Madison: University of Wisconsin Press.

———. 1998. *Dead End Kids*. Madison: University of Wisconsin Press.

Fligstein, N. 1991. "The Structural Transformation of American Industry: An Institutional Account of the Causes of Diversification in the Largest Firms, 1919–1979." In *The New Institutionalism in Organizational Analysis*, edited by W. Powell and P. J. DiMaggio, 311–336. Chicago: University of Chicago Press.

———. 2001. "Social Skill and the Theory of Fields." *Sociological Theory* 19 (2): 105–25.

Futrell, R., and P. Simi. 2004. "Free Spaces, Collective Identity, and the Persistence of U.S. White Power Activism." *Social Problems* 51 (1): 16–42.

Galaskiewicz, J. 1985. "Interorganizational Relations." *Annual Review of Sociology* 11:281–304.

Galen, B. R., and M. K. Underwood. 1997. "A Developmental Investigation of Social Aggression among Children." *Developmental Psychology* 33 (4): 589–600.

Garot, R. 2007a. "Non-violence in the Inner City: 'Decent' and 'Street' as Strategic Resources." *Journal of African American Studies* 10 (4): 94–111.

———. 2007b. "'Where You From!': Gang Identity as Performance." *Journal of Contemporary Ethnography* 36 (1): 50–84.

———. 2009. "Reconsidering Retaliation: Structural Inhibitions, Emotive Dissonance, and the Acceptance or Ambivalence among Inner-city Young Men." *Ethnography* 10 (1): 63–90.

———. 2010. *Who You Claim?: Performing Gang Identity in School and on the Streets.* New York: New York University Press.

Gatti, U., R. E. Tremblay, F. Vitaro, and P. McDuff. 2005. "Youth Gangs, Delinquency and Drug Use: A Test of the Selection, Facilitation, and Enhancement Hypotheses." *Journal of Child Psychology and Psychiatry* 46 (11): 1178–1190.

Geertz, C. 1973. "Thick Description: Toward and Interpretive Theory of Culture." In *The Interpretation of Culture,* 3–30. New York: Basic Books.

Gieryn, T. F. 1983. "Boundary-Work and the Demarcation of Science from Non-science: Strains and Interests in Professional Interests of Scientists." *American Sociological Review* 48 (6): 781–795.

———. 1999. *Cultural Boundaries of Science: Credibility on the Line.* Chicago: University of Chicago Press.

Glaser, B. G., and A. L. Strauss. 2006. *The Discovery of Grounded Theory: Strategies for Qualitative Research.* Chicago: Aldine.

Gluckman, M. 1963. "Papers in Honor of Melville J. Herskovits: Gossip and Scandal." *Current Anthropology* 4 (3): 307–316.

Goffman, E. 1959. *The Presentation of Self in Everyday Life.* New York: Doubleday/Anchor Books.

———. 1967. *Interaction Ritual: Essays in Face-to-Face Behavior.* New Brunswick, NJ: Transaction.

———. 1974. *Frame Analysis.* New York: Harper Colophon Books.

Gold, R. L. 1958. "Roles in Sociological Field Observations." *Social Forces* 36:217–223.

Goodwin, M. H. 1980. "He-said-she-said: Formal Cultural Procedures for the Construction of a Gossip Dispute Activity." *American Ethnologist* 7 (4): 674–695.

Gordon, R. A., B. B. Lahey, E. Kawai, R. Loeber, M. Stouthamer-Loeber, and D. P. Farrington. 2004. "Antisocial Behavior and Youth Gang Membership: Selection and Socialization." *Criminology* 42 (1): 55–87.

Granovetter, M. S. 1973. "The Strength of Weak Ties." *American Journal of Sociology* 78 (6): 1360–1380.

———. 1983. "The Strength of Weak Ties: A Network Theory Revisited." *Sociological Theory* 1:201–33.

Greene, J. R. 2003. "Gangs, Community Policing, and Problem Solving." In *Policing Gangs and Youth Violence,* edited by S. H. Decker, 3–16. Belmont, CA: Thompson/Wadsworth.

Hagan, J., and B. McCarthy. 1997. *Mean Streets: Youth Crime and Homelessness.* New York: Cambridge University Press.

Hagedorn, J. M. 1998a. *People and Folks.* 2nd ed. Chicago: Lakeview Press.

———. 1998b. "Gang Violence in the Postindustrial Era." In *Youth Violence,* edited by M. Tonry and M. H. Moore, 364–420. Chicago: University of Chicago Press.

———. 2008. *A World of Gangs: Armed Young Men and Gangsta Culture.* Minneapolis: University of Minnesota Press.

Hammersley, M., and P. Atkinson. 1995. *Ethnography: Principles in Practice.* 2nd ed. New York: Routledge.

Hannerz, U. 1969. *Soulside: Inquiries in the Ghetto Culture and Community.* New York: Columbia University Press.

Harding, D. J. 2007. "Culture Context, Sexual Behavior, and Romantic Relationships in Disadvantaged Neighborhoods." *American Sociological Review* 72 (3): 341–364.

———. 2010. *Living the Drama: Community, Conflict, and Culture among Inner City Boys.* Chicago: University of Chicago Press.

Hawker, D.S.J., and M. J. Boulton. 2000. "Twenty Years' Research on Peer Victimization and Psychological Maladjustment: A Meta-analytic Review of Cross Sectional Studies." *Journal of Child Psychology & Psychiatry & Allied Disciplines* 41 (4): 441–455.

Hepburn, J. R. 1973. "Violent Behavior in Interpersonal Relationships." *Sociological Quarterly* 14 (3): 419–429.

Hermanowicz, J. C., and H. P. Morgan. 1999. "Ritualizing the Routine: Collective Identity Affirmation." *Sociological Forum* 14 (2): 194–214.

Hill, K. G., J. C. Howell, J. D. Hawkins, and S. R. Battin-Pearson. 1999. "Childhood Risk Factors for Adolescent Gang Membership: Results from the Seattle Social Development Project." *Journal of Research in Crime and Delinquency* 36 (3): 300–322.

Hirschi, T. 2006. *Causes of Delinquency.* New Brunswick, NJ: Transaction.

Hollander, J. A., and H. R. Gordon. 2006. "The Processes of Social Construction in Talk." *Symbolic Interaction* 29 (2): 183–212.

Homans, G. C. 1992. *The Human Group.* New York: Harcourt, Brace and World.

Horowitz, R. 1983. *Honor and the American Dream: Culture and identity in a Chicano Community.* New Brunswick, NJ: Rutgers University Press.

———. 1986. "Remaining an Outsider: Membership as a Threat to Research Rapport." *Journal of Contemporary Ethnography* 14 (4): 409–430.

Horowitz, R., and G. Schwartz. 1974. "Honor, Normative Ambiguity and Gang Violence." *American Sociological Review* 39 (2): 238–251.

Huff, C. R. 2004. "Comparing the Criminal Behavior of Youth Gangs and At-Risk Youth. In *American Youth Gangs at the Millennium,* edited by F. Esbensen, S. G. Tibbetts, and L. Gaines, 77–89. Long Grove, IL: Waveland Press.

Hughes, L. A., and J. F. Short. 2005. "Disputes Involving Street Gang Members: Micro-Social Contexts." *Criminology* 43(1): 43–76.

Indiana Black Expo, Inc. 2010. About Indianapolis Black Expo. http://www.indianablackexpo.com/about-statements.asp. Accessed April 12, 2011.

Indiana.gov. 2012. Twenty-first Century Scholars. State Student Assistance Commission of Indiana. http://www.in.gov/ssaci/2345.htm. Accessed January 4, 2012.

Indianapolis Metropolitan Police Department. 2009. 2008 Homicide Information. Prepared by Lt. R. L. Spurgeon.

Indianapolis Star Homicide Map. 2008. http://www.indystar.com/article/99999999/NEWS02/80304038/Interactive-Marion-County-homicide-map. Accessed December 16, 2011.

Jacobs, B. A. 1999. *Dealing Crack: The Social World of Street Corner Selling.* Boston: Northeastern University Press.

Jacobs, B. A., and R. Wright. 1999. "Stick-Up, Street Culture, and Offender Motivation." *Criminology* 37 (1): 149–173.

———. 2006. *Street Justice: Retaliation in the Criminal Underworld.* New York: Cambridge University Press.

Jansyn, L. R. 1966. "Solidarity and Delinquency in a Street Corner Group." *American Sociological Review* 31 (5): 600–614.

Jargowski, P. A. 1997. *Poverty and Place: Ghettos, Barrios, and the American City.* New York: Russell Sage.

Junker, B. H. 1960. *Field Work: An Introduction to the Social Sciences.* Chicago: University of Chicago Press

Katz, J. 1988. *Seductions of Crime: Moral and Sensual Attractions of Doing Evil.* New York: Basic Books.

Kautt, P. M., and C. C. Spohn. 2007. "Assessing Blameworthiness and Assigning Punishment: Theoretical Perspectives on Judicial Decision Making." In *Criminal Justice Theory: Explaining the Nature and Behavior of Criminal Justice,* edited by D. E. Duffee and E. R. Maguire, 155–180. New York: Routledge.

Kenis, P., and D. Knoke. 2002. "How Organizational Field Networks Shape Interorganizational Tie-Formation Rates." *Academy of Management Review* 27 (2): 275–293.

Kennedy, D. M., A. A. Braga, and A. M. Piehl. 2001. "Reducing Gun Violence: The Boston Gun Project's Operation Ceasefire." U.S. Department of Justice, Office of Justice Programs, National Institute of Justice. www.ncjrs.gov/pdffiles1/nij/188741.pdf. Accessed December 16, 2011.

Kirk, D. S., and A. V. Papachristos. 2011. "Cultural Mechanisms and the Persistence of Neighborhood Violence." *American Journal of Sociology* 116 (4): 1190–1233.

Klein, M. W. 1971. *Street Gangs and Street Workers.* Englewood Cliffs, NJ: Prentice Hall.

———. 1995. *The American Street Gang.* New York: Oxford University Press.

———. 2005. "The Value of Comparisons in Street Gang Research." *Journal of Contemporary Criminal Justice* 21 (2): 135–152.

Klein, M. W., and L. Y. Crawford. 1968. "Groups, Gangs, and Cohesiveness." In *Gang Delinquency and Delinquent Subcultures,* edited by J. F. Short, 256–272. New York: Harper and Row.

Klein, M. W., and C. L Maxson. 2006. *Street Gangs Patterns and Policy.* New York: Oxford University Press.

Knox, G. W. 2006. *An Introduction to Gangs.* 6th ed. Chicago: New Chicago School Press.

Knox, G. W., and A. V. Papachristos. 2002. *The Vice Lords: A Gang Profile Analysis.* Chicago: New Chicago School Press.

Korbin, S., J. Puntil, and E. Peluso. 1967. "Criteria of Status among Street Groups." *Journal of Research in Crime and Delinquency* 4 (1): 98–118.

Kostova, T., and S. Zaheer. 1999. "Organizational Legitimacy under Conditions of Complexity: The Case of the Multinational Enterprise." *Academy of Management Review* 24 (1): 64–81.

Kozol, Jonathan. 1992. *Savage Inequalities: Children in America's Schools*. New York: HarperPerennial.

——. 2006. *The Shame of a Nation: The Restoration of Apartheid Schooling in America*. New York: Three Rivers Press.

Kubrin, C. E. 2005. "Gangstas, Thugs, and Hustlas: Identity and the Code of the Street in Rap Music." *Social Problems* 52 (3): 360–378.

Lacourse, E., D. Nagin, R. E. Tremblay, F. Vitaro, and M. Claes. 2003. "Developmental Trajectories of Boys' Delinquent Group Membership and Facilitation of Violent Behaviors during Adolescence." *Development and Psychopathology* 15 (1): 183–187.

Lamont, M., and V. Molnar. 2002. "The Study of Boundaries in the Social Sciences." *Annual Review of Sociology* 28:167–195.

Leary, M. R., and R. M. Kowalski. 1990. "Impression Management: A Literature Review and Two-Component Model." *Psychological Bulletin* 107 (1): 34–47.

Levitt, S. D., and S. A. Venkatesh. 2000. "An Economic Analysis of a Drug-Selling Gang's Finances." *Quarterly Journal of Economics* 115 (3): 755–789.

Liebow, E. 1967. *Tally's Corner*. Boston: Little, Brown.

Loftland, J. 1970. "Interactionist Imagery and Analytic Interruptus." In *Human Nature and Collective Behavior*, edited by T. Shibutani, 35–45. Englewood Cliffs, NJ. Prentice Hall.

Luckenbill, D. F. 1977. "Criminal Homicide as a Situated Transaction." *Social Problems* 25 (2): 176–186.

Lune, H., and M. Martinez. 1999. "Old Structures, New Relations: How Community Development Credit Unions Define Organizational Boundaries." *Sociological Forum* 14 (4): 609–634.

Massey, D. S., and N. A. Denton. 1993. *American Apartheid: Segregation and the Making of the Underclass*. Cambridge, MA: Harvard University Press.

Matsueda, R. L. 1992. "Reflected Appraisals, Parental Labeling, and Delinquency: Specifying a Symbolic Interactionist Theory." *American Journal of Sociology* 97 (6): 1577–1611.

Maxson, C. L., M. L. Whitlock, and M. W. Klein. 1998. "Vulnerability to Street Gang Membership: Implications for Practice." *Social Service Review* 72 (1): 70–91.

McCorkle, R. C., and T. D. Miethe. 1998. "The Political and Organizational Response to Gangs: An Examination of a 'Moral Panic' in Nevada." *Justice Quarterly* 15 (1): 41–64.

McGarrell, E. F., and S. Chermak. 2003. "Problem Solving to Reduce Gang and Drug-Related Violence in Indianapolis." In *Policing Street Gangs and Youth Violence*, edited by S. H. Decker, 77–101. Belmont, CA: Thompson/Wadsworth.

McGloin, J. M. 2005. "Policy and Intervention Considerations of Network Analysis of Street Gangs." *Criminology and Public Policy* 4 (3): 607–636.

Melde, C., T. J. Taylor, and F. Esbensen. 2009. "'I got your back': An Examination of the Protective Function of Gang Membership in Adolescence." *Criminology* 47 (2): 565–594.

Melucci, A. 1995. "The Process of Collective Identity." In *Social Movements and Culture*, edited by H. Johnson, and B. Klandermans, 41–63. Minneapolis: University of Minnesota Press.

Merry, S. E. 1979. "Going to Court: Strategies of Dispute Management in an American Urban Neighborhood." *Law and Society Review* 13 (4): 891–925.

Mieczkowski, T. 1986. "'Geeking Up' and Throwing Down: Heroin Street Life in Detroit." *Criminology* 24 (4): 645–666.

Miller, J. 1998. "Gender and Victimization Risk among Young Women in Gangs." *Journal of Research in Crime and Delinquency* 35 (4): 429–453.

———. 2001. *One of the Guys: Girls, Gangs, and Gender.* New York: Oxford University Press.

———. 2008. *Getting Played: African American Girls, Urban Equality, and Gendered Violence.* New York: New York University Press.

Miller, J., and R. K. Brunson. 2000. "Gender Dynamics in Youth Gangs: A Comparison of Males' and Females' Accounts." *Justice Quarterly* 17 (3): 419–448.

Miller, J., and S. H. Decker. 2001. "Young Women and Gang Violence: Gender, Street Offending, and Violent Victimization in Gangs." *Justice Quarterly* 18 (1): 115–140.

Monti, D. J. 1992. "On the Risks and Rewards of 'Going Native.'" *Sociological Quarterly* 15 (3): 325–332.

———. 1994. *Wannabe: Gangs in Suburbs and Schools.* Cambridge, MA: Wiley Blackwell.

Moore, J. W. 1978. *Homeboys: Gangs, Drugs, and Prison in the Barrios of Los Angeles.* Philadelphia: Temple University Press.

———. 1991. *Going Down to the Barrio: Homeboys and Homegirls in Change.* Philadelphia: Temple University Press.

Muir, W. K. Jr. 1977. *Police: Streetcorner Politicians.* Chicago: University of Chicago Press.

National Youth Gang Center. 2011a. "National Youth Gang Survey Analysis: Measuring Extent of Gang Problems." U.S. Department of Justice, Office of Juvenile Justice and Delinquency Prevention. http://www.nationalgangcenter.gov/Survey-Analysis/Measuring-the-Extent-of-Gang-Problems#estimated gangmembers. Accessed December 16, 2011.

———. 2011b. "National Youth Gang Survey Analysis: Prevalence of Gang Problems." U.S. Department of Justice, Office of Juvenile Justice and Delinquency Prevention. http://www.nationalgangcenter.gov/Survey-Analysis/Prevalence-of-Gang-Problems. Accessed December 16, 2011.

Oliver, W. 1994. *The Violent Social World of Black Men.* San Francisco: Jossey Bass.

———. 2006. "'The Streets': An Alternative Black Male Socialization Institution." *Journal of Black Studies* 36 (6): 918–937.

Padilla, F. M. 1996. *The Gang as an American Enterprise.* New Brunswick, NJ: Rutgers University Press.

Paine, R. 1967. "What Is Gossip About? An Alternative Hypothesis." *Man* 2 (2): 278–285.

Papachristos, A. V. 2007 "Reciprocity, Balance, and Hierarchy in Gang Homicide Networks." Paper presented at the annual meeting of the American Sociological Association, August 10–14. New York City. http://www.allacademic.com/meta/p183748_index.html. Accessed December 16, 2011.

———. 2009. "Murder by Structure: Dominance Relations and the Social Structure of Gang Homicide." *American Journal of Sociology* 115 (1): 74–128.

Pelak, C. F. 2002. "Women's Collective Identity Formation in Sports: A Case Study from Women's Ice Hockey." *Gender and Society* 16 (1): 93–114.

Pfeffer, J., and G. R. Salancik. 1978. *The External Control of Organizations: A Resource Dependence Perspective.* Stanford, CA: Stanford University Press.

Pierce, R. B. 2005. *Polite Protest: The Political Economy of Race in Indianapolis, 1920–1970.* Bloomington: Indiana University Press.

Polletta, F., and J. M. Jasper. 2001. "Collective Identity and Social Movements." *Annual Review of Sociology* 27:283–305.

Prinstein, M. J., J. Boergers, and E. M. Vernberg, 2001. "Overt and Relational Aggression in Adolescents: Social-Psychological Adjustment of Aggressors and Victims." *Journal of Child Clinical Psychology* 30 (4): 479–491.

ProximityOne: Information, Resources, and Solutions. 2010. American Community Survey Data Access and Use. http://www.proximityone.com/acs.htm. Accessed April 12, 2011.

Sanchez-Jankowski, M. 1991. *Islands in the Street.* Berkeley: University of California Press.

———. 2001. "Gangs and Social Change." *Theoretical Criminology* 7 (2): 191–216.

———. 2008. *Cracks in the Pavement: Social Change and Resilience in Poor Neighborhoods.* Berkeley: University of California Press.

Schram, P. J., and L. K. Gaines. 2005. "Examining Delinquent Nongang Members and Delinquent Gang Members: A Comparison of Juvenile Probationers at Intake and Outcomes." *Youth Violence and Juvenile Justice* 3 (2): 99–115.

Scott, W. R., and J. W. Meyer 1991. "The Organization of Societal Sectors: Propositions and Early Evidence." In *The New Institutionalism in Organizational Analysis,* edited by W. W. Powell and P. J. DiMaggio, 108–140. Chicago: University of Chicago Press.

Shackley, S., and B. Wynne. 1996. "Representing Uncertainty in Global Climate Change Science and Policy: Boundary-Ordering Devices and Authority." *Science, Technology, and Human Values* 21 (3): 275–302.

Sherman, L. W., P. R. Gartin, and M. E. Bueger. 1989. "Hot Spots of Predatory Crime: Routine Activities and the Criminology of Place." *Criminology* 27 (1): 27–55.

Sherman, L. W., and D. P. Rogan. 1995. "Effects of Gun Seizures on Gun Violence: Hot Spots Patrol in Kansas City." *Justice Quarterly* 12 (4): 673–693.

Short, J. F., and F. L. Strodtbeck. 1974. *Group Process and Gang Delinquency.* Chicago: University of Chicago Press.

Shover, N., and D. Honaker. 1992. "The Socially Bounded Decision Making of Persistent Property Offenders." *Howard Journal* 31 (4): 276–293.

Small, M. L. 2002. "Culture, Cohorts, and Social Organization Theory: Understanding Participation in a Latino Housing Project." *American Journal of Sociology* 108 (1): 1–54.

Snow, D. A., C. Morrill, and L. Anderson. 2003. "Elaborating Analytic Ethnography: Linking Fieldwork and Theory." *Ethnography* 4 (2): 181–200.

Snow, D. A., E. B. Rochford, Jr., S. K. Worden, and R. D. Benford. 1986. "Frame Alignment Processes, Micromobilization, and Movement Participation." *American Sociological Review* 51 (4): 464–481.

Spergel, I. A. 1984. "Violent Gang in Chicago: In Search of Social Policy." *Social Service Review* 58 (2): 199–226.

Spergel, I. A., and G. D. Curry. 1993. "The National Youth Gang Survey: A Research and Development Program." In *The Gang Intervention Handbook*, edited by A. P. Goldstein, and C. R. Huff, 359–400. Champaign, IL: Research Press.

Spergel, I. A., and S. F. Grossman. 1997. "The Little Village Project: A Community Approach to the Gang Problem." *Social Work* 42 (5): 456–470.

Spergel, I. A., K. M. Wa, and R. V. Sosa. 2005. "Evaluation of the Tucson Comprehensive Community-Wide Approach to Gang Prevention, Intervention, and Suppression Program." Report submitted to the U.S. Department of Justice, National Institute of Justice. https://www.ncjrs.gov/pdffiles1/ojjdp/grants/209190.pdf. Accessed December 16, 2011.

Star, S. L., and J. R. Griesemer. 1989. "Institutional Ecology, 'Translations' and Boundary Objects: Amateurs and Professions in Berkeley's Museum of Vertebrate Zoology." *Social Studies of Science* 19 (3): 387–420.

Strauss, A., and J. Corbin. 1990. *Basics of Qualitative Research*. Newbury Park, CA: Sage.

Stryker, S. 1968. Identity Salience and Role Performance: The Relevance of Symbolic Interactionist Theory for Family Research. *Journal of Marriage and the Family* 30:558–564.

———. 1980. *Symbolic Interactionism*. Menlo Park, CA: Benjamin/Cummings.

Stryker, S., and E. A. Craft. 1982. "Deviance, Selves and Others Revisited." *Youth and Society* 14 (2): 159–183.

Suchman, M. C. 1995. "Managing Legitimacy: Strategic and Institutional Approaches." *Academy of Management Review* 20 (3): 571–610.

Sullivan, M. L. 1989. *Getting Paid: Youth Crime and Work in the Inner City*. Ithaca, NY: Cornell University Press.

———. 2005. "Maybe We Shouldn't Study 'Gangs': Does Reification Obscure Youth Violence?" *Journal of Contemporary Criminal Justice* 21 (2): 170–190.

———. 2006. "Are 'Gang' Studies Dangerous? Youth Violence, Local Context, and the Problem of Reification." In *Studying Youth Gang*, edited by J. F. Short Jr. and L. A. Hughes, 15–36. Lanham, MD: AltaMira Press.

Swidler, A. 1986. "Culture in Action: Symbols and Strategies." *American Sociological Review* 51 (2): 273–286.

Taylor, T. J. 2007. "The Boulevard Ain't Safe for Your Kids . . .: Youth GangMembership and Violent Victimization." *Journal of Contemporary Criminal Justice* 24 (2): 125–136.

Taylor, T. J., A. Freng, F. Esbensen, and D. Peterson. 2008. "Youth Gang Membership and Serious Violent Victimization. The Importance of Lifestyles and Routine Activities." *Journal of Interpersonal Violence* 23 (10): 1441–1464.

Taylor, T. J., D. Peterson, F. Esbensen, and A. Freng. 2008. "Gang Membership as a Risk Factor for Adolescent Violent Victimization." *Journal of Research in Crime and Delinquency* 44 (4): 351–380.

Thornberry, T. P., M. D. Krohn, A. J. Lizotte, C. A. Smith, and K. Tobin. 2003. *Gangs and Delinquency in Developmental Perspective*. New York: Cambridge University Press.

Thornberry, T. P., M. D. Krohn, A. J. Lizotte, and D. C. Wiershem. 1993. "The Role of Juvenile Gangs in Facilitating Delinquent Behavior." *Journal of Research in Crime and Delinquency* 30 (1): 55–87.

Thrasher, F. M. 1967. *The Gang.* Chicago: University of Chicago Press.

Tita, G., J. K. Riley, and P. Greenwood. 2001. "From Boston to Boyle Heights: The Process and Prospects of a 'Pulling Levers' Strategy in a Los Angeles Barrio." In *Policing Street Gangs and Youth Violence*, edited by S. H. Decker, 102–130. Belmont, CA: Thompson/Wadsworth.

Topalli, V. 1995. "When Being Good Is Bad: An Explanation of Neutralization Theory." *Criminology* 43 (3): 797–836.

Topalli, V., R. Wright, and R. Fornango. 2002. "Drug Dealers, Robbery, and Retaliation: Vulnerability, Deterrence, and the Contagion of Violence." *British Journal of Criminology* 42 (2): 337–351.

Underwood, M. K. 2003. *Social Aggression among Girls.* New York: New Guilford Press.

U.S. Census Bureau. 1995. Statistical Brief: Poverty Areas. http://www.census .gov/population/socdemo/statbriefs/povarea.html.

———. 2007. American Community Survey: Indianapolis. http://factfinder.census .gov/servlet/ADPTable?_bm=y&-geo_id=31200US269001836003&-qr _name=ACS_2007_1YR_G00_DP3&-ds_name=D&-_lang=en&- redoLog=false. Accessed January 10, 2012.

———. 2010a. State and County Quick Facts. http://quickfacts.census.gov. Accessed January 10, 2010.

———. 2010b. American FactFinder. http://factfinder.census.gov. Accessed January 10, 2010.

U.S. Department of Justice. 2009. "Crime in the United States, 2008: Expanded Homicide Data, Table 2, Murder Victims by Age, Sex, and Race." Federal Bureau of Investigation. http://www2.fbi.gov/ucr/cius2008/offenses/ expanded_information/data/shrtable_02.html. Accessed January 10, 2012.

———. 2010. "Crime in the United States, 2009: Expanded Homicide Data, Table 2, Murder Victims by Age, Sex, and Race." Federal Bureau of Investigation. http://www2.fbi.gov/ucr/cius2009/offenses/expanded_ information/data/shrtable_02.html. Accessed January 10, 2012.

Venkatesh, S. A. 2000. *American Ghetto: The Rise and Fall of a Modern Ghetto.* Cambridge, MA: Harvard University Press.

———. 2002. "'Doin' the Hustle': Constructing the Ethnographer in the American Ghetto." *Ethnography* 3 (1): 91–111.

———. 2006. *Off the Books: The Underground Economy of the Urban Poor.* Cambridge, MA: Harvard University Press.

Vigil, J. D. 1991. *Barrio Gangs: Street Life and Identity in Southern California.* Austin: University of Texas Press.

———. 2003. "Urban Violence and Street Gangs." *Annual Review of Anthropology* 32:225–42.

Warren, R. L. 1967. "The Interorganizational Field as a Focus for Intervention." *Administrative Science Quarterly* 12 (3): 396–419.

Wasserman, S., and K. Faust. 1999. *Social Network Analysis: Methods and Applications.* New York: Cambridge University Press.

Wiesburd, D., and L. Green. 1995. "Policing Drug Hot Spots: The Jersey City Drug Market Analysis Experiment." *Justice Quarterly* 12 (4): 711–735.

Whyte, W. F. 1981 [1941]. *Street Corner Society: The Social Structure of an Italian Slum.* 3rd ed. Chicago: University of Chicago.

Wilkinson, D. L. 2001. "Violent Events and Social Identity: Specifying the Relationship between Respect and Masculinity in Inner City Youth Violence." *Sociological Studies of Children and Youth* 8:231–265.

Wilkinson, D. L., and J. Fagan. 2003. "A Theory of Violent Events." In *The Process and Structure of Crime: Criminal Events and Crime Analysis. Advances in Criminological Theory*, vol. 9, edited by R. F. Meier, L. W. Kennedy, and V. F. Sacco, 169–196. New Brunswick, NJ: Transaction.

Wilson, W. J. 1987. *The Truly Disadvantaged: The Inner City, the Underclass, and Public Policy*. Chicago: University of Chicago Press.

———. 1996. *When Work Disappears: The World of the New Urban Poor*. New York: Vintage Books.

Winfree, T. L., K. Fuller, T. Vigil, and G. L. Mays. 1992. "The Definition and Measurement of 'Gang Status': Policy Implications for Juvenile Justice." *Juvenile and Family Court Journal* 43 (1): 29–38.

Wright, R. T., F. Brookman, and T. Bennett. 2006. "The Foreground Dynamics of Street Robbery in Britain." *British Journal of Criminology* 46 (1): 1–15.

Wright, R. T., and S. H. Decker. 1997. *Armed Robbers in Action: Stickups and Street Culture*. Boston: Northeastern University Press.

Yablonksy, L. 1959. "The Delinquent Gang as a Near-Group." *Social Problems* 7 (2): 108–117.

———. 1967. *The Violent Gang*. Baltimore: Penguin.

Zehr, S. C. 2000. "Public Representations of Scientific Uncertainty about Global Climate Change." *Public Understanding of Science* 9 (2): 85–103.

Index

About the Author

TIMOTHY R. LAUGER received his Ph.D. in criminal justice from Indiana University. He is currently an assistant professor of criminology and criminal justice at Niagara University in Lewiston, New York.

Robert H. Tillman and Michael L. Indergaard, *Pump and Dump: The Rancid Rules of the New Economy*

Mariana Valverde, *Law and Order: Images, Meanings, Myths*

Michael Welch, *Crimes of Power & States of Impunity: The U.S. Response to Terror*

Michael Welch, *Scapegoats of September 11th: Hate Crimes and State Crimes in the War on Terror*

Saundra D. Westervelt and Kimberly J. Cook, *Life after Death Row: Exonerees' Search for Community and Identity*